FOR[illegible]

In December of 1994, I pulled u[illegible] car. I rechecked the address b[illegible] enough. It was a nice house in a [illegible] leges, bordered tightly by similar [illegible]s parked in the drive. It would hav[illegible]d home for a professor from the local college. But I wasn[illegible]o-fessor from the local college; I was looking for Peter Drucker—the leading founder of the field of management, the most influential management thinker in the second half of the twentieth century, the founding father of the Peter F. Drucker Graduate School of Management.

But the address matched, so I ambled up to the front door and rang the bell. I waited. Nothing happened. So, I rang again. "Okay, okay, I'm coming," I heard a voice from inside the house. "I'm not so fast anymore." The voice sounded cranky, and I expected a curmudgeon to open the door, but instead found myself greeted with a gracious smile that made me feel that my host was really happy to see me, even though we'd never met. "Mr. Collins. So very pleased to meet you," said Drucker, with a handshake that warmly invited me across the threshold. "Please come inside."

We settled in the living room, with Drucker asking questions from his favorite wicker chair, probing, pushing, challenging. He gave freely of his wisdom, asking nothing in return. He simply wanted to contribute to my development at what was then a pivotal stage of my career; I was only thirty-six years of age with no significant reputation. His generosity of spirit explains much of Drucker's immense influence. I reflected back on his work, *The Effective Executive*, and his admonition to replace the quest for success with the quest for contribution. The critical question is not, "How can I achieve?" but "What can I contribute?"

Drucker's primary contribution is not a single idea, but rather an entire body of work that has one gigantic advantage: nearly all of it is essentially right. Drucker has an uncanny ability to develop insights about the workings of the social world, and to later be proved right by history. His first book, *The End of Economic Man*, published in 1939, sought to explain the origins of totalitarianism; after the fall of France in 1940, Winston Churchill made it a required part of the book kit issued to every graduate of the British Officer's Candidate School. His 1946 book *The Concept of the Corporation* analyzed the technocratic corporation, based upon an in-depth look at General Motors. It so rattled senior management in its accurate foreshadowing of future challenges to the corporate state that it was essentially banned at GM during the Sloan era. Drucker's 1964 book was so far ahead of its time in laying out the principles of corporate strategy that his publisher convinced him to abandon the title *Business Strategies* in favor of *Managing for Results,* because the term "strategy" was utterly foreign to the language of business.

There are two ways to change the world: with the pen (the use of ideas) and with the sword (the use of power). Drucker chooses the pen, and has rewired the brains of thousands who carry the sword. When in 1956 David Packard sat down to type out the objectives for the Hewlett-Packard Company, he'd been shaped by Drucker's writings, and very likely used *The Practice of Management*—which still stands as perhaps the most important management book ever written—as his guide. In our research for the book *Built to Last,* Jerry Porras and I came across a number of great companies whose leaders had been shaped by Drucker's writings, including Merck, Procter & Gamble, Ford, General Electric, and Motorola. Multiply this impact across thousands of organizations of all types—from police departments to symphony orchestras to government agencies and business corporations—and it is hard to escape the conclusion that Drucker is one of the most influential individuals of the twentieth century.

At one point during my day with Drucker, I asked, "Which of your twenty-six books are you most proud of?"

"The next one," snapped Drucker.

He was eighty-five years young at the time, cranking at a pace of nearly a book a year, plus significant articles. Over the next nine years, he added another eight books to the count and continues at age ninety-four to produce work highly relevant to the challenges of the twenty-first century. For

The Daily Drucker

The Daily Drucker

366 Days of Insight and Motivation for Getting the Right Things Done

PETER F. DRUCKER
with Joseph A. Maciariello

HARPER
BUSINESS

An Imprint of HarperCollins*Publishers*
www.harpercollins.com

HarperCollins books may be purchased for educational, business, or sales promotional use. For information please write: Special Markets Department, HarperCollins Publishers, Inc., 10 East 53rd Street, New York, NY 10022.

A hardcover edition of this book was published in 2004 by Harper Business, an imprint of HarperCollins Publishers.

FIRST HARPER BUSINESS INTERNATIONAL EDITION PUBLISHED 2011

Library of Congress Cataloging-in-Publication Data is available upon request.

ISBN 978-0-06-208924-3

11 12 13 14 15 DIX/RRD 10 9 8 7 6 5 4 3 2

"KNOW THY TIME."

Peter F. Drucker

Drucker, writing is a compulsion—a form of productive neurosis, which explains his grand output. "I started in journalism," he explained in response to the question of how he manages to write so much, so fast. "I had to write fast to make deadline. I was trained to be prolific." I do not know precisely how many pages Drucker has written so far in his career, but his books alone almost certainly exceed 10,000 pages. Drucker occupies a rare quadrant of genius, being both highly prolific and remarkably insightful.

Drucker's genius shines best in the short paragraph or single sentence that cuts through the clutter and messiness of a complex world and exposes a truth. Like a Zen poet, Drucker packs universal truth into just a few words; we can return to his teachings repeatedly, each time with a deeper level of understanding. This wonderful collection presents these pearls of insight in one place, where you can reflect upon them one at a time, without having to read all 10,000 pages. Professor Maciariello has masterfully culled the very best of Drucker and deserves our appreciation for this significant service.

Drucker likes to tell the story of a Greek sculptor from 500 BCE who was commissioned by the city of Athens to construct a set of statues to ring the top of a building. (Entitled "Pursuing Perfection," you may find this story on October 1.) The sculptor toiled for months longer than expected, making the backs of the statues as beautiful as the fronts. The city commissioners, angered by his extra work, asked: "Why did you make the backs of the statues as beautiful as the front? No one will ever see the backs!"

"Ah, but the Gods can see them," replied the sculptor.

This book is like getting all the fronts of the statues assembled in one place for us to enjoy. But what makes the fronts so beautiful is all the thinking and work that went into the entire statue—work you and I can never see, but without which the work would lack integrity. We know we can trust these wonderful gems because Drucker's entire body of work, the hundreds of thousands of hours of thinking and reflection by one of the piercing intellects of the modern age, stands behind this carefully selected set of words.

At the end of my day with Drucker in 1994, we pulled up to his home after a meal at his favorite local restaurant. "How can I thank you, how can I repay you?" I asked, knowing that the value of a day with Drucker was incalculable.

"You have already repaid me," said Drucker. "I have learned much from our conversation today." That's when I realized that what ultimately sets Peter Drucker apart is that he does not see himself as a guru; he remains a student. Most management gurus are driven to say something; Drucker is driven to learn something. Drucker's work is interesting—he is interesting—because, to borrow a phrase from the late John Gardner, he remains relentlessly interested.

"Just go out and make yourself useful," he finished. Then, without another word, he got out of the car and walked into his modest home, presumably back to his typewriter, to continue carving the fronts and backs of beautiful statues of great ideas.

JIM COLLINS
Boulder, Colorado
August 3, 2004

PREFACE

"Which of Peter Drucker's books should I read?" "Where in your work do I find the best discussion on how to place people?" Not a week goes by without my receiving half a dozen questions like these. With thirty-four books published over sixty-five years, even I find it difficult to answer these questions.

The Daily Drucker is intended to provide an answer. It presents in organized form—and directly from my own writings—a key statement of mine, followed by a few lines, also from my own works, of comment and explanation, on topics ranging across a great many fields of my work: management, business, and the world economy; a changing society; innovation and entrepreneurship; decision making; the changing workforce; the nonprofits and their management; and so on.

But the most important part of this book is the blank spaces at the bottom of its pages. They are what the readers will contribute, their actions, decisions and the results of these decisions. *For this is an action book.*

This book owes everything to my longtime friend and colleague, Professor Joseph A. Maciariello. It was his idea to bring together in one volume the best excerpts from my writings. He then selected both the appropriate quotes and the commentaries on them from my books, scripts, and articles. The result is a truly comprehensive guide to executive effectiveness. My readers and I owe a very great debt of gratitude to Professor Maciariello.

PETER F. DRUCKER
Claremont, California
Summer 2004

INTRODUCTION

In putting together *The Daily Drucker*, I have tried to distill and synthesize the "tapestry" that Peter Drucker has woven and continues to weave. I have done this by constructing 366 readings, each addressing a major topic, one for every day of the year, including February 29. Each reading starts with a topic and a "Drucker Proverb" or other quote capturing the essence of the topic. These proverbs, wise sayings, and quotes are mnemonic constructs that remind one of the teaching on each topic. Then follows a teaching taken directly from the works of Peter Drucker. Next comes the action step, where you are asked to "act on" the teaching and apply it to yourself and your organization.

After each reading, the original source or sources from which the reading was excerpted are cited as references. Unless indicated otherwise, the page references provided in "Sources by Day" refer to the latest edition of each book. The status of each reference is contained in the "Annotated Bibliography," at the end of the book. Most Drucker books referenced are in print, especially those referred to most often. If you wish to go deeper into a specific topic, you may.

One word of advice: Look for "the future that has already happened." If you can identify and act upon trends that are just now emerging, you will carry forward in practice the Drucker Tradition.

I have many times listened to Peter Drucker address executives, and I have on a few occasions seen him in action as a consultant. In his teaching and consulting he has impressed me most by the consistency and effectiveness of the approach he uses. First, he always makes sure he has defined the problem correctly. Next, he seems to weave a tapestry, bringing his vast knowledge to bear upon the specific problem, and putting in "stitches," or specific portions of the solution to the problem. Finally, once the problem has been circumscribed and the tapestry woven, he outlines the specific actions that should be taken to solve the problem. He then tells his audiences, "Don't tell me you enjoyed this; tell me what you will do differently on Monday morning."

While his approach is consistent, any single Drucker book or article is different. By the time Peter Drucker has worked through the many drafts, out comes a systematic and insightful discussion of a major topic "in society" or "in management." But, if one studies his many writings completed over the past sixty-five years, the same tapestry that I refer to as "The Tapestry of Drucker on Society and Management" is seen.

Since graduating from college in 1962, I have been studying and using Drucker's work. Even so, distilling and synthesizing Drucker's work and giving thought to appropriate Action Points for each reading has been a transformative experience for me. It is my wish that the book also will be transformative for you.

I am profoundly grateful to Peter Drucker for offering me an opportunity of a lifetime and for his advice and friendship over the years. Stephen Hanselman and Leah Spiro of HarperCollins have helped to turn this opportunity into a reality. Steve had the idea for *The Daily Drucker.* Leah Spiro provided detailed advice and support in writing the book. I am especially grateful for the help Leah provided in reviewing each reading and helping to draft the Action Points. Ceci Hunt copyedited the manuscript. I am grateful both for her skill and hard work. I also owe a debt of gratitude to Diane Aronson, copy chief, and to Knox Huston of HarperCollins for their help in preparing this book.

In addition to the help provided by HarperCollins, I am grateful to Dean de Kluyver of the Peter F. Drucker and Masatoshi Ito Graduate School of Management and to Claremont Graduate University for the sabbatical leave that allowed me to concentrate my time exclusively on this project for most of the year. Antonina Antonova served as my research assistant and Bernadette Lambeth as my assistant during this period. Diane Wallace, of the Peter F. Drucker Archive, assisted me in preparing the Annotated Bibliography. I am grateful to Antonina, Bernadette, and Diane for their help.

Finally, my wife, Judy, relieved me of all other responsibilities during this time and assisted me at every turn. It is hard to imagine a more loving wife.

JOSEPH A. MACIARIELLO
Claremont, California
Summer 2004

CONTENTS

January

1 ◈ Integrity in Leadership
2 ◈ Identifying the Future
3 ◈ Management Is Indispensable
4 ◈ Organizational Inertia
5 ◈ Abandonment
6 ◈ Practice of Abandonment
7 ◈ Knowledge Workers: Asset Not Cost
8 ◈ Autonomy in Knowledge Work
9 ◈ The New Corporation's Persona
10 ◈ Management as the Alternative to Tyranny
11 ◈ Management and Theology
12 ◈ Practice Comes First
13 ◈ Management and the Liberal Arts
14 ◈ The Managerial Attitude
15 ◈ The Spirit of an Organization
16 ◈ The Function of Management Is to Produce Results
17 ◈ Management: The Central Social Function
18 ◈ Society of Performing Organizations
19 ◈ The Purpose of Society
20 ◈ Nature of Man and Society
21 ◈ Profit's Function
22 ◈ Economics as a Social Dimension
23 ◈ Private Virtue and the Commonweal
24 ◈ Feedback: Key to Continuous Learning
25 ◈ Reinvent Yourself
26 ◈ A Social Ecologist
27 ◈ The Discipline of Management
28 ◈ Controlled Experiment in Mismanagement
29 ◈ Performance: The Test of Management
30 ◈ Terrorism and Basic Trends
31 ◈ A Functioning Society

Integrity in Leadership

The spirit of an organization is created from the top.

The proof of the sincerity and seriousness of a management is uncompromising emphasis on integrity of character. This, above all, has to be symbolized in management's "people" decisions. For it is character through which leadership is exercised; it is character that sets the example and is imitated. Character is not something one can fool people about. The people with whom a person works, and especially subordinates, know in a few weeks whether he or she has integrity or not. They may forgive a person for a great deal: incompetence, ignorance, insecurity, or bad manners. But they will not forgive a lack of integrity in that person. Nor will they forgive higher management for choosing him.

This is particularly true of the people at the head of an enterprise. For the spirit of an organization is created from the top. If an organization is great in spirit, it is because the spirit of its top people is great. If it decays, it does so because the top rots; as the proverb has it, "Trees die from the top." No one should ever be appointed to a senior position unless top management is willing to have his or her character serve as the model for subordinates.

ACTION POINT: Evaluate the character of the CEO and top management when considering a job offer. Align yourself with people who have integrity.

Management: Tasks, Responsibilities, Practices

Identifying the Future

The important thing is to identify the "future that has already happened."

Futurists always measure their batting average by counting how many things they have predicted that have come true. They never count how many important things come true that they did not predict. Everything a forecaster predicts may come to pass. Yet, he may not have seen the most meaningful of the emergent realities or, worse still, may not have paid attention to them. There is no way to avoid this irrelevancy in forecasting, for the important and distinctive are always the result of changes in values, perception, and goals, that is, in things that one can divine but not forecast.

But the most important work of the executive is to identify the changes that have already happened. The important challenge in society, economics, politics, is to exploit the changes that have already occurred and to use them as opportunities. The important thing is to identify the "future that has already happened"—and to develop a methodology for perceiving and analyzing these changes. A good deal of this methodology is incorporated in my 1985 book *Innovation and Entrepreneurship*, which shows how one systematically looks to the changes in society, in demographics, in meaning, in science and technology, as opportunities to make the future.

ACTION POINT: Identify the major trends in your market that have already appeared. Write a page on their likely longevity and impact on your life and organization.

The Ecological Vision
The Age of Discontinuity

Management Is Indispensable

Whoever makes two blades of grass grow where only one grew before deserves better of mankind than any speculative philosopher or metaphysical system builder.

Management will remain a basic and dominant institution perhaps as long as Western civilization itself survives. For management is not only grounded in the nature of the modern industrial system and in the needs of modern business enterprise, to which an industrial system must entrust its productive resources, both human and material. Management also expresses the basic beliefs of modern Western society. It expresses the belief in the possibility of controlling man's livelihood through the systematic organization of economic resources. It expresses the belief that economic change can be made into the most powerful engine for human betterment and social justice—that, as Jonathan Swift first overstated it three hundred years ago, whoever makes two blades of grass grow where only one grew before deserves better of mankind than any speculative philosopher or metaphysical system builder.

Management—which is the organ of society specifically charged with making resources productive, that is, with the responsibility for organized economic advance—therefore reflects the basic spirit of the modern age. It is, in fact, indispensable, and this explains why, once begotten, it grew so fast and with so little opposition.

ACTION POINT: Come up with a few examples of why management, its competence, its integrity, and its performance, is so decisive to the free world.

The Practice of Management

Organizational Inertia

All organizations need a discipline that makes them face up to reality.

All organizations need to know that virtually no program or activity will perform effectively for a long time without modification and redesign. Eventually every activity becomes obsolete. Among organizations that ignore this fact, the worst offender is government. Indeed, the inability to stop doing anything is the central disease of government and a major reason why government today is sick. Hospitals and universities are only a little better than government in getting rid of yesterday.

Businessmen are just as sentimental about yesterday as bureaucrats. They are just as likely to respond to the failure of a product or program by doubling the efforts invested in it. But they are, fortunately, unable to indulge freely in their predilections. They stand under an objective discipline, the discipline of the market. They have an objective outside measurement, profitability. And so they are forced to slough off the unsuccessful and unproductive sooner or later. In other organizations—government, hospitals, the military, and so on—economics is only a restraint.

All organizations must be capable of change. We need concepts and measurements that give to other kinds of organizations what the market test and profitability yardstick give to business. Those tests and yardsticks will be quite different.

ACTION POINT: Make sure your nonprofit organization has rigorous tests and yardsticks to measure performance.

The Age of Discontinuity

Abandonment

There is nothing as difficult and as expensive, but also nothing as futile, as trying to keep a corpse from stinking.

Effective executives know that they have to get many things done effectively. Therefore, they concentrate. And the first rule for the concentration of executive efforts is to slough off the past that has ceased to be productive. The first-class resources, especially those scarce resources of human strength, are immediately pulled out and put to work on the opportunities of tomorrow. If leaders are unable to slough off yesterday, to abandon yesterday, they simply will not be able to create tomorrow.

Without systematic and purposeful abandonment, an organization will be overtaken by events. It will squander its best resources on things it should never have been doing or should no longer do. As a result, it will lack the resources, especially capable people, needed to exploit the opportunities that arise. Far too few businesses are willing to slough off yesterday, and as a result, far too few have resources available for tomorrow.

ACTION POINT: Stop squandering resources on obsolete businesses and free up your capable people to take advantage of new opportunities.

The Effective Executive
Managing in Turbulent Times
Managing in a Time of Great Change
Management Challenges for the 21st Century

Practice of Abandonment

If we did not do this already, would we go into it now?

The question has to be asked—and asked seriously—"If we did not do this already, would we, knowing what we know, go into it now?" If the answer is no, the reaction must be "What do we do now?"

In three cases the right action is always outright abandonment. Abandonment is the right action if a product, service, market, or process "still has a few years of life." It is these dying products, services, or processes that always demand the greatest care and the greatest efforts. They tie down the most productive and ablest people. But equally, a product, service, market, or process should be abandoned if the only argument for keeping it is "It is fully written off." For *management* purposes there are no "cost-less assets." There are only "sunk costs." The third case where abandonment is the right policy—and the most important one—is the one where, for the sake of maintaining the old or declining product, service, market, or process the *new* and growing product, service, or process is being stunted or neglected.

ACTION POINT: Ask the questions posed above and if the answer is no, make the tough choice to abandon a cherished business.

Management Challenges for the 21st Century

Knowledge Workers: Asset Not Cost

Management's duty is to preserve the assets of the institution in its care.

Knowledge workers own the means of production. It is the knowledge between their ears. And it is a totally portable and enormous capital asset. Because knowledge workers own their means of production, they are mobile. Manual workers need the job much more than the job needs them. It may still not be true for all knowledge workers that the organization needs them more than they need the organization. But for most of them it is a symbiotic relationship in which the two need each other in equal measure.

Management's duty is to preserve the assets of the institution in its care. What does this mean when the knowledge of the individual knowledge worker becomes an asset and, in more and more cases, the *main* asset of an institution? What does this mean for personnel policy? What is needed to attract and to hold the highest-producing knowledge workers? What is needed to increase their productivity and to convert their increased productivity into performance capacity for the organization?

ACTION POINT: Attract and hold the highest-producing knowledge workers by treating them and their knowledge as the organization's most valuable assets.

Management Challenges for the 21st Century

Autonomy in Knowledge Work

Knowledge work requires both autonomy and accountability.

Demanding of knowledge workers that they define their own task and its results is necessary because knowledge workers must be autonomous. As knowledge varies among different people, even in the same field, each knowledge worker carries his or her own unique set of knowledge. With this specialized, unique knowledge, each worker should know more about his or her specific area than anyone else in the organization. Indeed, knowledge workers *must* know more about their areas than anyone else; they are paid to be knowledgeable in their fields. What this means is that once each knowledge worker has defined his or her own task and once the work has been appropriately restructured, each worker should be expected to work out his or her own course and to take responsibility for it. Knowledge workers should be asked to think through their own work plans and then to submit them. *What am I going to focus on? What results can be expected for which I should be held accountable? By what deadline?* Knowledge work requires both *autonomy* and *accountability*.

ACTION POINT: Write a work plan that includes your focus, desired results, and deadline. Submit it to your boss.

Management Challenges for the 21st Century
Knowledge Worker Productivity (Corpedia Online Program)

The New Corporation's Persona

In the Next Society's corporation, top management will be the company. Everything else can be outsourced.

Increasingly, in the Next Society's corporation, top management will, in fact, be the company. This top management's responsibilities will cover the entire organization's direction, planning, strategy, values, and principles; its structure and relationships between its various members; its alliances, partnerships, and joint ventures; and its research, design, and innovation.

Establishing a new corporate persona calls for a change in the corporation's values. And that may well be the most important task for top management. In the half century after the Second World War, the business corporation has brilliantly proven itself as an economic organization, as a creator of wealth and jobs. In the Next Society, the biggest challenge for the large company and especially for the multinational may be its social legitimacy—its values, its mission, its vision. Everything else can be outsourced.

ACTION POINT: Focus on your organization's values, mission, and vision, and consider outsourcing everything else.

Managing in the Next Society
The Next Society (Corpedia Online Program)

Management as the Alternative to Tyranny

The alternative to autonomous institutions that function and perform is not freedom. It is totalitarian tyranny.

If the institutions of our pluralist society of institutions do not perform in responsible autonomy, we will not have individualism and a society in which there is a chance for people to fulfill themselves. We will, instead, impose on ourselves complete regimentation in which no one will be allowed autonomy. We will have Stalinism rather than participatory democracy, let alone the joyful spontaneity of doing one's own thing. Tyranny is the only alternative to strong, performing autonomous institutions.

Tyranny substitutes one absolute boss for the pluralism of competing institutions. It substitutes terror for responsibility. It does indeed do away with the institutions, but only by submerging all of them in the one all-embracing bureaucracy of the *apparat*. It does produce goods and services, though only fitfully, wastefully, at a low level, and at an enormous cost in suffering, humiliation, and frustration. To make our institutions perform responsibly, autonomously, and on a high level of achievement is thus the only safeguard of freedom and dignity in the pluralist society of institutions. Performing, responsible management is the alternative to tyranny and our only protection against it.

ACTION POINT: What steps can you and others take now to improve the performance of the institution for which you are responsible?

Management: Tasks, Responsibilities, Practices

Management and Theology

Management always deals with the nature of Man, and with Good and Evil.

Management always lives, works, and practices in and for an institution, which is a human community held together by a bond: the work bond. And precisely because the object of management is a human community held together by the work bond for a common purpose, management always deals with the nature of Man and (as all of us with any practical experience have learned) with Good and Evil, as well. I have learned more theology as a practicing management consultant than when I taught religion.

ACTION POINT: Do you have any colleagues who are truly evil? Is there anything you can do about it?

"Teaching the Work of Management," *New Management*

Practice Comes First

Decision makers need to factor into their present decisions the "future that has already happened."

Decision makers—in government, in the universities, in business, in the labor unions, in churches—need to factor into their present decisions the *future that has already happened.* For this they need to know what events have already occurred that do not fit into their present-day assumptions, and thereby create new realities.

Intellectuals and scholars tend to believe that ideas come first, which then lead to new political, social, economic, psychological realities. This does happen, but it is the exception. As a rule, theory does not precede practice. Its role is to structure and codify already proven practice. Its role is to convert the isolated and "atypical" from exception to "rule" and "system," and therefore into something that can be learned and taught and, above all, into something that can be generally applied.

ACTION POINT: Are the premises that you base your decisions on obsolete? Do you need a new intellectual framework to win in the market, as it exists today?

The New Realities

Management and the Liberal Arts

Management is a liberal art.

Management is what tradition used to call a liberal art—"liberal" because it deals with the fundamentals of knowledge, self-knowledge, wisdom, and leadership; "art" because it deals with practice and application. Managers draw upon all of the knowledges and insights of the humanities and social sciences—on psychology and philosophy, on economics and history, on the physical sciences and ethics. But they have to focus this knowledge on effectiveness and results—on healing a sick patient, teaching a student, building a bridge, designing and selling a "user-friendly" software program.

ACTION POINT: What is your plan to develop yourself in the humanities and social sciences? Develop such a plan today.

The New Realities

The Managerial Attitude

The demands for a "managerial attitude" on the part of even the lowliest worker is an innovation.

No part of the productive resources of industry operates at a lower efficiency than the human resources. The few enterprises that have been able to tap this unused reservoir of human ability and attitude have achieved spectacular increases in productivity and output. In the better use of human resources lies the major opportunity for increasing productivity in the great majority of enterprises—so that the management of people should be the first and foremost concern of operating managements, rather than the management of things and techniques, on which attention has been focused so far.

We also know what makes for the efficiency and productivity of the human resources of production. It is not primarily skill or pay; it is, first and foremost, an attitude—the one we call the "managerial attitude." By this we mean an attitude that makes the individual see his job, his work, and his product the way a manager sees them, that is, in relation to the group and the product as a whole.

ACTION POINT: What actions can you take now to impart a sense of managerial responsibility into your workforce?

The New Society

The Spirit of an Organization

"It's the abilities, not the disabilities, that count."

Two sayings sum up the "spirit of an organization." One is the inscription on Andrew Carnegie's tombstone:

Here lies a man
Who knew how to enlist
In his service
Better men than himself

The other is the slogan of the drive to find jobs for the physically handicapped: "It's the abilities, not the disabilities, that count." A good example was President Franklin D. Roosevelt's confidential adviser in World War II, Harry Hopkins. A dying, almost a dead man for whom every step was torment, he could work only a few hours every other day or so. This forced him to cut out everything but truly vital matters. He did not lose effectiveness thereby; on the contrary, he became as Churchill called him once, "Lord Heart of the Matter" and accomplished more than anyone else in wartime Washington. Roosevelt broke every rule in the book to enable the dying Harry Hopkins to make his unique contribution.

ACTION POINT: Figure out what each of your employees' or colleagues' strengths are and develop these strengths to help people perform better.

The Practice of Management
The Effective Executive

The Function of Management Is to Produce Results

Above all management is responsible for producing results.

Management has to give direction to the institution it manages. It has to think through the institution's mission, has to set its objectives, and has to organize resources for the results the institution has to contribute. Management is, indeed, J. B. Say's "entrepreneur" and responsible for directing vision and resources toward greatest results and contributions.

In performing these essential functions, management everywhere faces the same problems. It has to organize work for productivity; it has to lead the worker toward productivity *and* achievement. It is responsible for the social impact of its enterprise. Above all, it is responsible for producing the results—whether economic performance, student learning, or patient care—for the sake of which each institution exists.

ACTION POINT: Is your organization delivering the results it should? If not, articulate your mission.

Management: Tasks, Responsibilities, Practices

Management: The Central Social Function

Noneconomic institutions need a yardstick that does for them what profitability does for business.

Nonbusiness institutions flock in increasing numbers to business management to learn from it how to manage themselves. The hospital, the armed service, the Catholic diocese, the civil service—all want to go to school for business management.

This does not mean that business management can be transferred to other, nonbusiness institutions. On the contrary, the first thing these institutions have to learn from business management is that management begins with the setting of objectives and that, therefore, noneconomic institutions, such as a university or a hospital, will also need very different management from that of a business. But these institutions are right in seeing business management as the prototype. Business, far from being exceptional, is simply the first of the species and the one we have studied the most intensively. Noneconomic institutions need a yardstick that does for them what profitability does for the business. "Profitability," in other words, rather than being the "exception" and distinct from "human" or "social" needs, emerges, in the pluralist society of organizations, as the prototype of the measurement needed by every institution in order to be managed and manageable.

ACTION POINT: What is the most important nonbusiness institution with which you are associated? Does it use a specific yardstick to assess performance? How successful is the organization?

The Ecological Vision

Society of Performing Organizations

"By their fruits ye shall know them."

Society in all developed countries has become *a society of organizations* in which most, if not all, social tasks are being done in and by an organization. Organizations do not exist for their own sake. They are means: each society's organ for the discharge of one social task. The organization's goal is a specific contribution to individual and society. The test of its performance, unlike that of a biological organism, therefore, always lies outside itself. This means that we must know what "performance" means for this or that institution.

Each institution will be the stronger the more clearly it defines its objectives. It will be more effective the more yardsticks and measurements there are against which its performance can be appraised. It will be more legitimate the more strictly it bases authority on justification by performance. "By their fruits ye shall know them"—this might well be the fundamental constitutional principle of the new pluralist society of institutions.

ACTION POINT: Are your performance yardsticks appropriate to your objectives?

Post-Capitalist Society
The Age of Discontinuity

The Purpose of Society

Society is only meaningful if its purpose and ideals make sense in terms of the individual's purposes and ideals.

For the individual there is no society unless he has social status and function. There must be a definite functional relationship between individual life and group life. For the individual without function and status, society is irrational, incalculable, and shapeless. The "rootless" individual, the outcast—for absence of social function and status casts a man from the society of his fellows—sees no society. He sees only demoniac forces, half sensible, half meaningless, half in light and half in darkness, but never predictable. They decide about his life and his livelihood without the possibility of interference on his part, indeed without the possibility of his understanding them. He is like a blindfolded man in a strange room playing a game of which he does not know the rules.

ACTION POINT: Make time to reach out to a "rootless" person who may be unemployed or retired. Drop them a note of support or take them out to lunch.

The Future of Industrial Man

Nature of Man and Society

Every organized society is built upon a concept of the nature of man and of his function and place in society.

Whatever its truth as a picture of human nature, this concept always gives a true picture of the nature of the society, which recognizes and identifies itself with it. It symbolizes the fundamental tenets and beliefs of society by showing the sphere of human activity, which it regards as socially decisive and supreme. The concept of man as "economic animal" is the true symbol of societies of bourgeois capitalism and of Marxist socialism, which see in the free exercise of man's economic activity the means toward the realization of their aims. Economic satisfactions alone appear socially important and relevant. Economic positions, economic privileges, and economic rights are those for which man works.

ACTION POINT: What is the socially supreme sphere in the U.S.? How does this affect you?

The End of the Economic Man

Profit's Function

Today's profitable business will become tomorrow's white elephant.

Joseph Schumpeter insisted that innovation is the very essence of economics and most certainly of a modern economy. Schumpeter's *Theory of Economic Development* makes profit fulfill an economic function. In the economy of change and innovation, a profit, in contrast to Karl Marx's theory, is not a "surplus value" stolen from the workers. On the contrary, it is the only source of jobs for workers and of labor income. The theory of economic development shows that no one except the innovator makes a genuine "profit"; and the innovator's profit is always quite short-lived.

But innovation, in Schumpeter's famous phrase, is also "creative destruction." It makes obsolete yesterday's capital equipment and capital investment. The more an economy progresses, the more capital formation will it therefore need. Thus, what the classical economist—or the accountant or the stock exchange—considers "profit" is a genuine cost, the cost of staying in business, the cost of a future in which nothing is predictable except that today's profitable business will become tomorrow's white elephant.

ACTION POINT: Insure that you are investing enough in innovation to prepare for the day when your profitable business becomes obsolete.

The Ecological Vision

Economics as a Social Dimension

Keynes was interested in the behavior of commodities, while I was interested in the behavior of people.

I do not accept the basic premise on which economics as a discipline is based and without which it cannot be sustained. I do not accept that the economic sphere is an independent sphere, let alone that it is the dominant one. It is surely an important sphere. And as Bertolt Brecht said, "first comes the belly and then morality"—and filling the belly is what economics is all about in the main. I not only am willing but insist that in all political and social decisions the economic costs are calculated and taken into account. To talk only of "benefits," I consider irresponsible and bound to lead to disaster. And I believe in free markets, having seen far too much of the alternative.

But still, for me the economic sphere is *one* sphere rather than *the* sphere. Economic considerations are restraints rather than overriding determinants. Economic wants and economic satisfactions are important but not absolutes. Above all, economic activities, economic institutions, economic rationality, are means to noneconomic (that is, human or social) ends rather than ends in themselves. And this means that I do not see economics as an autonomous "science." In short, it means that I am not an economist—something I have known since, in 1934 as a young economist in a London merchant bank, I sat in the John Maynard Keynes seminar in Cambridge. I suddenly realized that Keynes was interested in the behavior of commodities, while I was interested in the behavior of people.

ACTION POINT: Before you finalize a major budget or strategic decision, set aside half an hour to make sure you have really considered the impact it will have on your people in your organization and on your customers.

The Ecological Vision

Private Virtue and the Commonweal

In a moral society the public good must always rest on private virtue.

To make what is good for the country good for the enterprise requires hard work, great management skill, high standards of responsibility, and broad vision. It is a counsel of perfection. To carry it out completely would require the philosopher's stone that can translate the basest element into pure gold. But, if management is to remain a leading group, it must make this rule the lodestar of its conduct, must consciously strive to live up to it, and must actually do so with a fair degree of success. For in a good, a moral, a lasting society, the public good must always rest on private virtue. Every leading group must be able to claim that the public good determines its own interest. This assertion is the only legitimate basis for leadership; to make it a reality is the first duty of the leaders.

ACTION POINT: Make a list of three new products or services that have failed and will fail because you and your organization have ignored the public good.

The Practice of Management

Feedback: Key to Continuous Learning

To know one's strengths, to know how to improve them, and to know what one cannot do—are the keys to continuous learning.

Whenever a Jesuit priest or a Calvinist pastor does anything of significance (for instance, making a key decision), he is expected to write down what results he anticipates. Nine months later, he then feeds back from the actual results to these anticipations. This very soon shows him what he did well and what his strengths are. It also shows him what he has to learn and what habits he has to change. Finally it shows him what he is not gifted for and cannot do well. I have followed this method myself, now for fifty years. It brings out what one's strengths are—and this is the most important thing an individual can know about himself or herself. It brings out where improvement is needed and what kind of improvement is needed. Finally, it brings out what an individual cannot do and therefore should not even try to do. To know one's strengths, to know how to improve them, and to know what one cannot do—they are the keys to continuous learning.

ACTION POINT: List your strengths and the steps you are taking to improve them. Who knows you well enough to help identify your strengths?

Drucker on Asia

Reinvent Yourself

Knowledge people must take responsibility for their own development and placement.

In today's society and organizations, people work increasingly with knowledge, rather than with skill. Knowledge and skill differ in a fundamental characteristic—skills change very, very slowly. Knowledge, however, changes itself. It makes itself obsolete, and very rapidly. A knowledge worker becomes obsolescent if he or she does not go back to school every three or four years.

This not only means that the equipment of learning, of knowledge, of skill, of experience that one acquires early is not sufficient for our present *life* time and working time. People change over such a long time span. They become different persons with different needs, different abilities, different perspectives, and, therefore, with a need to "reinvent themselves." I quite intentionally use a stronger word than "revitalize." If you talk of fifty years of working life—and this, I think, is going to be increasingly the norm—you have to reinvent yourself. You have to make something different out of yourself, rather than just find a new supply of energy.

ACTION POINT: Ask those ahead of you in age how they went about "repotting themselves." What steps should you take now?

Drucker on Asia

A Social Ecologist

For me the tension between the need for continuity and the need for innovation and change was central to society and civilization.

I consider myself a "social ecologist," concerned with man's man-made environment the way the natural ecologist studies the biological environment. The term "social ecology" is my own coinage. But the discipline itself boasts an old and distinguished lineage. Its greatest document is Alexis de Tocqueville's *Democracy in America.* But no one is as close to me in temperament, concepts, and approach as the mid-Victorian Englishman Walter Bagehot. Living (as I have) in an age of great social change, Bagehot first saw the emergence of new institutions: civil service and cabinet government, as cores of a functioning democracy, and banking as the center of a functioning economy.

A hundred years after Bagehot, I was first to identify management as the new social institution of the emerging society of organizations and, a little later, to spot the emergence of knowledge as the new central resource, and knowledge workers as the new ruling class of a society that is not only "postindustrial" but postsocialist and, increasingly, postcapitalist. As it had been for Bagehot, for me too the tension between the need for continuity and the need for innovation and change was central to society and civilization. Thus, I know what Bagehot meant when he said that he saw himself sometimes as a liberal Conservative and sometimes as a conservative Liberal but never as a "conservative Conservative" or a "liberal Liberal."

ACTION POINT: Are you and your organization change agents? What steps can you take to both change and balance change with stability?

The Ecological Vision

The Discipline of Management

If you can't replicate something because you don't understand it, then it really hasn't been invented; it's only been done.

When I published *The Practice of Management*, fifty years ago, that book made it possible for people to learn how to manage, something that up until then only a few geniuses seemed to be able to do, and nobody could replicate it.

When I came into management, a lot of it had come out of the field of engineering. And a lot of it had come out of accounting. And some of it came out of psychology. And some more came out of labor relations. Each of those fields was considered separate, and each of them, by itself, was ineffectual. You can't do carpentry, you know, if you have only a saw, or only a hammer, or if you have never heard of a pair of pliers. It's when you put all of those tools into one kit that you invent. That's what I did in large part in *The Practice of Management*. I made a discipline of it.

ACTION POINT: Are your management practices ad hoc or systematic?

The Frontiers of Management

Controlled Experiment in Mismanagement

The story of Henry Ford, his rise and decline, and of the revival of his company is what one might call a controlled experiment in mismanagement.

The story of Henry Ford, his rise and decline, and of the revival of his company under his grandson, Henry Ford II, has been told many times. But it is not commonly realized that this dramatic story is far more than a story of personal success and failure. It is, above all, what one might call a controlled experiment in mismanagement.

The first Ford failed because of his firm conviction that a business did not need managers and management. All it needed, he believed, was the owner-entrepreneur with his "helpers." The only difference between Ford and most of his business contemporaries, in the U.S. as well as abroad, was that, as in everything else he did, Henry Ford stuck uncompromisingly to his convictions. The way he applied them—for example, by firing or sidelining any one of his "helpers," no matter how able, who dared act as a "manager," make a decision, or take action without orders from Ford—can only be described as a test of a hypothesis that ended up by fully disproving it. In fact, what makes the Ford story unique—but also important—is that Ford could test the hypothesis, in part because he lived so long and in part because he had a billion dollars to back his convictions. Ford's failure was not the result of personality or temperament but, first and foremost, the result of his refusal to accept managers and management as necessary and as grounded in task and function rather than in "delegation" from the "boss."

ACTION POINT: Are you an owner-executive who treats all your employees as your helpers? Are you an employee who is treated as a helper? List three ways your organization could be more profitable if employees were encouraged to assume responsibility.

Management: Tasks, Responsibilities, Practices

Performance: The Test of Management

Achievement rather than knowledge remains both the proof and aim of management.

The ultimate test of management is performance. Management, in other words, is a practice, rather than a science or profession, although containing elements of both. No greater damage could be done to our economy or to our society than to attempt to professionalize management by licensing managers, for instance, or by limiting access to management positions to people with a special academic degree. On the contrary, the test of good management is whether it enables the successful performer to do her work. And any serious attempt to make management "scientific" or a "profession" is bound to lead to the attempt to eliminate those "disturbing nuisances," the unpredictabilities of business life—its risks, its ups and downs, its "wasteful competition," the "irrational choices" of the consumer—and in the process, the economy's freedom and its ability to grow.

ACTION POINT: Which of your management practices have yielded good results? Which practices should you abandon now?

The Practice of Management

Terrorism and Basic Trends

Management of an institution has to be grounded in basic and predictable trends that persist regardless of today's headlines.

The terrorist attacks of September 2001 and America's response to them have profoundly changed world politics. We clearly face years of disorder, especially in the Middle East. Management of an institution—whether a business, a university, a hospital—has to be grounded in basic and predictable trends that persist regardless of today's headlines. It has to exploit these trends as opportunities. And these basic trends are the emergence of the Next Society and its new and unprecedented characteristics, especially

- the global shrinking of the youth population and the emergence of the "new workforce"
- the steady decline of manufacturing as a producer of wealth and jobs
- the changes in the form, the structure, and the function of the corporation and of its top management

In times of great and unpredictable surprises, even basing one's strategy and one's policies on these unchanging and basic trends does not automatically ensure success. But not to do so guarantees failure.

ACTION POINT: Write down three basic social trends that your business is based on. Are these trends still intact?

Managing in the Next Society

A Functioning Society

Unless power is legitimate there can be no social order.

A functioning society must always be capable of organizing the tangible reality of the social order. It must master the material world, make it meaningful and comprehensible for the individual, and it must establish legitimate social and political power.

No society can function unless it gives the individual member social status and function, and unless the decisive social power is legitimate power. The former establishes the basic frame of social life: the purpose and meaning of society. The latter shapes the space within the frame: it makes society concrete and creates its institutions. If the individual is not given social status and function, there can be no society but only a mass of social atoms flying through space without aim or purpose. And unless power is legitimate, there can be no social fabric; there is only a social vacuum held together by mere slavery or inertia.

ACTION POINT: What will the emerging government in Iraq have to do to become legitimate? What must a legitimate government do to create status and function for Iraqis?

A Functioning Society
The Future of Industrial Man

February

Crossing the Divide

Crossing the divide into the new realities.

Every few hundred years there occurs a sharp transformation. We cross a "divide." Within a few short decades, society rearranges itself—its worldview, its basic values, its social and political structure, its arts, its key institutions. Fifty years later, there is a new world. The people born after the transformation cannot even imagine the world in which their grandparents lived and into which their own parents were born.

But today's fundamental changes, these new realities visible thirty years ago, are actually only beginning and just about to have their full impacts. They underlie the worldwide restructuring of businesses, large and small—mergers, divestitures, alliances. They underlie the worldwide restructuring of the workforce—which, while largely an accomplished fact in the U.S., is still in its early stages in Japan and Europe. And they underlie the need for fundamental innovation in education and especially in higher education. These realities are different from the issues on which politicians, economists, scholars, businessmen, and union leaders still fix their attention, still write books, still make speeches.

ACTION POINT: Next time you hear colleagues pounding the table for something that is clearly yesterday's news, find a way to tell them they need to wake up and smell the coffee.

The New Realities
Post-Capitalist Society
The Age of Discontinuity

Face Reality

Exploit the new realities.

Today's new realities fit neither the assumptions of the Left nor those of the Right. They don't mesh at all with "what everybody knows." They differ even more from what everybody, regardless of political persuasion, still believes reality to be. "What is" differs totally from what both the Right and the Left believe "ought to be." The greatest and most dangerous turbulence today results from the collision between the delusions of the decision makers—whether in governments, in the top managements of businesses, or in union leadership—and the realities.

But a time of turbulence is also one of great opportunity for those who can understand, accept, and exploit the new realities. One constant theme is, therefore, the need for the decision maker in the individual enterprise to face up to reality and resist the temptation of what "everybody knows," the temptations of the certainties of yesterday, which are about to become the deleterious superstitions of tomorrow. To manage in turbulent times, therefore, means to face up to the new realities. It means starting with the question: "What is the world really like?" rather than with the assertions and assumptions that made sense only a few years ago.

ACTION POINT: List three new opportunities created by demographic shifts—changes in the composition of the population and workforce—and the shift from national to regional to transnational economies. Pursue them.

Managing in Turbulent Times

The Management Revolution

What matters is the productivity of nonmanual workers.

In 1881, an American, Frederick Winslow Taylor (1856–1915), first applied knowledge to the study of *work,* the analysis of work, and the engineering of work. This led to the *productivity revolution.* The Productivity Revolution has become a victim of its own success. From now on, what matters is the productivity of nonmanual workers. And that requires *applying knowledge to knowledge.*

But knowledge is now also being applied systematically and purposefully to define what new knowledge is needed, whether it is feasible, and what has to be done to make knowledge effective. It is being applied, in other words, to *systematic innovation.* This third change in the dynamics of knowledge can be called the Management Revolution. Supplying knowledge to find out how existing knowledge can best be applied to produce results is, in effect, what we mean by *management.*

ACTION POINT: What results are you being paid to achieve? List three tasks that you should eliminate to be productive.

Post-Capitalist Society

Knowledge and Technology

The new technology embraces and feeds off the entire array of human knowledges.

The search for knowledge, as well as the teaching thereof, has traditionally been dissociated from application. Both have been organized by subject, that is, according to what appeared to be the logic of knowledge itself. The faculties and departments of the university, its degrees, its specializations, indeed the entire organization of higher learning, have been subject-focused. They have been, to use the language of the experts on organization, based upon "product," rather than on "market" or "end use." Now we are increasingly organizing knowledge and the search for it around areas of application rather than around the subject areas of disciplines. Interdisciplinary work has grown everywhere.

This is a symptom of the shift in the meaning of knowledge from an end in itself to a resource, that is, a means to some result. Knowledge as the central energy of a modern society exists altogether in application and when it is put to work. Work, however, cannot be defined in terms of the disciplines. End results are interdisciplinary of necessity.

ACTION POINT: List results for which you are responsible. What specialists are you dependent on to get these results? How can you improve coordination among these specialists?

The Age of Discontinuity

Shrinking of the Younger Population

The next society will be with us shortly.

In the developed countries, the dominant factor in the next society will be something to which most people are only just beginning to pay attention: the rapid growth of the older population and the rapid shrinking of the younger generation. The shrinking of the younger population will cause an even greater upheaval than the growing number of older people, if only because nothing like this has happened since the dying centuries of the Roman Empire. In every single developed country, but also in China and Brazil, the birth rate is now well below the replacement rate of 2.2 live births per woman of reproductive age. Politically, this means that immigration will become an important—and highly divisive—issue in all rich countries. It will cut across all traditional political alignments.

Economically, the decline in the younger population will change markets in fundamental ways. Growth in family formation has been the driving force of all domestic markets in the developed world, but the rate of family formation is certain to fall steadily unless bolstered by large-scale immigration of younger people.

ACTION POINT: Determine whether your organization is betting on young people, older people, or immigrants. Make sure you have a plan for the gradual decrease in the youth market and the increase in newcomers and the aged.

Managing in the Next Society

The Transnational Company

Successful transnational companies see themselves as separate, nonnational entities.

Most companies doing international business today are still organized as traditional multinationals. But the transformation into transnational companies has begun, and it is moving fast. The products or services may be the same, but the structure is fundamentally different. In a transnational company there is only one economic unit, the world. Selling, servicing, public relations, and legal affairs are local. But parts, machines, planning, research, finance, marketing, pricing, and management are conducted in contemplation of the world market. One of America's leading engineering companies, for instance, makes one critical part for all its forty-three plants worldwide in one location outside of Antwerp, Belgium—and nothing else. It has organized product development for the entire world in three places and quality control in four. For this company, national boundaries have largely become irrelevant.

The transnational company is not totally beyond the control of national governments. It must adapt to them. But these adaptations are exceptions to policies and practices decided on for worldwide markets and technologies. Successful transnational companies see themselves as separate, nonnational entities. This self-perception is evidenced by something unthinkable a few decades ago: a transnational top management.

ACTION POINT: Ask the foreign technical-support center for your U.S.-purchased computer or printer a question about the operation of your equipment. How does the quality of this support compare with that of your local cable company?

"The Global Economy and the Nation-State," *Foreign Affairs, 75th Anniversary Edition*

The Educated Person

The educated person needs to bring knowledge to bear on the present, not to mention molding the future.

In his 1943 novel, published in English as *Magister Ludi* (1949), Hermann Hesse anticipated the sort of world the humanists want—and its failure. The book depicts a brotherhood of intellectuals, artists, and humanists who live a life of splendid isolation, dedicated to the Great Tradition, its wisdom and its beauty. But the hero, the most accomplished Master of the Brotherhood, decides in the end to return to the polluted, vulgar, turbulent, strife-torn, moneygrubbing reality—for his values are only fool's gold unless they have relevance to the world.

Postcapitalist society needs the educated person even more than any earlier society did, and access to the great heritage of the past will have to be an essential element. But liberal education must enable the person to understand reality and master it.

ACTION POINT: Read a book on politics, history, or anything that interests you. What did you learn? How can you put that knowledge to work?

Post-Capitalist Society

8 FEBRUARY

Balance Continuity and Change

Precisely because change is a constant, the foundations have to be extra strong.

The more an institution is organized to be a change leader, the more it will need to establish continuity internally and externally, the more it will need to balance rapid change and continuity. One way is to make partnership in change the basis of continuing relationships. Balancing change and continuity requires continuous work on information. Nothing disrupts continuity and corrupts relationships more than poor or unreliable information. It has to become routine for any enterprise to ask at any change, even the most minor one: "Who needs to be informed of this?" And this will become more and more important as more enterprises come to rely on people working together without actually working together—that is, on people using the new technologies of information. Above all, there is need for continuity in respect to the fundamentals of the enterprise: its mission, its values, its definition of performance and results.

Finally, the balance between change and continuity has to be built into compensation, recognition, and rewards. We will have to learn, similarly, that an organization will have to reward continuity—for instance, by considering people who deliver continuing improvement to be as valuable to the organization, and as deserving of recognition and reward, as the genuine innovator.

ACTION POINT: When you make a decision or a change, ask yourself, "Who needs to be informed of this?"

Management Challenges for the 21st Century

Organizations Destabilize Communities

In its culture, the organization always transcends the community.

Modern organizations have to operate in a community. Their results are in the community. Yet the organization cannot submerge itself in the community or subordinate itself to that community. Its "culture" has to *transcend* community. Companies on which local communities depend for employment close their factories or replace grizzled model-makers who have spent years learning their craft with twenty-five-year-old "whiz kids" who know computer simulation. Every one of such changes upsets the community. Every one is perceived as "unfair." Every one destabilizes.

It is the nature of the task that determines the culture of an organization, rather than the community in which that task is being performed. Each organization's value system is determined by its task. Every hospital, every school, every business, has to believe that what it is doing is an essential contribution on which all the others in the community depend in the last analysis. To perform its task successfully, it has to be organized and managed the same way. If an organization's culture clashes with the values of its community, the organization's culture will prevail—or else the organization will not be able to make its social contribution.

ACTION POINT: If Wal-Mart wishes to move into your neighborhood against the wishes of the neighborhood, what actions should Wal-Mart take? Under what conditions would it be wise for it to withdraw its move?

Post-Capitalist Society

Modern Organization Must Be a Destabilizer

Only a society in dynamic disequilibrium has stability and cohesion.

Society, community, and family are all conserving institutions. They try to maintain stability and to prevent, or at least to slow, change. And yet we also know that theories, values, and all the artifacts of human minds do age and rigidify, becoming obsolete, becoming afflictions.

Yet "revolutions" every generation, as was recommended by Thomas Jefferson, are not the solution. We know that "revolution" is not achievement and the new dawn. It results from senile decay, from the bankruptcy of ideas and institutions, from a failure of self-renewal. The only way in which an institution—whether a government, a university, a business, a labor union, an army—can maintain *continuity* is by building systematic, organized innovation into its very structure. Institutions, systems, policies, eventually outlive themselves, as do products, processes, and services. They do it when they accomplish their objectives, and they do it when they fail to accomplish their objectives. Innovation and entrepreneurship are thus needed in society as much as in the economy, in public service institutions as much as in business. The modern organization must be a destabilizer; it must be organized for innovation.

ACTION POINT: When is the last time you created or helped create a new product or service? Were you just copying a competitor, or did you actually hatch a fresh idea? Try again.

Managing in a Time of Great Change
The Ecological Vision
Innovation and Entrepreneurship

Human Factor in Management

Management is about human beings.

The task of management is to make people capable of joint performance, to make their strengths effective and their weaknesses irrelevant. This is what organization is all about, and it is the reason that management is the critical, determining factor.

Management must be built on communications and on individual responsibility. All members need to think through what they aim to accomplish—and make sure their associates know and understand that aim. All have to think through what they owe to others—and make sure that others understand. All have to think through what they, in turn, need from others—and make sure others know what is expected of them.

Management must enable the enterprise and each of its members to grow and to develop as needs and opportunities change.

ACTION POINT: Are you a great actor in a terrible play? What are you going to do about it?

The New Realities

Role of the Bystander

. . . the bystander sees things neither actor nor audience notices.

Bystanders have no history of their own. They are on the stage but are not part of the action. They are not even audience. The fortunes of the play and every actor in it depend on the audience, whereas the reaction of the bystander has no effect except on himself. But standing in the wings—much like the fireman in the theater—the bystander sees things neither actor nor audience notices. Above all, he sees differently from the way actors or audience see. Bystanders reflect, and reflection is a prism rather than a mirror; it refracts.

To watch and think for yourself is highly commendable. But "to shock people by shouting strange views from the rooftops is not." The admonition is well taken. But I have rarely heeded it.

ACTION POINT: Be a bystander to figure out what has to be done in your organization. Then act, but know you are running the risk of shocking people.

Adventures of a Bystander

The Nature of Freedom

Freedom is never a release and always a responsibility.

Freedom is not fun. It is not the same as individual happiness, nor is it security or peace or progress. It is a responsible choice. Freedom is not so much a right as a duty. Real freedom is not freedom from something; that would be license. It is freedom to choose between doing or not doing something, to act one way or another, to hold one belief or the opposite. It is not "fun" but the heaviest burden laid on man: to decide his own individual conduct as well as the conduct of society and to be responsible for both decisions.

ACTION POINT: List specific goals for your work. Think of goals that will meet your need for personal fulfillment, while also helping your boss meet his or her performance objectives. Sell these goals to your boss and keep the boss informed on your progress.

"The Freedom of Industrial Man," *The Virginia Quarterly Review*

Demands on Political Leadership

Beware charisma.

Charisma is "hot" today. There is an enormous amount of talk about it, and an enormous number of books are written on the charismatic leader. But, the desire for charisma is a political death wish. No century has seen more leaders with more charisma than the twentieth century, and never have political leaders done greater damage than the four giant leaders of the twentieth century: Stalin, Mussolini, Hitler, and Mao. What matters is not charisma. What matters is whether the leader leads in the right direction or misleads. The constructive achievements of the twentieth century were the work of completely uncharismatic people. The two military men who guided the Allies to victory in World War II were Dwight Eisenhower and George Marshall. Both were highly disciplined, highly competent, and deadly dull.

Perhaps the greatest cause for hope, for optimism is that to the new majority, the knowledge workers, the old politics make no sense at all. But proven competence does.

ACTION POINT: Seek out the most competent people in your organization, not necessarily those with the most charisma.

The New Realities

Salvation by Society

The end of the belief in salvation by society may even lead to a return to individual responsibility.

Surely the collapse of Marxism as a creed signifies the end of the belief in salvation by society. What will emerge next, we cannot know; we can only hope and pray. Perhaps nothing beyond stoic resignation? Perhaps a rebirth of traditional religion, addressing itself to the needs and challenges of the person in the knowledge society? The explosive growth of what I call "pastoral" Christian churches in America—Protestant, Catholic, nondenominational—might be a portent. But so might the resurgence of fundamentalist Islam. For the young people in the Muslim world who now so fervently embrace Islamic fundamentalism would, forty years ago, have been equally fervent Marxists. Or will there be new religions? Still, redemption, self-renewal, spiritual growth, goodness, and virtue—the "New Man," to use the traditional term—are likely to be seen again as existential rather than social goals or political prescriptions. The end of the belief in salvation by society surely marks an inward turning. It makes possible renewed emphasis on the individual, the person. It may even lead—at least we can so hope—to a return to individual responsibility.

ACTION POINT: The human resources department is not responsible for taking care of you; you are. Know what you are good at, make sure your results are equal to your expectations, and manage yourself. Continually ask yourself, "What should MY contribution be?"

Post-Capitalist Society

Need for a Harmony of Interests

The demand for harmony does not mean that society should abandon its right to limit the exercise of economic power on the part of the corporation.

Economic purpose does not mean that the corporation should be free from social obligations. On the contrary it should be so organized as to fulfill, automatically, its social obligations in the very act of seeking its own self-interest. An individual society based on the corporation can function only if the corporation contributes to social stability and to the achievement of social aims independent of the goodwill or the social consciousness of individual corporation managements.

At the same time, the demand for harmony does not mean that society should abandon its needs and aims and its right to limit the exercise of economic power on the part of the corporation. On the contrary, it is a vital function of rulership to set the frame within which institutions and individuals act. But, society must be organized so that there is no temptation to enact, in the name of social stability or social beliefs, measures that are inimical to the survival and stability of its representative institutions.

ACTION POINT: Until early in 2004 many well-known mutual funds permitted large customers to trade funds after the close of business, which gave these large customers the advantage of knowing the sell price at the time of sale, a benefit unavailable to the common shareholder. Send an e-mail to the chairman of a mutual fund in which you own shares and ask for proof that you were not harmed by this practice.

Concept of the Corporation

Social Purpose for Society

The absence of a basic social purpose for industrial society constitutes the core of our problem.

We already have given up the belief that economic progress is always and by necessity the highest goal. And once we have given up economic achievement as the highest value and have come to regard it as no more than one goal among many, we have, in effect, given up economic activity as the basis for social life. The abandonment of the economic as the socially constructive sphere has gone further. Western society has given up the belief that man is fundamentally Economic Man, that his motives are economic motives, and that his fulfillment lies in economic success and economic rewards.

We have to develop a free and functioning society on the basis of a new concept of man's nature and of the purpose and fulfillment of society. A basic ethical concept of social life must be developed. It lies in the philosophical or metaphysical field.

ACTION POINT: Define an organizational purpose that goes beyond next-quarter financial results and goes beyond maximization of shareholder wealth. Define a purpose that employees can believe in and challenges them to contribute their best work.

The Future of Industrial Man

Reinventing Government

Government has to regain a modicum of performance capacity.

Governments have become powerless against the onslaught of special-interest groups, have, indeed, become powerless to govern—to make decisions and to enforce them. The new tasks—protection of the environment, stamping out private armies and international terrorism, making arms control effective—all will require more rather than less government. But they will require a *different form* of government.

Government has to regain a modicum of performance capacity. It has to be *turned around.* To turn around any institution—whether a business, a labor union, a university, a hospital, or a government—always requires the same three steps:

1. Abandonment of the things that do not work, the things that have never worked, the things that have outlived their usefulness and their capacity to contribute.
2. Concentration on the things that do work, the things that produce results, the things that improve the organization's ability to perform.
3. Analysis of the half-successes, the half-failures.

A turnaround requires abandoning whatever does not perform and doing more of what does perform.

ACTION POINT: Can your business profit from government incompetence much like FedEx and UPS have profited from the shortcomings of the U.S. Postal Service? If you work for government, improve your effectiveness by concentrating on what works.

Post-Capitalist Society

Reprivatization

The strongest argument for private enterprise is the function of loss.

Reprivatization is a systematic policy of using the other, nongovernmental institutions of the society of organizations for the actual "doing," that is, the performance, operation, execution of tasks that flowed to government because the original private institution of society, the family, could not discharge them. What makes business especially appropriate for reprivatization is that, of all social institutions, it is predominately an organ of innovation. All other institutions were originally created to prevent, or at least to slow down, change. They become innovators only by necessity and most reluctantly.

Business has two advantages where government has a major weakness. Business can abandon an activity. Indeed, it is forced to do so if it operates in a market. What's more: of all institutions, business is the only one society will let disappear. The second strength of business: alone among all institutions, it has the test of performance. The consumer always asks: "And what will the product do for me tomorrow?" If the answer is "nothing," he will see its manufacturer disappear without the slightest regret. And so will the investor. The strongest argument for "private enterprise" is not the function of profit. The strongest argument is the function of loss. Because of it business is the most adaptable and the most flexible of the institutions around.

ACTION POINT: First prisons, now wars are being manned by private companies. Make a list of which sectors will privatize next and determine how you can benefit.

The Age of Discontinuity

Management and Economic Development

It can be said that there are no "underdeveloped countries." There are only "undermanaged" ones.

Management creates economic and social development. Economic and social development is the result of management. It can be said, without too much oversimplification, that there are no "underdeveloped countries." There are only "undermanaged" ones. Japan a hundred and forty years ago was an underdeveloped country by every material measurement. But it very quickly produced management of great competence, indeed, of excellence.

This means that management is the prime mover and that development is a consequence. All our experience in economic development proves this. Wherever we have only capital, we have not achieved development. In the few cases where we have been able to generate management energies, we have generated rapid development. Development, in other words, is a matter of human energies rather than of economic wealth. And the generation and direction of human energies is the task of management.

ACTION POINT: What impact does your company have in the developing world? Are your activities there raising the managerial standards of local companies?

The Ecological Vision

Failure of Central Planning

Any society in the era of the new technology would perish miserably were it to run the economy by central planning.

The new technology will greatly extend the management area; many people now considered rank-and-file will have to become capable of doing management work. And on all levels the demands on the manager's responsibility and competence, her vision, her capacity to choose between alternate risks, her economic knowledge and skill, her ability to manage managers and to manage worker and work, her competence in making decisions, will be greatly increased.

The new technology will demand the utmost in decentralization. Any society in the era of the new technology would perish miserably were it to attempt to get rid of free management of autonomous enterprise so as to run the economy by central planning. And so would any enterprise that attempted to centralize responsibility and decision making at the top. It would go under like the great reptiles of the saurian age who attempted to control a huge body by a small, centralized nervous system that could not adapt to rapid change in the environment.

ACTION POINT: Do you micromanage your employees? Start empowering them by making sure they are trained properly to do their jobs, and then give them responsibility to do it. Provide room for failure.

The Practice of Management

The Pork-Barrel State

Government becomes the master of civil society, able to mold and shape it.

Until World War I, no government in history was ever able to obtain from its people more than a very small fraction of the country's national income, perhaps 5 or 6 percent. As long as revenues were known to be limited, governments, whether democracies or absolute monarchies like that of the Russian czars, operated under extreme restraints. These restraints made it impossible for the government to act as either a social or an economic agency. But since World War I—and even more noticeably since World War II—the budgeting process has meant, in effect, saying yes to everything. Under the new dispensation, which assumes that there are no economic limits to the revenues it can obtain, government becomes the master of civil society, able to mold and shape it. Through the power of the purse, it can shape society in the politician's image. Worst of all, the fiscal state has become a "pork-barrel state."

The pork-barrel state thus increasingly undermines the foundations of a free society. The elected representatives fleece their constituents to enrich special-interest groups and thereby to buy their votes. This is a denial of the concept of citizenship—and is beginning to be seen as such.

ACTION POINT: Draft a ballot petition for a balanced-budget amendment in your city including a limit to annual increases in property taxes, like Proposition 13 in California. Then go to city council meetings and evaluate expenditures against budget limitations.

Post-Capitalist Society

The New Tasks of Government

The new tasks will require a different form of government.

The new tasks all will require more rather than less government. But they will require a different *form* of government. The greatest threat is damage to the human habitat. Second only to caring for the environment is the growing need for transnational action and institutions to abort the return of private armies and stamp out terrorism.

Terrorism is all the more threatening as very small groups can effectively hold even large countries to ransom. A nuclear bomb can easily be put into a locker or a postal box in any major city and exploded by remote control; so could a bacterial bomb, containing enough anthrax spores to kill thousands of people and to contaminate a big city's water supply, making it uninhabitable. What is needed to control the threat of terrorism is action that goes beyond any one sovereign state. The design of the necessary agencies is still ahead of us; so is the length of time it will take any of them to develop. It may well take major catastrophes to make national governments willing to accept subordination to such institutions and their decisions.

ACTION POINT: Get involved with industry-wide initiatives of importance to you and your company by partnering with multinational groups like the International Atomic Energy Agency, which fights nuclear terrorism.

Post-Capitalist Society

Legitimacy of the Corporation

Unless the power in the corporation can be organized on an accepted principle of legitimacy, it will disappear.

No social power can endure unless it is legitimate power. And no society can function unless it integrates the individual member. Unless the members of the industrial system are given the social status and function that they lack today, our society will disintegrate. The masses will not revolt; they will sink into lethargy; they will flee the responsibility of freedom, which without social meaning is nothing but a threat and a burden. We have only two alternatives: either to build a functioning industrial society or to see freedom itself disappear in anarchy and tyranny.

ACTION POINT: Decide whether it is worthwhile to you and your company to operate in parts of the world that are tyrannies or in anarchy, or if it is just too dangerous.

The Future of Industrial Man

Governance of the Corporation

What does capitalism mean when knowledge governs rather than money?

Within a fairly short period of time, we will face the problem of the governance of corporations again. We will have to redefine the purpose of the employing organization and of its management, to satisfy *both* the legal owners, such as shareholders, *and* the owners of the human capital that gives the organization its wealth-producing power, that is, the knowledge workers. For increasingly the ability of organizations to survive will come to depend on their "comparative advantage" in making the knowledge worker productive. And the ability to attract and hold the best of the knowledge workers is the first and most fundamental precondition.

What does capitalism mean when knowledge governs rather than money? And what do "free markets" mean when knowledge workers are the true assets? Knowledge workers can be neither bought nor sold. They do not come with a merger or an acquisition. It is certain that the emergence of the knowledge worker will bring about fundamental changes in the very structure and nature of the economic system.

ACTION POINT: What percentage of your workforce consists of people whose work requires advanced schooling? Tell these people you value their contributions and ask them to participate in decisions where their expertise is important. Make them feel like owners.

Management Challenges for the 21st Century

Balancing Three Corporate Dimensions

Shareholder sovereignty is bound to flounder. It is a fair-weather model.

An important task for top management in the next society's corporation will be to balance the three dimensions of the corporation: as an economic organization, as a human organization, and as an increasingly important social organization. Each of the three models of the corporation developed in the past half-century stressed one of these dimensions and subordinated the other two. The German model of the "social market economy" put the emphasis on the social dimension; the Japanese one, on the human dimension; and the American one, on the economic dimension.

None of the three is adequate on its own. The German model achieved both economic success and social stability, but at the price of high unemployment and dangerous labor-market rigidity. The Japanese model was strikingly successful for many years, but faltered at the first serious challenge; indeed, it was a major obstacle to recovery from Japan's recession of the 1990s. Shareholder sovereignty is also bound to flounder. It is a fair-weather model that works well only in times of prosperity. Obviously the enterprise can fulfill its human and social functions only if it prospers as a business. But now that knowledge workers are becoming the key employees, a company also needs to be a desirable employer to be successful.

ACTION POINT: Audit your organization's performance as an economic, human, and social entity. List five areas where it comes up short. Prepare a plan to correct these.

Managing in the Next Society

Defining Business Purpose and Mission

What is our business?

Nothing may seem simpler or more obvious than to know what a company's business is. A steel mill makes steel; a railroad runs trains to carry freight and passengers; an insurance company underwrites fire risks; a bank lends money. Actually, "What is our business?" is almost always a difficult question and the right answer is usually anything but obvious.

A business is not defined by the company's name, statutes, or articles of incorporation. It is defined by the want the customer satisfies when she buys a product or a service. To satisfy the customer is the mission and purpose of every business. The question "What is our business?" can, therefore, be answered only by looking at the business from the outside, from the point of view of the customer and the market. What the customer sees, thinks, believes, and wants, at any given time, must be accepted by management as an objective fact and must be taken as seriously as the reports of the salesperson, the tests of the engineer, or the figures of the accountant. And management must make a conscious effort to get answers from the customer herself rather than attempt to read her mind.

ACTION POINT: Talk to one customer every day this week. Ask them how they see your company, what they think of it, what kind of company they believe it is and what they want from it. Use this feedback to better define your company's mission.

Management: Tasks, Responsibilities, Practices

Defining Business Purpose and Mission: The Customer

Who is the customer?

"Who is the customer?" is the first and the crucial question in defining business purpose and business mission. It is not an easy, let alone an obvious question. How it is being answered determines, in large measure, how the business defines itself. The consumer—that is, the ultimate user of a product or a service—is always a customer.

Most businesses have at least two customers. Both have to buy if there is to be a sale. The manufacturers of branded consumer goods always have two customers at the very least: the housewife and the grocer. It does not do much good to have the housewife eager to buy if the grocer does not stock the brand. Conversely, it does not do much good to have the grocer display merchandise advantageously and give it shelf space if the housewife does not buy. To satisfy only one of these customers without satisfying the other means that there is no performance.

ACTION POINT: Take one product or service that you are responsible for and determine how many kinds of customers you have for it. Then figure out if you are satisfying all of your different kinds of customers, or if you are ignoring some category(ies) of customers.

Management: Tasks, Responsibilities, Practices

Understanding What the Customer Buys

What does the customer consider value?

The final question needed in order to come to grips with business purpose and business mission is: "What is value to the customer?" It may be the most important question. Yet it is the one least often asked. One reason is that managers are quite sure that they know the answer. Value is what they, in their business, define as quality. But this is almost always the wrong definition. The customer never buys a product. By definition the customer buys the satisfaction of a want. He buys value.

For the teenage girl, for instance, value in a shoe is high fashion. It has to be "in." Price is a secondary consideration and durability is not value at all. For the same girl as a young mother, a few years later, high fashion becomes a restraint. She will not buy something that is quite unfashionable. But what she looks for is durability, price, comfort and fit, and so on. The same shoe that represents the best buy for the teenager is a very poor value for her slightly older sister. What a company's different customers consider value is so complicated that it can be answered only by the customers themselves. Management should not even try to guess at the answers—it should always go to the customers in a systematic quest for them.

ACTION POINT: What do your customers consider most valuable about the product or service you provide? If you don't know, find out. If you do know, ask your customers if you are delivering.

Management: Tasks, Responsibilities, Practices

March

1 ◈ The Change Leader
2 ◈ Test of Innovation
3 ◈ Knowledge External to the Enterprise
4 ◈ In Innovation, Emphasize the Big Idea
5 ◈ Managing for the Future
6 ◈ Innovation and Risk Taking
7 ◈ Creating a True Whole
8 ◈ Turbulence: Threat or Opportunity?
9 ◈ Organize for Constant Change
10 ◈ Searching for Change
11 ◈ Piloting Change
12 ◈ The Purpose of a Business
13 ◈ Converting Strategic Plans to Action
14 ◈ Universal Entrepreneurial Disciplines
15 ◈ Managing for the Short Term and Long Term
16 ◈ Balancing Objectives and Measurements
17 ◈ The Purpose of Profit
18 ◈ Morality and Profits
19 ◈ Defining Corporate Performance
20 ◈ A Scorecard for Managers
21 ◈ Beyond the Information Revolution
22 ◈ Internet Technology and Education
23 ◈ The Great Strength of E-Commerce
24 ◈ E-Commerce: The Challenge
25 ◈ From Legal Fiction to Economic Reality
26 ◈ Management of the Multinational
27 ◈ Command or Partner
28 ◈ Information for Strategy
29 ◈ Why Management Science Fails to Perform
30 ◈ Nature of Complex Systems
31 ◈ From Analysis to Perception

1 MARCH

The Change Leader

The most effective way to manage change successfully is to create it.

One cannot manage change. One can only be ahead of it. In a period of upheavals, such as the one we are living in, change is the norm. To be sure, it is painful and risky, and above all it requires a great deal of very hard work. But unless it is seen as the task of the organization to *lead change,* the organization will not survive. In a period of rapid structural change, the only ones who survive are the *change leaders.* A change leader sees change as an opportunity. A change leader looks for change, knows how to find the right changes, and knows how to make them effective both outside the organization and inside it. To make the future is highly risky. It is less risky, however, than not to try to make it. A goodly proportion of those attempting to will surely not succeed. But predictably, no one else will.

ACTION POINT: Anticipate the future and be a change leader.

Management Challenges for the 21st Century
Managing in the Next Society

Test of Innovation

Measure innovations by what they contribute to market and customer.

The test of an innovation is whether it creates value. Innovation means the creation of new value and new satisfaction for the customer. A novelty only creates amusement. Yet, again and again, managements decide to innovate for no other reason than that they are bored with doing the same thing or making the same product day in and day out. The test of an innovation, as well as the test of "quality," is not "Do we like it?" It is "Do customers want it and will they pay for it?"

Organizations measure innovations not by their scientific or technological importance but by what they contribute to market and customer. They consider social innovation to be as important as technological innovation. Installment selling may have had a greater impact on economics and markets than most of the great scientific advances in this century.

ACTION POINT: Identify innovations in your organization that are novelties versus those that are creating value. Did you launch the novelties because you were bored with doing the same thing? If so, make sure your next new product or service meets your customers' needs.

The Frontiers of Management
Management Challenges for the 21st Century

Knowledge External to the Enterprise

The technologies that are likely to have the greatest impact on a company and an industry are technologies outside its own field.

Many changes that have transformed enterprises have originated outside the specific industry of that enterprise. Here are three notable examples. The zipper was originally invented to close bales of heavy goods, such as grain, particularly in seaports. Nobody thought of using it for clothing. The clothing industry did not think it could replace buttons. And the inventor never dreamed it would be successful in the clothing industry.

Commercial paper (that is, short-term notes originated by nonbank financial institutions) did not originate with banks, but had a tremendous negative impact on them. Under U.S. law, commercial paper is considered a security, which means that commercial banks cannot deal in it. Because financial services companies, such as Goldman Sachs, Merrill Lynch, GE Capital, and so on, discovered this, they have largely replaced commercial banks as the world's most important and leading financial institutions. Fiberglass cable, the invention that has revolutionized the telephone industry, did not come out of the great telephone research labs in the U.S., Japan, or Germany. It came, rather, from a glass company, Corning.

ACTION POINT: Identify at least one change that has originated outside your industry that either has transformed or has the potential to transform your enterprise. Look for ideas in other industries that can be used profitably in your industry.

Management Challenges for the 21st Century
From Data to Information Literacy (Corpedia Online Program)

In Innovation, Emphasize the Big Idea

Innovative ideas are like frogs' eggs: of a thousand hatched, only one or two survive to maturity.

The innovative organization understands that innovation starts with an idea. Ideas are somewhat like babies—they are born small, immature, and shapeless. They are promise rather than fulfillment. In the innovative organization executives do not say, "This is a damn-fool idea." Instead they ask, "What would be needed to make this embryonic, half-baked, foolish idea into something that makes sense, that is feasible, that is an opportunity for us?"

But an innovative organization also knows that the great majority of ideas will turn out not to make sense. Executives in innovative organizations therefore demand that people with ideas think through the work needed to turn an idea into a product, a process, a business, or a technology. They ask, "What work should we have to do and what would we have to find out and learn before we can commit the company to this idea of yours?" These executives know that it is as difficult and risky to convert a small idea into successful reality as it is to make a major innovation. They do not aim at "improvements" or "modifications" in products or technology. They aim at innovating a new business.

ACTION POINT: Make a list of your three best ideas. Then make a list of the key pieces of information you need to know and the major work that needs to be done before these ideas can blossom into a new business. Now pursue the best idea, or if none is practical, start again.

The Frontiers of Management

Managing for the Future

Prediction of future events is futile.

The starting point to *know the future* is the realization that there are two different, though complementary, approaches:

- Finding and exploiting the time lag between the appearance of a discontinuity in the economy and society and its full impact—one might call this *anticipation of a future that has already happened.*
- Imposing on the yet unborn future a new idea that tries to give direction and shape to what is to come. This one might call *making the future* happen.

The future that has already happened is not within the present business; it is outside: a change in society, knowledge, culture, industry, or economic structure. It is, moreover, a major trend, a break in the pattern rather than a variation within it. Looking for the future that has already happened and anticipating its impacts introduces new perception in the beholder. The need is to make oneself see it. What then could or should be done is usually not too difficult to discover. The opportunities are neither remote nor obscure. The pattern has to be recognized first.

Predicting the future can only get you in trouble. The task is to *manage* what is there and to work to create what could and should be.

ACTION POINT: Spot a discontinuity in the economy or society that has appeared and presents an opportunity for your enterprise. Determine how long it will take for this change to impact the business. Develop a business plan to cash in on this insight.

Managing for Results

Innovation and Risk Taking

Successful innovators are conservative.

I once attended a university symposium on entrepreneurship at which a number of psychologists spoke. Although their papers disagreed on everything else, they all talked about an "entrepreneurial personality," which was characterized by a "propensity for risk taking." A well-known and successful innovator and entrepreneur who had built a process-based innovation into a substantial worldwide business in the space of twenty-five years was then asked to comment. He said: "I find myself baffled by your papers. I think I know as many successful innovators and entrepreneurs as anyone, beginning with myself. I have never come across an 'entrepreneurial personality.' The successful ones I know all have, however, one thing—and only one thing—in common: they are *not* 'risk takers.' They try to define the risks they have to take and to minimize them as much as possible. Otherwise none of us could have succeeded."

This jibes with my own experience. I, too, know a good many successful entrepreneurs. Not one of them has a "propensity for risk taking." Most successful innovators in real life are colorless figures, and much more likely to spend hours on cash-flow projections than to dash off looking for "risks." They are not "risk-focused"; they are "opportunity-focused."

ACTION POINT: Determine which of your ideas presents the least risk and the most opportunity and focus on them.

Innovation and Entrepreneurship

Creating a True Whole

Create a true whole greater than the sum of its parts.

A manager has the task of creating a true whole that is larger than the sum of its parts. One analogy is the task of the conductor of a symphony orchestra, through whose effort, vision, and leadership individual instrumental parts become the living whole of a musical performance. But the conductor has the composer's score; he is only interpreter. The manager is both composer and conductor.

The task of creating a genuine whole also requires that the manager, in every one of her acts, consider simultaneously the performance and results of the enterprise as a whole and the diverse activities needed to achieve synchronized performance. It is here, perhaps, that the comparison with the orchestra conductor fits best. A conductor must always hear both the whole orchestra and, say, the second oboe. Similarly, a manager must always consider both the overall performance of the enterprise and, say, the market-research activity needed. By raising the performance of the whole, she creates scope and challenge for market research. By improving the performance of market research, she makes possible better overall business results. The manager must simultaneously ask two double-barreled questions: "What better business performance is needed and what does this require of what activities?" And "What better performances are the activities capable of and what improvement in business results will they make possible?"

ACTION POINT: Have you composed your symphony? Has your boss composed his or hers? Have you begun rehearsals with your players yet? Can you hear the second oboe? Are you ready for Carnegie Hall?

Management: Tasks, Responsibilities, Practices

Turbulence: Threat or Opportunity?

When it rains manna from heaven, some people put up an umbrella. Others reach for a big spoon.

The manager will have to look at her task and ask, "What must I do to be prepared for danger, for opportunities, and above all for change?" First, this is a time to make sure that your organization is lean and can move fast. So this is a time when one systematically abandons and sloughs off unjustifiable products and activities—and sees to it that the really important tasks are adequately supported. Second, she will have to work on the most expensive of resources—*time*—particularly in areas where it is people's *only* resource, as it is for highly paid, important groups such as research workers, technical service staffs, and all managers. And one must set goals for productivity improvement. Third, managers must learn to manage growth and to distinguish among kinds of growth. If productivity of your combined resources goes up with growth, it is healthy growth. Fourth, the development of people will be far more crucial in the years ahead.

ACTION POINT: Get rid of unjustifiable products and activities, set goals to improve productivity, manage growth, and develop your people.

The "How to" Drucker
Managing in Turbulent Times

Organize for Constant Change

Today's certainties always become tomorrow's absurdities.

One thing is certain for developed countries—and probably for the entire world—we face long years of profound changes. An organization must be organized for constant change. It will no longer be possible to consider entrepreneurial innovation as lying outside of management or even as peripheral to management. Entrepreneurial innovation will have to become the very heart and core of management. The organization's function *is* entrepreneurial, to *put knowledge to work*—on tools, products, and processes; on the design of work; on *knowledge itself*.

Deliberate emphasis on innovation may be needed most where technological changes are least spectacular. Everyone in a pharmaceutical company knows that the company's survival depends on its ability to replace three quarters of its products by entirely new ones every ten years. But how many people in an insurance company realize that the company's growth—perhaps even its survival—depends on the development of new forms of insurance? The less spectacular or prominent technological change is in a business, the greater the danger that the whole organization will ossify, and the more important, therefore, is the emphasis on innovation.

ACTION POINT: Are you and your organization in danger of ossification? Decide how you and your organization can systematically innovate, and build this into your management process.

Managing in a Time of Great Change
The Practice of Management
The Ecological Vision
Management Challenges for the 21st Century

Searching for Change

A change is something people do; a fad is something people talk about.

Entrepreneurs see change as the norm and as healthy. Usually they do not bring about the change themselves. But—and this defines *the entrepreneur and entrepreneurship—the entrepreneur always searches for change, responds to it, and exploits it as an opportunity.*

Look at every change, look out every window. And ask: "Could this be an opportunity?" "Is this new thing a genuine change or simply a fad?" The difference is very simple: A change is something people do, and a fad is something people talk about. An enormous amount of talk is a fad. You must also ask yourself if these transitions, these changes, are an opportunity or a threat. If you start out by looking at change as threat, you will never innovate. Don't dismiss something because this is not what you had planned. The unexpected is often the best source of innovation.

ACTION POINT: Take a half an hour to discuss with a colleague the changes sweeping your industry and identify the biggest genuine changes. Ignore the fads; figure out how to capitalize on the genuine changes.

Managing in the Next Society

Piloting Change

Neither studies nor market research nor computer modeling is a substitute for the test of reality.

Everything improved or new needs first to be tested on a small scale; that is, it needs to be piloted. The way to do this is to find somebody within the enterprise who really wants the new. Everything new gets into trouble. And then it needs a champion. It needs somebody who says, "I am going to make this succeed," and who then goes to work on it. And this person needs to be somebody whom the organization respects. This need not even be somebody within the organization.

Often a good way to pilot a new product or new service is to find a customer who really wants the new, and who is willing to work with the producer on making truly successful the new product or the new service. If the pilot test is successful—it finds the problems nobody anticipated but also finds the opportunities that nobody anticipated, whether in terms of design, of market, of service—the risk of change is usually quite small.

ACTION POINT: Make sure the best ideas in your organization have fierce advocates to see them through a test in the marketplace.

Management Challenges for the 21st Century

The Purpose of a Business

A business enterprise has two basic functions: marketing and innovation.

If we want to know what a business is, we have to start with its *purpose.* And the purpose must lie outside the business itself. In fact, it must lie in society, since a business enterprise is an organ of society. There is only one valid definition of business purpose: *to create a customer.* The customer is the foundation of a business and keeps it in existence. He alone gives employment. And it is to supply the customer that society entrusts wealth-producing resources to the business enterprise.

Because it is the purpose to create a customer, any business enterprise has two—and only two—basic functions: marketing and innovation. These are the entrepreneurial functions. Marketing is the distinguishing, the unique function of Business.

ACTION POINT: Find out what needs your customers want fulfilled today. Determine how well your products are meeting the needs of your customers.

The Practice of Management

Converting Strategic Plans to Action

The best plan is only good intentions unless it degenerates into work.

The distinction that marks a plan capable of producing results is the commitment of key people to work on specific tasks. Unless such commitment is made, there are only promises and hopes, but no plan. A plan needs to be tested by asking managers, "Which of your best people have you put on this work today?" The manager who comes back (as most of them do) and says, "But I can't spare my best people now. They have to finish what they are doing now before I can put them to work on tomorrow," is simply admitting that he does not have a plan.

Work implies accountability, a deadline, and finally, the measurement of results, that is, feedback from results on the work. What we measure and how we measure determine what will be considered relevant, and determine, thereby, not just what we see, but what we—and others—do.

ACTION POINT: Establish specific numerical criteria and goals to measure results. Set deadlines for yourself and your organization to achieve these results.

Management: Tasks, Responsibilities, Practices

Universal Entrepreneurial Disciplines

The entrepreneurial disciplines are not just desirable; they are conditions for survival today.

Every institution—and not only businesses—must build into its day-to-day management four entrepreneurial activities that run in parallel. One is organized abandonment of products, services, processes, markets, distribution channels, and so on that are no longer an optimal allocation of resources. Then any institution must organize for systematic, continuing improvement. Then it has to organize for systematic and continuous exploitation, especially of its successes. And finally, it has to organize systematic innovation, that is, create the different tomorrow that makes obsolete and, to a large extent, replaces even the most successful products of today in an organization. I emphasize that these disciplines are not just desirable; they are conditions for survival today.

ACTION POINT: Abandon what is about to be obsolete, develop a system to exploit your successes, and develop a systematic approach to innovation.

"Management's New Paradigms," *Forbes*
Management Challenges for the 21st Century
The Next Society (Corpedia Online Program)

Managing for the Short Term and Long Term

John Maynard Keynes's best-known saying is surely "In the long run we are all dead." It is a total fallacy that, as Keynes implies, optimizing the short term creates the right long-term future.

It is a value question whether a business should be run for short-term results or for "the long run." Financial analysts believe that businesses can be run for both, simultaneously. Successful businessmen know better. To be sure, everyone has to produce short-term results. But in any conflict between short-term results and long-term growth, one company decides in favor of long-term growth, and another company decides such a conflict in favor of short-term results. Again, this is not primarily a disagreement on economics. It is fundamentally a value conflict regarding the function of a business and the responsibility of management.

ACTION POINT: Does your organization sacrifice the long-term wealth-producing capacity of the enterprise to produce short-term results? Discuss how you can break out of this trap and still produce short-term profits.

The Ecological Vision
Management Challenges for the 21st Century

Balancing Objectives and Measurements

The traditional theorem of the maximization of profit has to be discarded.

To manage a business is to balance a variety of needs and goals. To emphasize only profit, misdirects managers to the point where they may endanger the survival of the business. To obtain profit today, they tend to undermine the future. They may push the most easily saleable product lines and slight those that are the market of tomorrow. They tend to short-change research, promotion, and other postponable investments. Above all, they shy away from any capital expenditure that may increase the investment capital base against which profits are measured; and the result is dangerous obsolescing of equipment. In other words, they are directed into the worst practices of management.

Objectives are needed in every area where performance and results directly and vitally affect the survival and prosperity of the business. There are eight areas in which performance and objectives have to be set: market standing, innovation, productivity, physical and financial resources, profitability, manager performance and development, worker performance and attitude, and public responsibility. Different key areas require different emphasis in different businesses—and different emphasis at different stages of the development of each business. But the areas are the same, whatever the business, whatever the economic conditions, whatever the business's size or stage of growth.

ACTION POINT: In addition to setting profit objectives, set objectives for your business in the following areas: market standing, innovation, productivity, physical and financial resources, profitability, manager performance and development, worker performance, and public responsibility.

The Practice of Management

The Purpose of Profit

Profit is the ultimate test of business performance.

Profit serves three purposes. One is it measures the net effectiveness and soundness of a business's efforts. Another is the "risk premium" that covers the costs of staying in business—replacement, obsolescence, market risk and uncertainty. Seen from this point of view, there is no such thing as "profit"; there are only "costs of being in business" and "costs of staying in business." And the task of a business is to provide adequately for these "costs of staying in business" by earning an adequate profit. Finally, profit ensures the supply of future capital for innovation and expansion, either directly, by providing the means of self-financing out of retained earnings, or indirectly, through providing sufficient inducement for new outside capital in the form in which it is best suited to the enterprise's objectives.

ACTION POINT: Decide to pull the plug on an unprofitable business if it is not covering the cost required to stay in business or providing enough capital for future growth.

The Practice of Management

Morality and Profits

Is there sufficient profit?

Joseph Schumpeter's "innovator," with his "creative destruction," is the only theory so far to explain why there is something we call "profit." The classical economists very well knew that their theory did not give any rationale for profit. Indeed, in the equilibrium economics of a closed economic system, there is no place for profit, no justification for it, no explanation of it. If profit is, however, a genuine cost, and especially if profit is the only way to maintain jobs and to create new ones, then capitalism becomes again a moral system.

The weakness on moral grounds of the profit incentive enabled Karl Marx at once to condemn the capitalist as wicked and immoral and assert "scientifically" that he serves no function. As soon, however, as one shifts from the axiom of an unchanging, self-contained, closed economy, what is called profit is no longer immoral. It becomes a moral imperative. Indeed the question then is no longer: "How can the economy be structured to minimize the bribe of the functionless surplus called profit that has to be handed over to the capitalist to keep the economy going?" The question in Schumpeter's economics is always: "Is there sufficient profit?" Is there adequate capital formation to provide for the costs of the future, the costs of staying in business, the costs of "creative destruction"?

ACTION POINT: Check to see if you are earning enough profit to cover the cost of capital and provide for innovation. If not, what are you going to do about it?

The Ecological Vision

Defining Corporate Performance

Maximize the wealth-producing capacity of the enterprise.

Ralph Cordiner, CEO of the General Electric Company from 1958 to 1963, asserted that top management in the large, publicly owned corporation was a "trustee." Cordiner argued that senior executives were responsible for managing the enterprise "in the best-balanced interest of shareholders, customers, employees, suppliers, and plant community cities." That is what we now call "stakeholders." Cordiner's answer still required a clear definition of results and of the meaning of "best" with respect to "balance." We no longer need to theorize about how to define performance and results in the large enterprise. We have successful examples.

Both the Germans and the Japanese have highly concentrated institutional ownership. How, then, do the institutional owners of German or Japanese industry define performance and results? Though they manage quite differently, they define them in the same way. Unlike Cordiner, they do not "balance" anything. They maximize. But they do not attempt to maximize shareholder value or the short-term interest of any one of the enterprise's "stakeholders." Rather, they maximize the wealth-producing capacity of the enterprise. It is this objective that integrates short-term and long-term results and that ties the operational dimensions of business performance—market standing, innovation, productivity, and people and their development—with financial needs and financial results. It is also this objective on which all the constituencies—whether shareholders, customers, or employees—depend for the satisfaction of their expectations and objectives.

ACTION POINT: Check the tradeoff your enterprise is making between long-term performance variables—market standing, innovation, productivity, and people development—and short-term profitability. Decide whether these tradeoffs are healthy for the enterprise.

A Functioning Society

A Scorecard for Managers

The things that the proponents of "management audits" talk about—integrity and creativity, for instance—are better left to the novelist.

The "bottom line" measures business performance rather than management performance. And the performance of a business today is largely a result of the performance of management in years past. Performance in management, therefore, means in large measure doing a good job of preparing today's business for the future. The future of a business is largely formed by present-management performance in four areas:

- *Performance in appropriating capital:* We need to measure the return on investment against the return expected.
- *Performance in people decisions:* Neither what is expected of a person's performance when he or she is put into the job, nor how the appointment works out, is "intangible." Both can be fairly easily judged.
- *Performance in innovation:* Research results can be appraised, and then projected backward on the promises and expectations at the time the research effort was started.
- *Strategies versus performance:* Did the things that the strategy expected to happen take place? And were the goals set the right goals in light of actual developments? Have they been attained?

ACTION POINT: Perform a management audit of yourself and the people who report directly to you. The criteria should include whether you/they made good people decisions, whether you/they have had any innovative ideas, and whether your/their strategic expectations came to pass.

Managing in Turbulent Times

Beyond the Information Revolution

There is a service *waiting to be born.*

The truly revolutionary impact of the information revolution is just beginning to be felt. But it is not "information" that fuels this impact. It is something that practically no one foresaw or even talked about fifteen or twenty years ago: *e-commerce*—that is, the explosive emergence of the Internet as a major, perhaps eventually *the* major, worldwide distribution channel for goods, for services, and, surprisingly, for managerial and professional jobs. This is profoundly changing economies, markets, and industry structures; products and services and their flow; consumer segmentation, consumer values, and consumer behavior; jobs and labor markets.

New and unexpected industries will no doubt emerge, and fast. There is a *service* waiting to be born.

ACTION POINT: Fast-forward to 2015. What are three entirely new businesses that will emerge in your industry from technological developments that you can identify today?

Managing in the Next Society

Internet Technology and Education

The medium not only controls how things are communicated, but what things are communicated.

In health care, information technology has already made a fabulous impact. In education, its impact will be greater. However, attempts to put ordinary college courses on the Internet are a mistake. Marshall McLuhan was correct. The medium controls not only how things are communicated, but what things are communicated. On the Web, you must do it differently.

You must redesign everything. Firstly, you must hold students' attention. Any good teacher has a radar system to get the class's reaction, but you don't have that online. Secondly, you must enable students to do what they can do in a college course, which is to go back and forth. So, online you must combine a book's qualities with a course's continuity and flow. Above all, you must put it in a context. In a college course, the college provides the context. In that online course you turn on at home, the course must provide the background, the context, the references.

ACTION POINT: Think about your organization's online services, from Web-based learning to health benefits to compliance. Ask a few employees who use these services whether they are satisfied with them. Hint: Bring earplugs!

Managing in the Next Society

The Great Strength of E-Commerce

Selling is tied no longer to production but to distribution.

E-commerce is to the information revolution what the railroad was to the industrial revolution. The railroad mastered distance—e-commerce eliminates it. The Internet provides the enterprise with the ability to link one activity to another and to make real-time data widely available, both within the company and to outside suppliers, outside channels of distribution, and customers. It strengthens the move to disintegrate the corporation.

But, the great strength of e-commerce is that it provides the consumer with a whole range of products, no matter who makes them. Examples include Amazon.com and CarsDirect.com. E-commerce separates, for the first time, selling and producing. Selling is tied no longer to production but to distribution. There is absolutely no reason why any e-commerce facility should limit itself to marketing and selling one maker's products or brands.

ACTION POINT: Is your business the equivalent of Amazon.com or the local bookstore? If the latter, determine how you can use e-commerce to fight back.

Managing in the Next Society
The Next Society (Corpedia Online Program)

E-Commerce: The Challenge

It is going to CANNIBALIZE our business.

We don't know yet which goods and services will turn out to be most suitable for e-commerce. But we do know that any success in selling through e-commerce, whether business-to-business or business-to-consumer, is going to be seen as a threat by the traditional distribution channels, such as the supermarkets or the local offices of the brokerage houses. "It is going to CANNIBALIZE our business," the traditional distributors will scream. Actually, if past experience is any guide, it may, in many cases, ADD traditional business and actually, increase their business and their profits. That's very often the result of a new distribution channel.

But we won't know that for a good many years. Nor will we know for some years which goods and services will lend themselves to distribution through e-commerce. And there's no point in trying to guess. So the decision to push e-commerce is a risky one. And yet, no business can risk NOT pushing e-commerce if there's the slightest indication that it will become an important distribution channel for its goods and services, if not the most important one.

ACTION POINT: List the three main ways e-commerce has changed your distribution channels and the three ways it will change those channels in the next few years.

Managing in a Time of Great Change
The Five Deadly Business Sins (Corpedia Online Program)

From Legal Fiction to Economic Reality

Where do activities belong?

Increasingly, the economic process depends on structures built upon alliances, joint ventures, and outsourcing. Structures that are built upon strategy, rather than ownership and control, are becoming the models for growth in the global economy. Executives in these partnership structures should organize and manage corporate strategy, product planning, and product costing as one economic whole.

Take for example, a leading global manufacturer of consumer goods. Formerly the company assumed that the more in-house manufacturing it did, the better. Now it is asking, "Where do activities belong?" So, it has decided to place finishing activities into many of the 180 countries where the customer is located. But it produces itself fundamental compounds for the products only in a few regions of the world. For example, a large plant in Ireland serves all of Europe and Africa. The company is in-sourcing the basic compounds to achieve quality control, but it is outsourcing final assembly. It is looking at the entire value chain and decides where to place various activities.

ACTION POINT: Think about your job. Could someone else do it cheaper and better? If so, develop a plan to get new skills to move up the food chain, by reading, doing research, and talking to people.

Management Challenges for the 21st Century
From Data to Information Literacy (Corpedia Online Program)

Management of the Multinational

The multinationals of 2025 are likely to be held together and controlled by strategy.

Statistically, multinational companies play much the same part in the world economy today as they did in 1913. But they have become very different animals. Multinationals in 1913 were domestic firms with subsidiaries abroad, each of them self-contained, in charge of a politically defined territory, and highly autonomous. Multinationals now tend to be organized globally along product or service lines. But like the multinationals of 1913, they are held together and controlled by ownership. By contrast, the multinationals of 2025 are likely to be held together and controlled by strategy. There will still be ownership, of course. But alliances, joint ventures, minority stakes, know-how agreements and contracts, will increasingly be the building blocks of a confederation.

This kind of organization will need a new kind of top management. In most countries, and even in a good many large and complex companies, top management is still seen as an extension of operating management. Tomorrow's top management, however, is likely to be a distinct and separate organ: it will stand for the company.

ACTION POINT: Is your expertise or your boss's expertise in the nuts and bolts of operating a division or in knitting together a far-flung confederation of strategic partners? Do two things that will improve your personal attractiveness as a strategic partner, such as reading a book about another business or culture or talking to an executive who has partnering expertise.

Managing in the Next Society

Command or Partner

The axiom that an enterprise should aim for maximum integration is obsolete.

The traditional axiom that an enterprise should aim for maximum integration is becoming obsolete in the new corporation. There are two explanations for the "disintegration" of the enterprise. First, knowledge has become increasingly specialized. Knowledge is therefore increasingly expensive, and also it is increasingly difficult to maintain enough critical mass for every major task within an enterprise. And because knowledge rapidly deteriorates unless it is used constantly, maintaining within an organization an activity that is used only intermittently guarantees incompetence.

Second, by now the new information technologies—Internet and e-mail—have practically eliminated the physical costs of communication. This has meant that often the most productive and most profitable way to organize is to disintegrate and to partner. This is being extended to more and more activities. Outsourcing the management of an institution's information technology, data processing, and computer system has become routine, for instance.

ACTION POINT: Think about whether you are about to be "disintegrated" out of a job by your employer outsourcing your function. Prepare a backup plan.

Managing in the Next Society
The Next Society (Corpedia Online Program)

Information for Strategy

The only profit center of a business is a customer whose check hasn't bounced.

Strategy has to be based on information about markets, customers, and noncustomers, about technology in one's own industry and others', about worldwide finance, and about the changing world economy. For that is where the results are. Inside an organization there are only cost centers.

Major changes always start outside an organization. A retailer may know a great deal about the people who shop at its stores. But no matter how successful, no retailer ever has more than a small fraction of the market as its customers; the great majority are noncustomers. It is always with noncustomers that basic changes begin and become significant. At least half of the important new technologies that have transformed an industry in the past fifty years came from outside the industry itself.

ACTION POINT: Set up a system for your organization to collect and organize relevant information on the environment, including information about markets, customers, noncustomers, and technology in and outside of your industry.

Management Challenges for the 21st Century

Why Management Science Fails to Perform

Parts exist in contemplation of the whole.

There is one fundamental insight underlying all management science. It is that the business enterprise is a *system* of the highest order: a system whose parts are human beings contributing voluntarily of their knowledge, skill, and dedication to a joint venture. And one thing characterizes all genuine systems, whether they be mechanical like the control of a missile, biological like a tree, or social like the business enterprise: it is interdependence. The whole of a system is not necessarily improved if one particular function or part is improved or made more efficient. In fact, the system may well be damaged thereby, or even destroyed. In some cases the best way to strengthen the system may be to weaken a part—to make it less precise or less efficient. For what matters in any system is the performance of the whole; this is the result of growth and of dynamic balance, adjustment, and integration, rather than of mere technical efficiency.

Primary emphasis on the efficiency of parts in management science is therefore bound to do damage. It is bound to optimize precision of the tool at the expense of the health and performance of the whole.

ACTION POINT: Determine what parts of your company, such as finance or engineering, might be weakened to improve overall performance.

Landmarks of Tomorrow
Management: Tasks, Responsibilities, Practices

Nature of Complex Systems

In respect to short-term phenomena, there is no system. There is only chaos.

The fastest growing field of modern mathematics is the theory of complexity. It shows, with rigorous mathematical proof, that complex systems do not allow prediction; they are controlled by factors that are not statistically significant. This has become known as the "butterfly effect": a whimsical but mathematically rigorous (and experimentally proven) theorem shows that a butterfly flapping its wings in the Amazon rain forest can and sometimes does control the weather in Chicago a few weeks or months later. In complex systems, the climate is predictable and has high stability; the "weather" is not predictable and is totally unstable. And no complex system can exclude anything as "external." In respect to the weather, that is, in respect to short-term phenomena, there is no system. There is only chaos.

Economics and economic policy deal with short-term phenomena. They deal with recessions and changes in prices. Contemporary economics and economic policy assume that the system, the long term, is made by short-term policies, for example, changes in interest rates, government spending, tax rates, and so on. For a complex system this is simply not true, as modern mathematics has now proven.

ACTION POINT: Identify the long-term phenomena affecting your organization. How will these affect your organization in both the short term and the long term?

The New Realities

From Analysis to Perception

In an ecology, the "whole" has to be seen and understood and the "parts" exist only in contemplation of the whole.

In the world of the mathematicians and philosophers, perception was "intuition" and either spurious or mystical, elusive, mysterious. Perception, the mechanical worldview asserts, is not "serious" but is relegated to the "finer things of life," that is to things we can do without. In the biological universe, however, perception is at the center. And of course any "ecology" is perception rather than analysis. In an ecology, the "whole" has to be seen and understood and the "parts" exist only in contemplation of the whole. Three hundred years ago, Descartes said, "I think, therefore I am." We will now have to say also, "I see therefore I am."

Indeed, the new realities with which this book deals are *configurations* and, as such, call for perception as much as analysis: the dynamic disequilibrium of the new pluralisms, for instance; the multinational and transnational economy and the transnational ecology; the new archetype of the "educated person" that is so badly needed.

ACTION POINT: What are the roles of both perception and analysis in the following statement about an organization?: "For what matters in any system is the performance of the whole; this is the result of growth and of dynamic balance, adjustment, and integration rather than of mere technical efficiency."

The New Realities

April

Management as a Human Endeavor

Management is about human beings.

The modern enterprise is a human and social organization. Management as a discipline and as a practice deals with human and social values. To be sure, the organization exists for an end beyond itself. In the case of business enterprise, the end is *economic;* in the case of the hospital, it is the care of the patient and his or her recovery; in the case of the university, it is teaching, learning, and research. To achieve these ends, the peculiar modern invention we call management organizes human beings for joint performance and creates social organization. But only when management succeeds in making the human resources of the organization productive is it able to attain the desired outside objectives and results.

Management is no more a science than is medicine: both are practices. A practice feeds from a large body of true sciences. Just as medicine feeds off biology, chemistry, physics, and a host of other natural sciences, so management feeds off economics, psychology, mathematics, political theory, history, and philosophy. But like medicine, management is also a discipline in its own right, with its own assumptions, its own aims, its own tools, and its own performance goals and measurements.

ACTION POINT: Are you by background an engineer, economist, psychologist, mathematician, political scientist, historian, or philosopher? List three ways your background influences your approach to management.

The Frontiers of Management

The Responsible Worker

The responsible worker has a personal commitment to getting results.

But there also is the task of building and leading organizations in which every person sees *herself* as a "manager" and accepts the full burden of what is basically *managerial* responsibility: responsibility for her own job and work group, for her contribution to the performance and results of the entire organization, and for the social tasks of the work community.

Responsibility, therefore, is both external and internal. Externally it implies accountability *to* some person or body and accountability *for* specific performance. Internally it implies commitment. The Responsible Worker is a worker who not only is accountable for specific results but also has authority to do whatever is necessary to produce these results and, finally, is committed to these results as a personal achievement.

ACTION POINT: Are you personally committed to getting results at work, or are you just going through the motions? Do you lack the authority to produce results? Either get it, or look for another job.

Management: Tasks, Responsibilities, Practices
(second paragraph from a letter to Jack Beatty; *The World According to Peter Drucker*)

Spirit of Performance

The purpose of an organization is to enable common men to do uncommon things.

Morality, to have any meaning at all, must not be exhortation, sermon, or good intentions. *It must be practices.* Specifically:

1. The focus of the organization must be on *performance*. The first requirement of the spirit of performance is high performance standards, for the group as well as for each individual.
2. The focus of the organization must be on *opportunities* rather than on problems.
3. The decisions that affect *people*—their placement, pay, promotion, demotion, and severance—must express the values and beliefs of the organization.
4. Finally, in its people decisions, management must demonstrate that it realizes that *integrity* is one absolute requirement of any manager, the one quality that he has to bring with him and cannot be expected to acquire later on.

ACTION POINT: Focus on performance, opportunities, people, and integrity.

Management: Tasks, Responsibilities, Practices

Organizations and Individuals

The more the organization grows, the more the individual can grow.

The more the individual in an organization grows as a person, the more the organization can accomplish—this is the insight underlying all our attention to manager development and advanced manager education today. The more the organization grows in seriousness and integrity, objectives and competence, the more scope there is for the individual to grow and to develop as a person.

ACTION POINT: Keep learning. Take full advantage of your company's educational benefits.

Landmarks of Tomorrow

5 APRIL

Picking a Leader

I always ask myself, would I want one of my sons to work under that person?

What would I look for in picking a leader of an institution? First, I would look at what the candidates have done, what their strengths are. You can only perform with strength—and what have they done with it? Second, I would look at the institution and ask: "What is the one immediate key challenge?" I would try to match the strength with the needs.

Then I would look for integrity. A leader sets an example, especially a strong leader. He or she is somebody on whom people, especially younger people, in the organization model themselves. Many years ago I learned from a very wise old man, who was the head of a very large, worldwide organization. He was in his late seventies, famous for putting the right people into the right enterprises, all over the globe. I asked him: "What do you look for?" And he said: "I always ask myself, would I want one of my sons to work under that person? If he is successful, then young people will imitate him. Would I want my son to look like this?" This, I think, is the ultimate question.

ACTION POINT: Next time you hire someone, ask yourself whether you would want your son or daughter to work for him or her.

Managing the Non-Profit Organization

Qualities of a Leader

Leadership is the lifting of a man's vision to higher sights.

The leader who basically focuses on himself or herself is going to mislead. The three most charismatic leaders in this century inflicted more suffering on the human race than almost any other trio in history: Hitler, Stalin, and Mao. What matters is not the leader's charisma. For leadership is not magnetic personality—that can just as well be demagoguery. It is not "making friends and influencing people"—that is flattery.

Leadership is the lifting of a man's vision to higher sights, the raising of a man's performance to a higher standard, the building of a man's personality beyond its normal limitations. Nothing better prepares the ground for such leadership than a spirit of management that confirms in the day-to-day practices of the organization strict principles of conduct and responsibility, high standards of performance, and respect for the individual and his work.

ACTION POINT: Set strict principles of conduct and high standards of performance, and respect people and their work.

Managing the Non-Profit Organization
Management: Tasks, Responsibilities, Practices

Base Leadership on Strength

The distance between the leaders and the average is a constant.

In human affairs, the distance between the leaders and the average is a constant. If leadership performance is high, the average will go up. The effective executive knows that it is easier to raise the performance of one leader than it is to raise the performance of a whole mass. She therefore makes sure that she puts into the leadership position, into the standard-setting, the performance-making position, the person who has the strength to do the outstanding, the pacesetting job. This always requires focus on the one strength of a person and dismissal of weaknesses as irrelevant unless they hamper the full deployment of the available strength.

The task of an executive is not to change human beings. Rather, as the Bible tells us in the parable of the talents, the task is to multiply the performance capacity of the whole by putting to use whatever strength, whatever health, whatever aspiration there is in individuals.

ACTION POINT: To raise the performance of a business unit, put a strong leader at the helm.

The Effective Executive

Leadership Is Responsibility

Not enough generals were killed.

All the effective leaders I have encountered—both those I worked with and those I merely watched—knew four simple things: a leader is someone who has *followers*; popularity is not leadership, *results are*; leaders are highly visible, they set *examples*; leadership is not rank, privilege, titles, or money, it is *responsibility*.

When I was in my final high school years, our excellent history teacher—himself a badly wounded war veteran—told each of us to pick several of a whole spate of history books on World War I and write a major essay on our selections. When we then discussed these essays in class, one of my fellow students said, "Every one of these books says that the Great War was a war of total military incompetence. *Why was it?*" Our teacher did not hesitate a second but shot right back, "Because not enough generals were killed; they stayed way behind the lines and let others do the fighting and dying." Effective leaders delegate, but they do not delegate the one thing that will set the standards. *They do it.*

ACTION POINT: Don't expect to retain the respect of your employees if you completely delegate the central function of your enterprise, whether it's healing patients or selling bonds.

The Leader of the Future
The Essential Drucker
Managing the Non-Profit Organization

Absence of Integrity

An executive should be a realist; and no one is less realistic than the cynic.

Integrity may be difficult to define, but what constitutes lack of integrity is of such seriousness as to disqualify a person for a managerial position. A person should never be appointed to a managerial position if his vision focuses on people's weaknesses rather than on their strengths. The person who always knows exactly what people cannot do, but never sees anything they can do, will undermine the spirit of her organization. An executive should be a realist; and no one is less realistic than the cynic.

A person should not be appointed if that person is more interested in the question "Who is right?" than in the question "What is right?" To ask "Who is right?" encourages one's subordinates to play it safe, if not to play politics. Above all, it encourages subordinates to "cover up" rather than to take corrective action as soon as they find out that they have made a mistake. Management should not appoint a person who considers intelligence more important than integrity. It should never promote a person who has shown that he or she is afraid of strong subordinates. It should never put into a management job a person who does not set high standards for his or her own work.

ACTION POINT: Define integrity. Work on those attributes of integrity that you require in a new employee.

Management: Tasks, Responsibilities, Practices

Crisis and Leadership

Leadership is a foul-weather job.

The most successful leader of the twentieth century was Winston Churchill. But for twelve years, from 1928 to Dunkirk in 1940, he was totally on the sidelines, almost discredited—because there was no need for a Churchill. Things were routine or, at any rate, looked routine. When the catastrophe came, thank goodness he was available. Fortunately or unfortunately, the one predictable thing in any organization is the crisis. That always comes. That's when you *do* depend on the leader.

The most important task of an organization's leader is to anticipate crisis. Perhaps not to avert it, but to anticipate it. To wait until crisis hits is abdication. One has to make the organization capable of anticipating the storm, weathering it, and in fact, being ahead of it. You cannot prevent a major catastrophe, but you can build an organization that is battle-ready, that has high morale, that knows how to behave, that trusts itself, and where people trust one another. In military training, the first rule is to instill soldiers with trust in their officers, because without trust they won't fight.

ACTION POINT: Confront the major problems facing your organization. Communicate their essence frankly and fully. Gather support for taking the steps necessary to solve them.

Managing the Non-Profit Organization

The Four Competencies of a Leader

Keep your eye on the task, not on yourself.
The task matters, and you are a servant.

Most organizations need somebody who can lead regardless of the weather. What matters is that he or she works on the basic competencies. As the first such basic competence, I would put the willingness, ability, and self-discipline to *listen*. Listening is not a skill; it is a discipline. Anybody can do it. All you have to do is to keep your mouth shut. The second essential competence is the willingness to *communicate*, to make yourself understood. That requires infinite patience. The next important competence is *not to alibi*. Say: "This doesn't work as well as it should. Let's take it back and reengineer it." The last basic competence is the willingness to realize how unimportant you are compared to the task. Leaders subordinate themselves to the *task*.

When effective leaders have the capacity to maintain their personality and individuality, even though they are totally dedicated, the task will go on after them. They also have a human existence outside of the task. Otherwise they do things for personal aggrandizement, in the belief that this furthers the cause. They become self-centered and vain. And above all, they become jealous. One of the great strengths of Winston Churchill was that Churchill, to the very end, pushed and furthered young politicians.

ACTION POINT: Set aside ten minutes every Friday afternoon to give yourself a weekly report card on all four skills: listening, communicating, reengineering mistakes, and subordinating your ego to the task at hand.

Managing the Non-Profit Organization

Fake Versus True Leaders

All one could do in 1939 was pray and hope.

But this is hindsight. Winston Churchill appears in *The End of Economic Man* and is treated with great respect. Indeed, reading now what I then wrote, I suspect that I secretly hoped that Churchill would indeed emerge into leadership. I also never fell for the *ersatz* leaders to whom a good many well-informed contemporaries—a good many members of Franklin Roosevelt's entourage in Washington, for instance—looked for deliverance. Yet in 1939 Churchill was a might-have-been: a powerless old man rapidly approaching seventy; a Cassandra who bored his listeners in spite (or perhaps because) of his impassioned rhetoric; a two-time loser who, however magnificent in opposition, had proven himself inadequate to the demands of office. I know that it is hard to believe today that even in 1940 Churchill was by no means the inevitable successor when the "Men of Munich" were swept out of office by the fall of France and the retreat at Dunkirk.

Churchill's emergence in 1940, more than a year after the book was first published, was the reassertion of the basic moral and political values for which *The End of Economic Man* had prayed and hoped. But all one could do in 1939 was pray and hope. The reality was the absence of leadership, the absence of affirmation, the absence of men and values and principle.

ACTION POINT: Face your own reality. What threats have you been avoiding? Put a plan in place today to solve these problems.

A Functioning Society

Churchill the Leader

What Churchill gave was moral authority, belief in values, and faith in the rightness of rational action.

The last reality of the thirties, which *The End of Economic Man* clearly conveys, is the total absence of leadership. The political stage was full of characters. Never before, it seems, had there been so many politicians, working so frenziedly. Quite a few of these politicians were decent men, some even very able ones. But excepting the twin Princes of Darkness, Adolf Hitler and Joseph Stalin, they were all pathetically small men; even mediocrities were conspicuous by their absence. "But," today's reader will protest, "there was Winston Churchill." To be sure, Churchill's emergence as the leader in Europe's fight against the evil forces of totalitarianism was the crucial event. It was, to use a Churchillian phrase, "the hinge of fate."

Today's reader is indeed likely to underrate Churchill's importance. Until Churchill took over as leader of free peoples everywhere, after the retreat at Dunkirk and the fall of France, Hitler had moved with apparent infallibility. After Churchill, Hitler was "off" for good, never retaining his sense of timing or his uncanny ability to anticipate every opponent's slightest move. The shrewd calculator of the thirties became the wild, uncontrolled plunger of the forties. It is hard to realize today, sixty-five years after the event, that without Churchill the United States might have resigned itself to Nazi domination of Europe. What Churchill gave was precisely what Europe needed: moral authority, belief in values, and faith in the rightness of rational action.

ACTION POINT: Record the key values that are operative in your organization. Compare these to values espoused by your leaders. Recommend steps to bring espoused values in line with operating values to produce the right action.

A Functioning Society

Alfred Sloan's Management Style

"A Chief Executive Officer who has 'friendships' within the company . . . cannot remain impartial."

Rarely has a chief executive of an American corporation been as respected and revered as Alfred P. Sloan, Jr., was at General Motors during his long tenure at the top. Many GM managers felt a deep personal gratitude to him for his quiet but decisive acts of kindness, of help, of advice, or just warm sympathy when they were in trouble. At the same time, however, Sloan kept aloof from the entire management group in GM.

"It is the duty of the Chief Executive Officer to be objective and impartial," Sloan said, explaining his management style. "He must be absolutely tolerant and pay no attention to how a man does his work, let alone whether he likes a man or not. The only criteria must be performance and character. And that is incompatible with friendship and social relations. A Chief Executive Officer who has 'friendships' within the company, has 'social relations' with colleagues, or discusses anything with them except the job, cannot remain impartial—or at least, which is equally damaging, he will not appear as such. Loneliness, distance, and formality may be contrary to his temperament—they have always been contrary to mine—but they are his duty."

ACTION POINT: Focus on your employees' performance and character, not on whether you like them.

Management Cases

People Decisions

No organization can do better than the people it has.

People decisions are the ultimate—perhaps the only—control of an organization. People determine the performance capacity of an organization. No organization can do better than the people it has. The yield from the human resource really determines the organization's performance. And that's decided by the basic people decisions: whom we hire and whom we fire, where we place people, and whom we promote. The quality of these human decisions largely determines whether the organization is being run seriously, whether its mission, its values, and its objectives are real and meaningful to people, rather than just public relations and rhetoric.

Any executive who starts out believing that he or she is a good judge of people is going to end up making the worst decisions. To be a judge of people is not a power given to mere mortals. Those who have a batting average of almost a thousand in such decisions start out with a very simple premise: that they are not judges of people. They start out with a commitment to a diagnostic process. Medical educators say their greatest problem is the brilliant young physician who has a good eye. He has to learn not to depend on that alone but to go through the patient process of making a diagnosis; otherwise he kills people. An executive, too, has to learn not to depend on insight and knowledge of people but on a mundane, boring, and conscientious step-by-step process.

ACTION POINT: Don't hire people based on your instincts. Have a process in place to research and test applicants thoroughly.

Managing the Non-Profit Organization

Attracting and Holding People

The first sign of decline of an industry is loss of appeal to able people.

In the area of people genuine marketing objectives are required. "What do our jobs have to be to attract and hold the kind of people we need and want? What is the supply available on the job market? And, what do we have to do to attract it?" It is highly desirable to have specific objectives for manager supply, development, and performance, but also specific objectives for major groups within the nonmanagerial workforce. There is need for objectives for employee attitudes as well as for employee skills.

The first sign of decline of an industry is loss of appeal to qualified, able, and ambitious people. The American railroads, for instance, did not begin their decline after World War II—it only became obvious and irreversible then. The decline actually set in around the time of World War I. Before World War I, able graduates of American engineering schools looked for a railroad career. From the end of World War I on—for whatever reason—the railroads no longer appealed to young engineering graduates, or to any educated young people. As a result, there was nobody in management capable and competent to cope with new problems when the railroads ran into heavy weather twenty years later.

ACTION POINT: Set objectives for attracting and retaining the best people, including goals for performance standards and employee attitudes and skills.

Management: Tasks, Responsibilities, Practices

Picking People: An Example

Don't hire a person for what they can't do; hire them for what they can *do.*

A very great leader of men, General George C. Marshall, chief of staff of the U.S. Army during World War II, had the most remarkable record of putting people into the right place at the right time. He appointed something like six hundred people to positions as general officer, division commander, and so on, almost without a dud. And not one of these people had ever commanded troops before. A discussion would come up, and Marshall's aides would say, "Colonel So-and-So is the best trainer of people we have, but he has never gotten along with his boss. If he has to testify before Congress, he'll be a disaster. He is so rude." Marshall would then ask, "What is the assignment? To train a division? If he is first-rate as a trainer, put him in. The rest is my job." As a result, he created the largest army the world had ever seen, thirteen million people, in the shortest possible time, with very few mistakes. The lesson is to focus on strengths.

ACTION POINT: Know the strengths of each person you hire.

Managing the Non-Profit Organization

Decision Steps for Picking People

The most important thing is that the person and the assignment fit each other.

General George C. Marshall followed Five Simple Decision Steps in making people decisions. First, Marshall carefully thought through the *assignment.* Job descriptions may last a long time, but job assignments change all the time. Second, Marshall always looked at *several qualified people.* Formal qualifications, such as those listed in a résumé, are no more than a starting point. Their absence disqualifies a candidate. However, the most important thing is that *the person and the assignment fit each other.* To find the best fit, you must consider *at least three to five candidates.* Third, Marshall studied *the performance records* of all three to five candidates to find what each did well. He looked for the candidate's strengths. The things a person cannot do are of little importance; instead, you must concentrate on the things they can do and determine whether they are the right strengths for this particular assignment. Performance can only be built on strengths. Fourth, Marshall *discussed the candidates with others who had worked with them.* The best information often comes through informal discussions with a candidate's former bosses and colleagues. And fifth, once the decision was made, Marshall made sure the appointee *understood the assignment.* Perhaps the best way to do this is to ask the new person to carefully think over what they have to do to be a success, and then, ninety days into the job, have the person commit it to writing.

ACTION POINT: Follow these five decision steps when hiring someone: Understand the job, consider three to five people, study candidates performance records to find their strengths, talk to the candidates' colleagues about them, and once hired, explain the assignment to the new employee.

The Essential Drucker
People Decisions (Corpedia Online Program)

Placements That Fail

The soldier has a right to competent command.

There is no such thing as a perfect record in making people decisions. Successful executives follow five ground rules. First, the executive must accept responsibility for any placement that fails. To blame the nonperformer is a cop-out. The executive made a mistake in selecting that particular person. But second, the executive does have the responsibility to remove people who do not perform. The incompetent or poor performer, when left in his or her job, penalizes all others and demoralizes the entire organization. Third, just because a person doesn't perform in the job he or she was put in doesn't mean that that person is a bad worker whom the company should let go. It only means that he or she is in the wrong job. Fourth, the executive must try to make the right people decisions for every position. An organization can only perform to the capacity of its individual workers; thus people decisions must be right. And fifth, newcomers best be put in an established position where the expectations are known and help is available. New major assignments should mainly go to people whose behaviors and habits are well known and who have already earned trust and credibility.

ACTION POINT: Accept responsibility for placements that fail. Remove people who do not perform.

Managing the Non-Profit Organization
People Decisions (Corpedia Online Program)

The Succession Decision

The most critical people decision, and the one that is hardest to undo, is the succession to the top.

The succession to the top decision is the most difficult because every such decision is a gamble. The only test of performance in the top position is performance in the top position—and there is very little preparation for it. What not to do is fairly simple. You don't want a carbon copy of the outgoing CEO. If the outgoing CEO says, "Joe [or Mary] is just like me thirty years ago," that's a carbon copy—and carbon copies are always weak. Be a little leery, too, of the faithful assistant who for eighteen years has been at the boss's side anticipating his or her every wish, but has never made a decision alone. By and large, people who are willing and able to make decisions don't stay in the assistant role very long. Stay away, too, from the anointed prince. Nine times out of ten that's a person who has managed to avoid ever being put in a position where performance is essential, measured, and where he or she might make a mistake. They are media events rather than performers.

What are the positive ways to handle the succession decision? Look at the assignment. In this institution, what is going to be the biggest challenge over the next few years? Then look at the people and their performance. Match the need against proven performance.

ACTION POINT: Determine what the single biggest challenge facing your organization is going to be over the next five years and choose someone who has a proven track record of surmounting those challenges.

Managing the Non-Profit Organization

Sloan on People Decisions

"If we didn't spend four hours on placing a man and placing him right, we'd spend four hundred hours on cleaning up after our mistake."

During the years in which I attended the meetings of GM's top committees, the company made basic decisions on postwar policies such as capital investments; overseas expansion; the balance between automotive businesses, accessory businesses, and nonautomotive businesses; union relations; and financial structure. . . . I soon realized that a disproportionate amount of time was taken up with decisions on people compared to the time spent on decisions on policy. On one occasion the committee spent hours discussing the work and assignment of a position way down the line. . . . As we went out, I turned and said, "Mr. Sloan, how can you afford to spend four hours on a minor job like this?" "This corporation pays me a pretty good salary," he said, "for making the important decisions, and for making them right. . . . If that master mechanic in Dayton is the wrong man, our decisions might as well be written on water. He converts them into performance. And as for taking a lot of time, that's horse apples" (his strongest and favorite epithet). . . . "If we didn't spend four hours on placing a man and placing him right, we'd spend four hundred hours on cleaning up after our mistake—and *that* time I wouldn't have. The decision," he concluded, "about people is the only truly crucial one. You think and everybody thinks that a company can have 'better' people. All it can do is place people right—and then it'll have performance."

ACTION POINT: Make decisions on people—selection, placement, and evaluation—your top priority.

Adventures of a Bystander

A Good Judge of People?

"There are only people who make people decisions right . . . and people who make people decisions wrong and then repent at leisure."

"I know," Mr. Sloan continued, "you think I should be a good judge of people. Believe me, there's no such person. There are only people who make people decisions right, and that means slowly, and people who make people decisions wrong and then repent at leisure. We do make fewer mistakes, not because we're good judges of people but because we're conscientious."

Decisions on people usually provoked heated debate in the General Motors executive committee. But on one occasion the whole committee seemed to be agreed on one candidate—he had handled this crisis superbly, solved that problem beautifully, quenched yonder fire with great aplomb—when suddenly Mr. Sloan broke in. "A very impressive record your Mr. Smith has," he said, "but do explain to me how he gets into all those crises he then so brilliantly surmounts?" Nothing more was heard of Mr. Smith. However, on occasion Mr. Sloan could also say, "You know all the things Mr. George cannot do—how come he got as far as he did? What *can* he do?" And when Mr. Sloan was told, he would say, "Alright, he's not brilliant, and not fast, and looks drab. But hasn't he always *performed?*" And Mr. George turned into a most successful general manager in a big division at a difficult time.

ACTION POINT: Make decisions on people your top priority. Spend more time on these decisions so that you will not have to "repent at leisure."

Adventures of a Bystander

The Crucial Promotions

The crucial promotion is into the group from which tomorrow's top people will have to be selected.

If a company is to obtain the needed contributions, it must reward those who make them. Decisions on people and especially its promotions affirm what an organization really believes in, really wants, really stands for. They speak louder than words and tell a clearer story than any figures.

The crucial promotion is not a person's first—though it may be the most important one to her and to her career. Nor is it the final one into the top position; there a management must choose from a small, already preselected group. The crucial promotion is into the group from which tomorrow's top people will have to be selected. It is the decision at the point where the pyramid in an organization narrows abruptly. Up to this point, there are in a large organization usually forty to fifty people to choose from for every vacant spot. Above it, the choice narrows to one out of three or four. Up to this point also, a person usually works in one area or function. Above it, she works in the business.

ACTION POINT: Use your influence to ensure that promotions to positions of senior leadership affirm what your organization really stands for.

Managing for Results

Social Responsibility

Good intentions are not always socially responsible.

A business that does not show a profit at least equal to its cost of capital is irresponsible; it wastes society's resources. Economic profit performance is the base without which business cannot discharge any other responsibilities, cannot be a good employer, a good citizen, a good neighbor. But economic performance is not the only responsibility of a business any more than educational performance is the only responsibility of a school or health care the only responsibility of a hospital.

Every organization must assume responsibility for its impact on employees, the environment, customers, and whomever and whatever it touches. That is social responsibility. But we also know that society will increasingly look to major organizations, for-profit and nonprofit alike, to tackle major social ills. And there we had better be watchful, because good intentions are not always socially responsible. It is irresponsible for an organization to accept—let alone to pursue—responsibilities that would impede its capacity to perform its main task and mission or to act where it has no competence.

ACTION POINT: When it comes to corporate philanthropy, make sure your company doesn't take its eye off the ball.

Managing in a Time of Great Change

Sloan on Social Responsibility

Authority without responsibility is illegitimate;
but so is responsibility without authority.

"Public" responsibility was to Alfred Sloan worse than unprofessional; it was irresponsible, a usurpation of power. "We have a responsibility toward higher education," a chief executive of a major American corporation once said at a meeting both Sloan and I attended. "Do we in business have any authority over higher education?" Sloan asked. "Should we have any?" "Of course not," was the answer. "Then let's not talk about 'responsibility,' " said Sloan with asperity. "You are a senior executive in a big company and you know the first rule: authority and responsibility must be congruent and commensurate to each other. If you don't want authority and shouldn't have it, don't talk about responsibility. And if you don't want responsibility and shouldn't have it, don't talk about authority."

Sloan based this on management principles. But of course it is the first lesson of political theory and political history. Authority without responsibility is illegitimate; but so is responsibility without authority. Both lead to tyranny. Sloan wanted a great deal of authority for his professional manager, and was ready to take high responsibility. But for that reason he insisted on limiting authority to the areas of professional competence, and refused to assert or admit responsibility in areas outside them.

ACTION POINT: Do your areas of responsibility match your authority? Make recommendations for achieving a closer match.

Adventures of a Bystander

Corporate Greed and Corruption

Every boom puts crooks in at the top.

It is easy to look good in a boom. But also, every boom—and I have lived and worked through four or five—puts crooks in at the top. In January 1930, my first assignment as a young journalist was to cover the trial of the top management of what had been Europe's biggest and proudest insurance company, who had systematically plundered their company—and so it goes *after* every boom. The only thing new is that the last boom considerably increased the temptation to fake the books—the exclusive emphasis on quarterly figures, the overemphasis on the stock price, the well-meant but idiotic belief that executives should have major financial stakes in the company, the stock options (which I have always considered an open invitation to mismanagement), and so on. Otherwise there's no difference.

ACTION POINT: Beware: economic booms bring financial predators, as well as prosperity.

"An Interview with Peter Drucker," *The Academy of Management Executive*

What Is Business Ethics?

Business ethics assumes that for some reason the ordinary rules of ethics do not apply to business.

The fundamental axiom on which the Western tradition of ethics has always been based is: There is only one code of ethics, that of individual behavior, for prince and pauper, for rich and poor, for the mighty and the meek alike. Ethics, in the Judeo-Christian tradition, is the affirmation that all men and women are alike creatures—whether the Creator be called God, Nature, or Society. There is only one ethics, one set of rules of morality, one code, that of individual behavior in which the same rules apply to everyone alike. And this fundamental axiom business ethics denies. Business ethics, in other words, is not ethics at all, as the term has commonly been used by Western philosophers and Western theologians. Business ethics assumes that for some reason the ordinary rules of ethics do not apply to business. What is business ethics then?

ACTION POINT: Do not separate personal values of what is right and wrong from the values you put into practice at work.

The Ecological Vision

The Ethics of Social Responsibility

What is business ethics? "It's casuistry."

What is business ethics? "It's casuistry," the historian of Western philosophy would answer. Casuistry asserted that rulers, because of their responsibility, have to strike a balance between the ordinary demands of ethics that apply to them as individuals and their social responsibility to their kingdom. But this implies that the rules that decide what is ethical for ordinary people do not apply equally, if at all, to those with social responsibility. Ethics for them is instead a cost-benefit calculation involving the demands of individual conscience and the demands of position—and that means that the rulers are exempt from the demands of ethics, if only their behavior can be argued to confer benefits on other people.

A great horror story of business ethics would, to the casuist, appear as an example of business virtue if not of unselfish business martyrdom. In the "electrical apparatus conspiracy" of the late 1950s, several high-ranking General Electric executives were sent to jail. They were found guilty of a criminal conspiracy in violation of antitrust because orders for heavy generating equipment, such as turbines, were parceled out among the three electrical apparatus manufacturers in the United States—General Electric, Westinghouse, and Allis Chalmers. The purpose of the cartel was the protection of the weakest and most dependent of the companies, Allis Chalmers. As soon as government action destroyed the cartel, Allis Chalmers had to go out of the turbine business and had to lay off several thousand people.

ACTION POINT: Document two decisions in your career where casuistry has been the basis of the ethics behind these decisions. What decisions *should* have been made in these cases?

The Ecological Vision

Business Ethics

"Primum non nocere — *'First do no harm.'* "

The first responsibility of a professional was spelled out clearly, 2,500 years ago, in the Hipprocratic oath of the Greek physician: *primum non nocere*, "above all, not knowingly to do harm." No professional, be she doctor, lawyer, or manager, can promise that she will indeed do good for her client. All she can do is try. But she can promise that she will not knowingly do harm. And the client, in turn, must be able to trust the professional not knowingly to do the client harm. Otherwise he cannot trust her at all. And *primum non nocere*, "not knowingly to do harm," is the basic rule of professional ethics, the basic rule of an ethics of public responsibility.

ACTION POINT: First do no harm.

Management: Tasks, Responsibilities, Practices

Psychological Insecurity

Insecurity permeates the entire industrial situation.

Insecurity—not economic but psychological insecurity—permeates the entire industrial situation. It creates fear; and since it is fear of the unknown and the unpredictable, it leads to a search for scapegoats and culprits. Only if we restore the worker's belief in the rationality and predictability of the forces that control his job, can we expect any policies in the industrial enterprise to be effective. In no other area can we hope to achieve so much so fast. All the basic forces—the objective requirements of society, the objective requirements of the enterprise, and the objective needs and requirements of the individual—work in the direction of making the industrial enterprise a functioning institution.

ACTION POINT: Set up a plan to stay on top of your knowledge area. If your employer cannot provide you with the training and experiences to maintain your employability, consider changing jobs.

The New Society

May

1 ◈ Managing Knowledge Workers
2 ◈ The Network Society
3 ◈ Global Competitiveness
4 ◈ Characteristics of the Next Society
5 ◈ The New Pluralism
6 ◈ Knowledge Does Not Eliminate Skill
7 ◈ A Knowledge Society and Society of Organizations
8 ◈ Price of Success in the Knowledge Society
9 ◈ The Center of the Knowledge Society
10 ◈ Sickness of Government
11 ◈ Managing Foreign Currency Exposure
12 ◈ The Manufacturing Paradox
13 ◈ Protectionism
14 ◈ Splintered Nature of Knowledge Work
15 ◈ Use of PEOs and BPOs
16 ◈ Managing Nontraditional Employees
17 ◈ The Corporation as Confederation
18 ◈ The Corporation as a Syndicate
19 ◈ People as Resources
20 ◈ Making Manual Work Productive
21 ◈ Productivity of Service Work
22 ◈ Raising Service-Worker Productivity
23 ◈ Knowledge-Worker Productivity
24 ◈ Defining the Task in Knowledge Work
25 ◈ Defining Results in Knowledge Work
26 ◈ Defining Quality in Knowledge Work
27 ◈ Management: A Practice
28 ◈ Continuous Learning in Knowledge Work
29 ◈ Raise the Yield of Existing Knowledge
30 ◈ Rank of Knowledge Workers
31 ◈ Post–Economic Theory

Managing Knowledge Workers

The management of people is a "marketing job."

The key to maintaining leadership in the economy and the technologies that are emerging is likely to be the social position of the knowledge professionals and social acceptance of their values. Today, however, we are trying to straddle the fence—to maintain the traditional mind-set, in which capital is the key resource and the financier is the boss, while bribing knowledge workers to be content to remain employees by giving them bonuses and stock options. But this, if it can work at all, can work only as long as the emerging industries enjoy a stock-market boom, as did the Internet companies.

The management of knowledge workers is a "marketing job." And in marketing one does not begin with the question: "What do we want?" One begins with the questions: "What does the other party want? What are its values? What are its goals? What does it consider results?" What motivates knowledge workers is what motivates volunteers. Volunteers have to get *more* satisfaction from their work than paid employees, precisely because they don't get a paycheck. They need, above all, challenges.

ACTION POINT: Provide your best employees with satisfying challenges.

Management Challenges for the 21st Century
Managing in the Next Society

The Network Society

The developed countries are moving fast toward a Network Society.

For well over a hundred years, all developed countries were moving steadily toward an *employee society of organizations*. Now the developed countries, with the United States in the lead, are moving fast toward a *Network Society* in respect to the relationship between organizations and individuals who work for them, and in respect to the relationships between different organizations.

Most adults in the U.S. labor force do work *for* an organization. But increasingly they are not *employees* of that organization. They are contractors, part-timers, temporaries. And relations between organizations are changing just as fast as the relations between organizations and the people who work for them. The most visible example is "outsourcing," in which a company, a hospital, or a government agency turns over an entire activity to an independent firm that specializes in that kind of work. Even more important may be the trend toward *alliances*. Individual professionals and executives will have to learn that they must take responsibility for placing themselves. This means above all they must know their strengths *and* look upon themselves as "products" that have to be *marketed*.

ACTION POINT: Make a list of the top ten reasons you are attractive as a partner in an alliance.

Managing in a Time of Great Change

Global Competitiveness

"Think globally, act locally."

Strategy has to accept a new fundamental. Any institution—and not just businesses—has to measure itself against the standards set by each industry's leaders anyplace in the world. Given the ease and speed at which information travels, every institution in the knowledge society has to be globally competitive, even though most organizations will continue to be local in their activities and markets. This is because the Internet will keep customers everywhere informed on what is available anywhere in the world, and at what price. E-commerce will create new global channels for commerce and wealth distribution.

Here is an example. An entrepreneur developed a highly successful engineering design firm in Mexico. He complains that one of his toughest jobs is to convince associates and colleagues that the competition is no longer merely Mexican. Even without the physical presence of competitors, the Internet allows customers to stay abreast of global offerings and demand the same quality of designs in Mexico. This executive must convince his associates that the competition faced by the firm is global and the performance of the firm must be compared against global competitors, not just those in Mexico.

ACTION POINT: Look at your domestic and foreign competitors' Web sites and compare them to your organization's Web site. If you don't like what you see, invest more in e-commerce.

Management Challenges for the 21st Century
The Next Society (Corpedia Script for Online Program)

Characteristics of the Next Society

Every institution in the knowledge society has to be globally competitive.

The next society will be a knowledge society. Its three main characteristics will be:

- Borderlessness, because knowledge travels even more effortlessly than money.
- Upward mobility, available to everyone through easily acquired formal education.
- The potential for failure as well as success. Anyone can acquire the "means of production," that is, the knowledge required for the job, but not everyone can win.

Together, those three characteristics will make the knowledge society a highly competitive one, for organizations and individuals alike.

Information technology, although only one of many new features of the next society, is already having one hugely important effect: it is allowing knowledge to spread near-instantly, and making it accessible to everyone. Given the ease and speed at which information travels, every institution in the knowledge society—not only businesses, but also schools, universities, hospitals, and increasingly, government agencies, too—has to be globally competitive, even though most organizations will continue to be local in their activities and in their markets. This is because the Internet will keep customers everywhere informed on what is available anywhere in the world, and at what price.

ACTION POINT: Find out how many customers you are losing because the Internet is making them more savvy about price. Decide whether to cut your prices to compete.

Managing in the Next Society

The New Pluralism

Each of the new institutions perceives its own purpose as central, as ultimate value, and as the one thing that really matters.

The new pluralist organization of society has no interest in government or governance. Unlike the earlier pluralist institutions, it is not a "whole." As such, its results are entirely on the outside. The product of a business is a satisfied customer. The product of a hospital is a cured patient. The "product" of the school is a student who ten years later puts to work what he or she has learned.

In some ways the new pluralism is thus far more flexible, far less divisive than the old pluralism. The new institutions do not encroach on political power as did the old pluralist institutions, whether the medieval church, feudal baron, or free city. The new institutions, however, unlike the old ones, do not share identical concerns or see the same world. Each of the new institutions perceives its own purpose as central, as ultimate value, and as the one thing that really matters. Every institution speaks its own language, has its own knowledge, its own career ladder, and above all, its own values. No one of them sees itself as responsible for the community as a whole. That is somebody else's business. But whose?

ACTION POINT: Reflect on the political disease of single-interest pluralism of our society.

The New Realities

Knowledge Does Not Eliminate Skill

Knowledge without skill is unproductive.

At present, the term "knowledge worker" is widely used to describe people with considerable theoretical knowledge and learning: doctors, lawyers, teachers, accountants, chemical engineers. But, the most striking growth will be in "knowledge technologists": computer technicians, software designers, analysts in clinical labs, manufacturing technologists, paralegals. These people are as much manual workers as they are knowledge workers; in fact, they usually spend far more time working with their hands than with their brains.

So, knowledge does not eliminate skill. On the contrary, knowledge is fast becoming the foundation for skill. We are using knowledge more and more to enable people to acquire skills of a very advanced kind fast and successfully. Only when knowledge is used as a foundation for skill does it become productive. For example, surgeons preparing for an operation to correct a brain aneurysm before it produces a lethal brain hemorrhage spend hours in diagnosis before they cut—and that requires specialized knowledge of the highest order. The surgery itself, however, is manual work—and manual work consisting of repetitive manual operations in which the emphasis is on speed, accuracy, uniformity. And these operations are studied, organized, learned, and practiced exactly like any other manual work.

ACTION POINT: Outline the skills required in your work. Analyze and refine these skills for optimum quality and productivity.

The Age of Discontinuity
Management Challenges for the 21st Century
Managing in the Next Society

A Knowledge Society and Society of Organizations

Specialized knowledge by itself produces nothing.

Postcapitalist society is both a knowledge society and a society of organizations, each dependent on the other and yet each very different in its concepts, views, and values. Specialized knowledge by itself produces nothing. It can become productive only when it is integrated into a task. And this is why the knowledge society is also a society of organizations: the purpose and function of every organization, business and nonbusiness alike, is the integration of specialized knowledges into a common task. It is only the organization that can provide the basic continuity that knowledge workers need to be effective. It is only the organization that can convert the specialized knowledge of the knowledge worker into performance.

Intellectuals see the organization as a tool; it enables them to practice their *techne*, their specialized knowledge. Managers see knowledge as a means to the end of organizational performance. Both are right. They are opposites; but they relate to each other as poles rather than as contradictions. If the two balance each other there can be creativity and order, fulfillment and mission.

ACTION POINT: Write a letter to your boss and colleagues describing the contributions you expect to make. Indicate your understanding of how your contributions integrate into the contributions of your colleagues to produce results for the organization.

Managing in a Time of Great Change
Post-Capitalist Society

Price of Success in the Knowledge Society

The fear of failure has already permeated the knowledge society.

The upward mobility of the knowledge society comes at a high price: the psychological pressures and emotional traumas of the rat race. There can be winners only if there are losers. This was not true of earlier societies.

Japanese youngsters suffer sleep deprivation because they spend their evenings at a crammer to help them pass their exams. Otherwise they will not get into the prestige university of their choice, and thus into a good job. Other countries, such as America, Britain, and France, are also allowing their schools to become viciously competitive. That this has happened over such a short time—no more than thirty or forty years—indicates how much the fear of failure has already permeated the knowledge society. Given this competitive struggle, a growing number of highly successful knowledge workers—business managers, university teachers, museum directors, doctors—"plateau" in their forties. If their work is all they have, they are in trouble. Knowledge workers therefore need to develop some serious outside interest.

ACTION POINT: Develop a serious satisfying outside interest.

Managing in the Next Society

The Center of the Knowledge Society

Education will become the center of the knowledge society, and schooling its key institution.

Throughout history, the craftsman who had learned a trade after five or seven years of apprenticeship had learned, by age eighteen or nineteen, everything he would ever need to use during his lifetime. Today the new jobs require a good deal of formal education and the ability to acquire and apply theoretical and analytical knowledge. They require a different approach to work and a different mind-set. Above all they require a habit of continuous learning.

What mix of knowledges is required for everybody? What is "quality" in learning and teaching? All these will, of necessity, become central concerns of the knowledge society, and central political issues. In fact, it may not be too fanciful to anticipate that the acquisition and distribution of formal knowledge will come to occupy the place in the politics of the knowledge society that the acquisition of property and income have occupied in the two or three centuries that we have come to call the Age of Capitalism.

ACTION POINT: Make learning a lifelong habit.

Managing in a Time of Great Change

Sickness of Government

Our love affair with government is over, although we keep the old mistress around.

Rarely has there been a more torrid political love affair than that between government and the generations that reached adulthood between 1918 and 1960. Anything anyone felt needed doing during this period was to be turned over to government—and this, everyone seemed to believe, made sure that the job was already done.

But now our attitudes are in transition. We are rapidly moving to doubt and distrust of government. We still, if only out of habit, turn social tasks over to government. We still revise unsuccessful programs over and over again, and assert that nothing is wrong with them that a change in procedures will not cure. But we no longer believe these promises when we reform a bungled program for the third time. We no longer expect results from government. Who, for instance, believes anymore that changes in the foreign aid program of the United States (or of the United Nations) will really produce rapid worldwide development? What was a torrid romance between the people and government for so very long has now become a tired, middle-aged liaison that we do not know how to break off but that only becomes exacerbated by being dragged out.

ACTION POINT: Propose a program to your congressional representative that applies logic from the work of your enterprise to solve a social problem and that doesn't require new government funds.

The Age of Discontinuity

Managing Foreign Currency Exposure

Foreign exchange risks make speculators out of the most conservative managements.

Old and amply tested wisdom holds that unless a company's business is primarily the trading of currencies or commodities, the firm inevitably will lose, and heavily, if it speculates in either. Yet foreign exchange risks make speculators out of the most conservative managements.

Executives will have to learn to protect their enterprises against several kinds of foreign exchange risks: losses on sales or purchases in foreign currencies, and loss of sales and market standing in both foreign and domestic markets. These risks cannot be eliminated. But they can be minimized or at least contained. Above all, they can be converted into a known, predictable, and controlled cost of doing business not too different from any other insurance premium by the use of hedging and options. "Internationalizing" the company's finances is also the best—perhaps the only—way in which a purely domestic firm can protect itself to some degree against foreign competition based on currency rates.

ACTION POINT: Protect your business against foreign-exchange risk by hedging your exposure.

The Frontiers of Management
The New Realities

The Manufacturing Paradox

How do you get far more output with far fewer workers?

The most believable forecast for 2020 suggests that manufacturing output in the developed countries will at least double, while manufacturing employment will shrink to 10 to 12 percent of the total workforce. What has changed manufacturing, and sharply pushed up productivity, are new concepts, such as "lean manufacturing." Information and automation are less important than new theories of manufacturing, which are an advance comparable to the arrival of mass production eighty years ago.

The decline in manufacturing as a creator of wealth and jobs will inevitably bring about a new protectionism, once again echoing what happened earlier in agriculture. The fewer farm voters there are, the more important the "farm vote" has become. As numbers have shrunk, farmers have become a unified special-interest group that carries disproportionate clout in all rich countries.

ACTION POINT: Determine the rate of growth in output per person in your manufacturing or operations functions. Is your organization experiencing the manufacturing paradox? Recommend programs for retraining excess manufacturing workers.

Managing in the Next Society

Protectionism

Some of the greatest impediments to effectiveness are the issues of yesterday, which still confine our vision.

The decline in manufacturing as a creator of wealth and jobs will inevitably bring about a new protectionism. For the first reaction to a period of turbulence is to try to build a wall that shields one's own garden from the cold winds outside. But such walls no longer protect institutions—and especially businesses—that do not perform up to world standards. It will only make them more vulnerable.

The best example is Mexico, which for fifty years from 1929 on had a deliberate policy of building its domestic economy independent of the outside world. It did this not only by building high walls of protectionism to keep foreign competition out. It did it—and this was uniquely Mexican in the twentieth-century world—by practically forbidding its own companies to export. This attempt to create a modern but purely Mexican economy failed dismally. Mexico actually became increasingly dependent on imports, both of food and of manufactured products, from the outside world. It was finally forced to open itself to the outside world, since it simply could no longer pay for the needed imports. And then Mexico found that a good deal of its industry could not survive.

ACTION POINT: When manufacturing jobs decline, is the country's manufacturing base threatened? Why is it so difficult to accept that society and the economy are no longer dominated by manual work in developed economies?

Management Challenges for the 21st Century
The New Realities
Managing in the Next Society

Splintered Nature of Knowledge Work

Knowledge work is deeply splintered in most organizations.

Knowledge work is specialized, and because it is so specialized, it is deeply splintered in most organizations. Managing all of these specialties effectively is a big challenge for knowledge-based organizations. For example, hospitals may use outsourcing, PEOs (Professional Employer Organizations), and temp agencies to manage, place, and satisfy the highly specialized knowledge worker. This results in outsourcing part of the management task. The modern hospital provides a great example of the management complexities created by the splintering of knowledge work and the resultant use of outsourcing, PEOs as well as temp agencies.

Even a fair-size community hospital with 275 to 300 beds will have approximately 3,000 people working for it. Close to half will be knowledge workers of one kind or another. Two of these groups, nurses and specialists in the business departments, are fairly large, numbering several hundred people each. But there are around thirty "paramedic specialties": the physical therapists and the people in the clinical lab; the psychiatric case workers; the oncological technicians; the two dozen people who prepare people for surgery; the people in sleep clinics; the ultrasound technicians; the cardiac-clinic technicians; and many, many more. Managing all these specialties makes the modern hospital the most complex of modern organizations.

ACTION POINT: Identify functions in your organization that could be outsourced. Make plans to outsource these functions and to monitor performance and quality.

Managing in the Next Society
The Next Society (Corpedia Online Program)

Use of PEOs and BPOs

Outsourcing human resources management can save up to 30 percent of the cost and increase employee satisfaction as well.

Companies are experiencing important changes in human resources management and the Professional Employer Organizations, or PEOs, have been one response to these changes. Primary factors driving the growth of the industry include an increase in the complexity of laws and regulations governing the human resource function and the subsequent need for professional expertise to manage and maintain a workforce to deal with these new realities. PEOs concentrate mainly on small- and medium-size companies. The use of PEOs frees up managers to focus on their core competencies rather than on employment-related rules, regulations, and paperwork. This industry, which twenty years ago barely existed, is now growing at a rate of 30 percent a year.

In contrast to PEOs, Business Process Outsourcing firms, or BPOs, assume full responsibility for performing the work of the human resource function in large enterprises, companies typically with twenty thousand or more employees. The innovator and leader in the BPO industry, Exult, founded in 1998, now manages the full spectrum of employee process such as payroll, recruiting and staffing, training administration, employee-data management, relocation, and severance administration for a number of Global Fortune 500 companies. According to a study by McKinsey, the management consultancy, outsourcing human resources management in these ways can save up to 30 percent of the cost and increase employee satisfaction as well.

ACTION POINT: Are you outsourcing part of your human resource function? Why or why not?

Managing in the Next Society
The Next Society (Corpedia Online Program)

Managing Nontraditional Employees

The challenge to executives is to coordinate efforts of all categories of workers.

Along with full-time employees, PEOs, and temp workers, there may also be a closely linked but separately managed organization made up of nontraditional employees in the new corporation. Increasingly, employees take early retirement but they do not stop working. Instead, their "second career" often takes an unconventional form. They may work freelance, or part-time, or as temporaries, or for an outsourcing contractor, or as contractors themselves. Such "early retirement to keep on working" is particularly common among knowledge workers.

Attracting and holding these diverse groups will become the central tasks of people management in the new corporation. These people do not have permanent relationships with the business. They may not have to be managed, but they have to be made productive. They will therefore have to be deployed where their specialized knowledge can make the greatest contribution. Managers need to work closely with their counterparts in the outsource contractor organization on the professional development, motivation, satisfaction, and productivity of these nontraditional workers.

ACTION POINT: Attract and integrate nontraditional employees effectively into your organization.

Managing in the Next Society
The Next Society (Corpedia Online Program)

The Corporation as Confederation

From corporation to confederation.

Here are two prominent examples of the corporation as a confederation. Eighty years ago General Motors first developed both the organizational concepts and the organizational structure upon which today's large corporations everywhere are based. And it was based for seventy-five of these eighty years on two basic principles. We own as much as possible of whatever we manufacture and we own everything we do. Now it is experimenting with becoming the minority partner in competing companies: Saab in Sweden, Suzuki and Isuzu in Japan, and it's about to become the controlling minority partner of Fiat. At the same time, it has divested itself of 70 or 80 percent of what it manufactures.

The second example goes exactly the other way. It's Toyota, which for the last twenty years or so has been the most successful automotive company. It is restructuring itself around its core competency—manufacturing. It is moving away from having multiple suppliers of parts and accessories to having only one or two everyplace. At the same time, it uses its manufacturing competence to manage these suppliers. They remain independent companies but they are basically part of Toyota in terms of management.

ACTION POINT: Understand the structure of your industry by analyzing whether your organization and its competitors are more like GM or Toyota.

Managing in the Next Society
The Next Society (Corpedia Online Program)

The Corporation as a Syndicate

The model for the syndicate is the nineteenth-century farmers' cooperative.

The approaches at GM and Toyota, however different, still take the traditional corporation as their point of departure. But there are also some new ideas that do away with the corporate model altogether.

One example is a "syndicate" being tested by several noncompeting manufacturers in the European Union. Each of the constituent companies is medium-sized, family-owned, and owner-managed. Each is a leader in a narrow, highly engineered product line. Each is heavily export-dependent. The individual companies intend to remain independent, and to continue to design their products separately. They will also continue to make them in their own plants for their main markets, and to sell them in these markets. But for other markets, and especially for emerging or less-developed countries, the syndicate will arrange for the making of the products, either in syndicate-owned plants producing for several of the members or by local contract manufacturers. The syndicate will handle the delivery of all members' products, and service them in all markets. Each member will own a share of the syndicate, and the syndicate, in turn, will own a small share of each member's capital. If this sounds familiar, it is because the model is the nineteenth-century farmers' cooperative.

ACTION POINT: Decide whether your organization would benefit from being part of an existing or a new syndicate.

Managing in the Next Society

People as Resources

People are a resource and not just a cost.

The Japanese heeded first and best my point of view that people must be viewed as your colleagues and as one of your prime resources. It is only through such respect of the workers that true productivity is achieved.

People are a resource and not just a cost. The most enlightened managers have started to understand what could be realized by managing people toward a desired end or goal. Management is so much more than exercising rank and privilege; it's so much more than "making deals." Management affects people and their lives, both in business and in many other aspects as well.

ACTION POINT: Look at people as resources to be developed. Take steps to expose your people and yourself to the best ideas and see to it that they are trained in how to apply them.

Managing in a Time of Great Change

Making Manual Work Productive

Knowledge work includes manual operations that require industrial engineering.

Frederick Winslow Taylor's principles sound deceptively simple. The first step in making the manual worker productive is to look at the task and to analyze its constituent motions. The next step is to record each motion, the physical effort it takes and the time it takes. Then motions that are not needed can be eliminated. Then each of the motions that remain as essential to obtaining the finished product is set up so as to be done the simplest way, the easiest way, the way that puts the least physical and mental strain on the operator, the way that requires the least time. Then these motions are put together again into a "job" that is in logical sequence. Finally, the tools needed to do the motions are redesigned.

Taylor's approach is still going to be the organizing principle in countries in which manual work is the growth sector of society and economy. In developed countries the challenge is no longer to make manual work productive. The central challenge will be to make knowledge workers productive. But, there is a tremendous amount of knowledge work—including work requiring highly advanced and theoretical knowledge—that includes *manual* operations. And the productivity of these operations also requires Industrial Engineering, the name by which Taylor's methodology now goes.

ACTION POINT: Figure out the mix of knowledge work and manual work in your job. Apply the basic principles of industrial engineering to the latter.

Management Challenges for the 21st Century

Productivity of Service Work

Raising the productivity of service work is the first social responsibility *of management.*

The need to raise the productivity of *service* work is a social priority in developed countries. Unless it is met, the developed world faces increasing social tensions, increasing polarization, increasing radicalization. It may increasingly face a new class war. Unless the productivity of service work is rapidly improved, both the social and economic position of a large class—as large a group as people making and moving things ever were at their peak—must steadily go down. Real incomes cannot for any length of time be higher than productivity. The service workers may use their numerical strength to get higher wages than their economic contribution justifies. But this only impoverishes all of society with everybody's real income going down and unemployment going up. Or the incomes of the unskilled workers are allowed to go down in relation to the steadily rising wages of the affluent knowledge workers, with an increasing gulf between the two groups, an increasing polarization into classes. In either case the service workers must become alienated, increasingly bitter, increasingly see themselves as a *class apart*.

We know *how to raise* service work productivity. This is production work and what we have learned during the past hundred years about increasing productivity applies to such work with minimum adaptation. The task is known and doable, but the urgency is great. It is, in fact, the first *social responsibility* of management in the knowledge society.

ACTION POINT: Set annual targets for raising the productivity of your service staff. Reward those who are successful in meeting these new targets.

The Ecological Vision

Raising Service-Worker Productivity

Sell the mailroom.

Improving the productivity of service workers will demand fundamental changes in the structure of organizations. Service work in many cases will be contracted out of the organization to whom the service is being rendered. This applies particularly to support work, such as maintenance, and to a good deal of clerical work. "Outsourcing," moreover, will be applied increasingly to such work as drafting for architects and to the technical or professional library. In fact, American law firms already contract out to an outside computerized "database" most of what their own law library used to do.

The greatest need for increased productivity is in activities that do not lead to promotion into senior management within the organization. But nobody in senior management is likely to be much interested in this kind of work, know enough about it, care greatly for it, or even consider it important. Such work does not fit the organization's value system. In the hospital, for instance, the value system is that of the doctors and nurses. They are concerned with patient care. No one therefore pays much attention to maintenance work, support work, clerical work. We should therefore expect within a fairly short period of years to find such work contracted out to independent organizations, which compete and get paid for their own effectiveness in making this kind of work more productive.

ACTION POINT: Make your backroom service activities someone else's front room.

Post-Capitalist Society
Managing for the Future

Knowledge-Worker Productivity

Knowledge-worker productivity requires that the knowledge worker be both seen and treated as an asset *rather than a* cost.

Work on the productivity of the knowledge worker has barely begun. But we already know a good many of the answers. We also know the challenges to which we do not yet know the answers.

Six major factors determine knowledge-worker productivity.

1. Knowledge-worker productivity demands that we ask the question: "What is the task?"
2. It demands that we impose the responsibility for their productivity on the individual knowledge workers themselves. Knowledge workers have to manage themselves. They have to have autonomy.
3. Continuing innovation has to be part of the work, the task, and the responsibility of knowledge workers.
4. Knowledge work requires continuous learning on the part of the knowledge worker, but equally continuous teaching on the part of the knowledge worker.
5. Productivity of the knowledge worker is not—at least not primarily—a matter of the quantity of output. Quality is at least as important.
6. Finally, knowledge-worker productivity requires that the knowledge worker be both seen and treated as an "asset" rather than a "cost." It requires that knowledge workers want to work for the organization in preference to all other opportunities.

ACTION POINT: Apply steps one through five to your knowledge work.

Management Challenges for the 21st Century

Defining the Task in Knowledge Work

In knowledge work, the how *only comes after the* what *has been answered.*

In manual work the task is always given. Wherever there still are domestic servants, the owner of the house tells them what to do. The machine or the assembly line programs the factory worker. But, in knowledge work, *what to do* becomes the first and decisive question. For knowledge workers are not programmed by the machine. They largely are in control of their own tasks and must be in control of their own tasks. For they, and only they, own and control the most expensive of the means of production—their education—and their most important tool—their knowledge. They do use other tools, of course, whether the nurse's IV or the engineer's computer. But their knowledge decides how these tools are being used and for what. They know what steps are most important and what methods need to be used to complete the tasks; and it is their knowledge that tells them *what chores are unnecessary and should be eliminated.*

Work on knowledge-worker productivity therefore begins with asking the knowledge workers themselves: *What is your task? What should it be? What should you be expected to contribute?* and *What hampers you in doing your task and should be eliminated?* The *how* only comes after the *what* has been answered.

ACTION POINT: Define your task as a knowledge worker by asking yourself: "What do I get paid for?" and "What should I get paid for?"

Management Challenges for the 21st Century
Knowledge Worker Productivity (Corpedia Online Program)

Defining Results in Knowledge Work

Results for a scientist—the advancement of scientific knowledge—may be quite irrelevant to the organization.

Defining the task makes it possible to define what the results of a given task should be. There is often more than one right answer to the question of what the right results are. Salespeople are right when they define results as the largest sale per customer, and they are also right when they define results as customer retention.

Hence the next and crucial step in making the knowledge worker productive is to define what *results* are or should be in a particular knowledge worker's task. This is—and should be—a controversial decision. It is also a risk-taking decision. Above all, it is the point where the individual worker's task and the mission of the organization converge and have to be harmonized. It is up to management to decide whether the department store aims at maximum sales per transaction or at maximum sales per customer. It is up to management to decide whether the patient or the physician is the primary customer of the hospital. And this decision is going to be one of the permanent challenges for managers and executives in the knowledge organization.

ACTION POINT: Define results for your position. Harmonize any conflict between the way you define results and the way the organization defines results for your position.

Management Challenges for the 21st Century
Knowledge Worker Productivity (Corpedia Online Program)

Defining Quality in Knowledge Work

Measuring quality in knowledge work sounds formidable.
In practice, it defines itself.

In some knowledge work—and especially in some work requiring a high degree of knowledge—we already measure quality. Surgeons, for instance, are routinely measured, by their success rates in difficult and dangerous procedures, for example, by the survival rates of their open-heart surgical patients. But by and large we have, so far, mainly *judgments* rather than *measures* regarding the quality of a great deal of knowledge work. The main trouble is, however, not the difficulty of measuring quality. It is the difficulty in defining what the task is and what it should be.

The best example is the American school. Public schools in the American inner city have become disaster areas. But next to them—in the same location and serving the same kinds of children—are private schools in which the kids behave well and learn well. There is endless speculation to explain these enormous quality differences. But a major reason is surely that the two kinds of schools define their tasks differently. The typical public school defines its task as "helping the underprivileged"; the typical private school (and especially the parochial schools of the Catholic church) define their task as "enabling those who want to learn, to learn." One therefore is governed by its scholastic failures, the other one by its scholastic successes.

ACTION POINT: Define quality for your job.

Management Challenges for the 21st Century

Management: A Practice

The test of any policy in management . . . is not whether the answer is right or wrong, but whether it works.

The GM executives believed that they had discovered principles and that those principles were absolutes, like laws of nature. I, by contrast, have always held that principles of this kind, being man-made, are at best heuristic. This has been the one point on which my approach to management has always differed from that of the writers or theoreticians on the subject—and the reason, perhaps, that I have never been quite respectable in the eyes of academia. I do believe that there are basic values, especially human ones. But I do not believe that there is "one correct answer." There are answers that have a high probability of being the wrong ones—at least to the point where one does not even try them unless all else has failed. But the test of any policy in management or in any other social discipline is not whether the answer is right or wrong, but whether it works. Management, I have always believed, is not a branch of theology but, at bottom, a clinical discipline. The test, as in the practice of medicine, is not whether the treatment is "scientific" but whether the patient recovers.

ACTION POINT: List three "rules of thumb" you have found helpful for improving performance. Cite a "textbook principle" that has not worked for you.

Concept of the Corporation

Continuous Learning in Knowledge Work

A knowledge organization has to be both a learning organization and a teaching organization.

Knowledge workers must have continuous learning built into their tasks. And a knowledge organization has to be both a *learning organization* and a *teaching organization.* Knowledge today, in all areas, changes so fast that knowledge workers become obsolete pretty soon unless they build *continuous learning into their work.* And that is not just true of high knowledge such as that of the engineer, the chemist, the biologist, or the accountant. It's increasingly just as true of the cardiac nurse, the person who handles payroll records, and the computer repair person. But also, a knowledge organization depends on knowledge specialists understanding what their colleagues are doing or trying to do. And each of them has a different specialty. Knowledge workers need, therefore, to hold themselves responsible for educating their colleagues, especially when the knowledge base of their own specialty changes.

This means that knowledge workers are well advised to sit down and answer two questions:

1. What do I need to learn to keep abreast of the knowledge I am being paid to know?
2. And what do my associates have to know and understand about my knowledge area and about what it can and should contribute to the organization and to their own work?

ACTION POINT: Answer the two questions at the end of this reading.

Management Challenges for the 21st Century
Knowledge Worker Productivity (Corpedia Online Program)

Raise the Yield of Existing Knowledge

"Only connect."

In learning and teaching, we do have to focus on the tool. In usage, we have to focus on the end result, on the task, on the work. "Only connect" was the constant admonition of a great English novelist, E. M. Forster. It has always been the hallmark of the artist, but equally of the great scientist. At their level, the capacity to connect may be inborn and part of that mystery we call "genius." But to a large extent, the ability to connect and thus to raise the yield of existing knowledge is learnable. Eventually, it should become teachable. It requires a methodology for problem definition—even more urgently perhaps than it requires the methodology for "problem solving." It requires systematic analysis of the kind of knowledge and information a given problem requires, and a methodology for organizing the stages in which a given problem can be tackled—the methodology that underlies what we now call "systems research." It requires what might be called "Organizing Ignorance"—and there is always so much more ignorance around than there is knowledge.

Specialization into knowledges has given us enormous performance potential in each area. But because knowledges are so specialized, we need also a methodology, a discipline, a process to turn this potential into performance. Otherwise, most of the available knowledge will not become productive; it will remain mere information. To make knowledge productive, we will have to learn to connect.

ACTION POINT: Spend sufficient time on the definition of a problem prior to making a decision.

Post-Capitalist Society

Rank of Knowledge Workers

"Philosophy is the queen of the sciences," says an old tag. But to remove a kidney stone, you want a urologist rather than a logician.

Knowledge workers can work only because there is an organization for them to work in. In that respect, they are dependent. But at the same time, they own the "means of production," that is, their knowledge. The knowledge worker sees herself as just another "professional," no different from the lawyer, the teacher, the preacher, the doctor, the government servant of yesterday. She has the same education. She may realize that she depends on the organization for access to income and opportunity, and without the investment the organization has made, there would be no job for her. But she also realizes, and rightly so, that the organization equally depends on her.

No knowledge "ranks" higher than another. The position of each in an organization is determined by its contribution to the common task rather than by any inherent superiority or inferiority.

ACTION POINT: Determine how your knowledge can be used to make the maximum contribution to your organization. Get agreement from your boss and colleagues on how you can maximize your contribution.

Post-Capitalist Society
The Age of Discontinuity

Post–Economic Theory

We have an approach that relates economics to human values.

Tomorrow's economics must answer the questions: "How do we relate the way we run a business to results? What *are* results?" The traditional answer—"the bottom line"—is treacherous. Under a bottom-line philosophy, we cannot relate the short run to the long term, and yet the balance between the two is a crucial test of management.

The beacons of productivity and innovation must be our guideposts. If we achieve profits at the cost of downgrading productivity or not innovating, they aren't profits. We're destroying capital. On the other hand, if we continue to improve productivity of all key resources and improve our innovative standing, we are going to be profitable. Not only today, but tomorrow. In looking at knowledge applied to human work as the source of wealth, we also see the function of the economic organization. For the first time we have an approach that makes economics a human discipline and relates it to human values, a theory that gives a businessperson a yardstick to measure whether she's still moving in the right direction and whether her results are real or delusions. We are on the threshold of posteconomic theory, grounded in what we know and understand about the generation of wealth.

ACTION POINT: Measure or assess your organization's performance on the two economic guideposts—productivity and innovation.

The Ecological Vision

June

1 ◈ Managing Oneself
2 ◈ A Successful Information-Based Organization
3 ◈ The "Score" in Information-Based Organizations
4 ◈ Taking Information Responsibility
5 ◈ Rewards for Information Specialists
6 ◈ Hierarchy Versus Responsibility
7 ◈ Sudden Incompetence
8 ◈ Self-Renewal
9 ◈ Individual Development
10 ◈ What to Do in a Value Conflict?
11 ◈ Place Yourself in the Right Organization
12 ◈ Management Education
13 ◈ Attracting Knowledge Workers
14 ◈ Pension-Fund Shareholders
15 ◈ Pension-Fund Regulation
16 ◈ Pension-Fund Capitalism
17 ◈ Test of Pension-Fund Socialism
18 ◈ The Business Audit
19 ◈ Inflation Versus Unemployment
20 ◈ When Regulation Is Required
21 ◈ Work
22 ◈ Goal and Vision for Work
23 ◈ Self-Governing Communities
24 ◈ Civilizing the City
25 ◈ Human Dignity and Status
26 ◈ Enjoying Work
27 ◈ Legitimacy of Management
28 ◈ Economic Progress and Social Ends
29 ◈ The Social Sector
30 ◈ Effective Management of Nonprofits

Managing Oneself

Knowledge workers must take responsibility for managing themselves.

Knowledge workers are likely to outlive their employing organization. Their average working life is likely to be fifty years. But the average life expectancy of a successful business is only thirty years. Increasingly, therefore, knowledge workers will outlive any one employer, and will have to be prepared for more than one job. And this means most knowledge workers will have to MANAGE THEMSELVES. They have to place themselves where they can make the greatest contribution; they will have to learn to develop themselves. They will have to learn how and when to change what they do, how they do it, and when they do it.

The key to managing oneself is to know: *Who am I? What are my strengths? How do I work to achieve results? What are my values? Where do I belong? Where do I* not *belong?* Finally, a crucial step in successfully managing oneself is FEEDBACK ANALYSIS. Record what you expect the results to be of every key action or key decision you take, and then compare ACTUAL RESULTS nine months or a year later to your expectations.

ACTION POINT: Manage yourself by knowing your strengths, values, and where you do best. Then use feedback analysis by, first, recording what you expect the results of key actions or decisions to be, and then nine months or a year later, comparing the actual results to those expectations.

Management Challenges for the 21st Century
Managing Oneself (Corpedia Online Program)

A Successful Information-Based Organization

The system worked because it was designed to ensure that each of its members had the information he needed to do his job.

The best example of a large and successful information-based organization, and one without any middle management at all, was the British civil administration in India. The British ran the Indian subcontinent for two hundred years, from the middle of the eighteenth century through World War II. The Indian civil service never had more than one thousand members to administer the vast and densely populated subcontinent. Most of the Britishers lived alone in isolated outposts with their nearest countryman a day or two of travel away, and for the first hundred years there was no telegraph or railroad.

The organization structure was totally flat. Each district officer reported directly to the "COO," the provincial political secretary. And since there were nine provinces, each political secretary had at least one hundred people reporting directly to him. Each month the district officer spent a whole day writing a full report to the political secretary in the provincial capital. He discussed each of his principal tasks. He put down in detail what he had expected would happen with respect to each of them, what actually did happen, and why, if there was a discrepancy, the two differed. Then he wrote down what he expected would happen in the ensuing month with respect to each key task and what he was going to do about it, asked questions about policy, and commented on long-term opportunities, threats, and needs. In turn, the political secretary wrote back a full comment.

ACTION POINT: Reflect on any similarities between your organization and the British civil administration in India.

The Ecological Vision

The "Score" in Information-Based Organizations

All the specialists in the hospital share a common "score": the care and cure of the sick.

What can we say about the requirements of the information-based organization? Several hundred musicians and their CEO, the conductor, can play together because they all have the same score. Similarly, all the specialists in the hospital share a common mission: the care and cure of the sick. The diagnosis is their "score"; it dictates specific action for the X-ray lab, the dietitian, the physical therapist, and the rest of the medical team. Information-based organizations, in other words, require clear, simple, common objectives that translate into particular actions.

Because the "players" in an information-based organization are specialists, they cannot be told how to do their work. There are probably few orchestra conductors who could coax even one note out of a French horn, let alone show the horn player how to do it. But the conductor can focus the horn player's skill and knowledge on the musicians' joint performance. And this focus is what the leaders of an information-based business must be able to achieve. An information-based business must be structured around goals that clearly state management's performance expectations for the enterprise and for each part and specialist and around organized feedback that compares results with these performance expectations so that every member can exercise self-control.

ACTION POINT: Have a common "score" for your organization that clearly states management's performance expectations for the enterprise and for each specialist, and that compares expectations to results.

The Ecological Vision

Taking Information Responsibility

Information specialists are tool makers. They can tell us what tool to use to hammer upholstery nails into a chair. We need to decide whether we should be upholstering a chair at all.

A requirement of an information-based organization is that everyone take information responsibility. The bassoonist in the orchestra takes *information responsibility* every time he plays a note. Doctors and paramedics work with an elaborate system of reports and an information center, the nurses' station on the patient's floor. The district officer in India acted on this responsibility every time he filed a report. The key to such a system is that everyone asks: "Who in this organization depends on me for what information? And on whom, in turn, do I depend?" Each person's list will always include superiors and subordinates. But the most important names on it will be those of colleagues, people with whom one's primary relationship is coordination. The relationship of the internist, the surgeon, and the anesthesiologist is one example. But the relationship of a biochemist, a pharmacologist, the medical director in charge of clinical testing, and a marketing specialist in a pharmaceutical company is no different. It, too, requires each party to take the fullest information responsibility.

ACTION POINT: Take information responsibility by getting the right information to the right people at the right time. Make a list of whom you depend on for what information and, in turn, who depends on you.

The Ecological Vision

Rewards for Information Specialists

Advancement into "management" will be the exception, for the simple reason that there will be far fewer middle-management positions to move into.

Opportunities for specialists in an information-based business organization should be more plentiful than they are in an orchestra or hospital, let alone in the Indian civil service. But as in these organizations, they will primarily be opportunities for advancement within the specialty, and for limited advancement at that. Advancement into "management" will be the exception, for the simple reason that there will be far fewer middle-management positions to move into.

But to professional specialists—and to their management colleagues—the only meaningful opportunities are promotions into management. And the prevailing compensation structure in practically all businesses reinforces this attitude because it is heavily biased toward managerial positions and titles. There are no easy answers to this problem. Some help may come from looking at large law and consulting firms, where even the most senior partners tend to be specialists and associates who will not make partner are outplaced fairly early on. But whatever scheme is eventually developed will work only if the values and compensation structure of business are drastically changed.

ACTION POINT: How can you alter the compensation-and-reward structure of your organization to reflect the reality that promotions are either horizontal or outside of the organization?

The Ecological Vision

Hierarchy Versus Responsibility

Traditional organizations rest on command authority. Information-based organizations rest on responsibility.

When a company builds its organization around modern information technology, it *must* ask the questions: "Who requires what information, when and where?" And then those management positions and management layers whose duty it has been *to report* rather than *to do* can be scrapped.

But, the information-based organization demands self-discipline and upward responsibility from the first-level supervisor all the way to top management. Traditional organizations rest on command authority. Information-based organizations rest on responsibility. The flow is circular from the bottom up and then down again. The information-based system can, therefore, function only if each individual and each unit accepts responsibility: for their goals and their priorities, for their relationships, and for their communications. This in turn makes possible fast decisions and quick responses. These advantages will be obtained only if there are understanding, shared values, and, above all, mutual respect. If every player needs to know the score, there has to be a common language, a common core of unity. If the organization is information-based, diversification in which financial control is the only language is bound to collapse into the confusion of the Tower of Babel.

ACTION POINT: Is your organization held together by financial controls or by understanding, shared values, and mutual respect? Accept responsibility for yourself and your unit, including your goals, your relationships, and your communications.

The Frontiers of Management

7 JUNE

Sudden Incompetence

The greatest waste of resources in all the organizations I have seen is the failed promotion.

Why should people who, for ten or fifteen years, have been competent suddenly become incompetent? The reason in practically all cases I have seen, is that people continue in their new assignment to do what made them successful in the old assignment and what earned them the promotion. Then they turn incompetent, not because they have *become* incompetent, but because they are doing the wrong things.

What the new assignment requires is not superior knowledge or superior talent. It requires concentration on the things that the new assignment requires, the things that are crucial to the new challenge, the new job, the new task.

ACTION POINT: Do not continue to do in your new assignment what made you successful in the old one. When you enter a new assignment, ask "What new things should I be doing in my new assignment to be effective?"

Drucker on Asia

Self-Renewal

"What do you want to be remembered for?"

When I was thirteen I had an inspiring teacher of religion who one day went right through the class of boys asking each one, "What do you want to be remembered for?" None of us, of course, could give an answer. So, he chuckled and said, "I didn't expect you to be able to answer it. But if you still can't answer it by the time you're fifty, you will have wasted your life."

I'm always asking that question: "What do you want to be remembered for?" It is a question that induces you to renew yourself, because it pushes you to see yourself as a different person—the person you can become. If you are fortunate, someone with moral authority will ask you that question early enough in your life so that you will continue to ask it as you go through life. It is a question that induces you to renew yourself, because it pushes you to see yourself as a different person—the person you can *become.*

ACTION POINT: What do *you* want to be remembered for?

Managing the Non-Profit Organization

Individual Development

The important thing is not that you have rank, but that you have responsibility.

The person with the most responsibility for an individual's development is the person himself—not the boss. The first priority for one's own development is to *strive for excellence.* Workmanship counts, not just because it makes such a difference in the quality of the job done, but because it makes such a difference in the person doing the job. Expect the job to provide stimulus only if you work on your own self-renewal, only if you create the excitement, the challenge, the transformation that makes an old job enriching over and over again. The most effective road to self-renewal is to look for the *unexpected success* and run with it.

The critical factor for success is accountability—holding *yourself* accountable. Everything else flows from that. The important thing is not that you have rank, but that you have responsibility. To be accountable, you must take the job seriously enough to recognize: *I've got to grow up to the job.* By focusing on accountability, people take a bigger view of themselves.

ACTION POINT: Strive for excellence.

Managing the Non-Profit Organization

What to Do in a Value Conflict?

I saw no point in being the richest man in the cemetery.

There rarely is a conflict between a person's strengths and the way that person performs. The two are complementary. But there is sometimes a conflict between a person's values and that same person's strengths. What one does well—even very well—and successfully may not fit with one's value system. It may not appear to that person as making a contribution and as something to which to devote one's life (or even a substantial portion thereof).

I, too, many years ago, had to decide between what I was doing well and successfully, and my values. I was doing extremely well as a young investment banker in London in the mid-1930s; it clearly fitted my strengths. Yet I did not see myself making a contribution as an asset manager of any kind. People, I realized, were my values. And I saw no point in being the richest man in the cemetery. I had no money, no other job in a deep Depression, and no prospects. But I quit—and it was the right thing. Values, in other words, are and should be the ultimate test.

ACTION POINT: Does what you do well fit with your value system?

Management Challenges for the 21st Century

Place Yourself in the Right Organization

Where do I belong as a person?

To develop yourself, you have to be doing the right work in the right kind of organization. The basic question is: "Where do I belong as a person?" This requires understanding what kind of work environment you need to do your best: A big organization or a small one? Working with people or alone? In situations of uncertainty or not? Under pressures of deadlines?

If the thoughtful answer to the question "Where do I belong?" is that you don't belong where you currently work, the next question is why? Is it because you can't accept the values of the organization? Is the organization corrupt? That will certainly damage you, because you become cynical and contemptuous of yourself if you find yourself in a situation where the values are incompatible with your own. Or you might find yourself working for a boss who corrupts because he's a politician or because he's concerned only with his career. Or—most tricky of all—a boss whom you admire fails in the crucial duty of a boss: to support, foster, and promote capable subordinates. The right decision is to quit if you are in the wrong place, if it is basically corrupt, or if your performance is not being recognized.

ACTION POINT: Are you in the right organization? Why or why not? If not, should you quit?

Managing the Non-Profit Organization

Management Education

Management courses for people without a few years of management experience are a waste of time.

What I would like to see—and what I have practiced now for many years in my own teaching—is:

- Management education *only* for already successful people. I believe management courses for people without a few years of management experience are a waste of time.
- Management education for people from the private, the public, and the not-for-profit sectors *together.*
- Planned, systematic work by the students while at school in *real* work assignments in real organizations—the equivalent to the MD residency.
- Far more emphasis on government, society, history, and the political process.
- Teachers with real management experience and enough of a consulting practice to know real challenges.
- Major emphasis on the *nonquantifiable* areas that are the real challenges—and especially on the nonquantifiable areas *outside* the business—at the same time much greater quantitative skills, that is, in understanding both the limitations of the available numbers and *how to use* numbers.

ACTION POINT: Take executive development courses that pertain to your current position and the position to which you aspire. Apply the concepts directly to your work assignments.

"An Interview with Peter Drucker," *The Academy of Management Executive*

Attracting Knowledge Workers

In attracting and holding knowledge workers, we already know what does not work: bribery.

Attracting and holding knowledge workers have become two of the central tasks of people management. We already know what does not work: bribery. In the past ten or fifteen years many businesses in America have used bonuses or stock options to attract and keep knowledge workers. It always fails when falling profits eliminate the bonus or falling stock prices make the option worthless. Then both the employee and the spouse feel bitter and betrayed. Of course knowledge workers need to be satisfied with their pay, because dissatisfaction with income and benefits is a powerful disincentive. The incentives, however, are different.

Knowledge workers know they can leave. They have both mobility and self-confidence. This means they have to be treated and managed as volunteers, in the same way as volunteers who work for not-for-profit organizations. The first thing such people want to know is what the company is trying to do and where it is going. Next, they are interested in personal achievement and personal responsibility—which means they have to be put in the right job. Knowledge workers expect continuous learning and continuous training. Above all, they want respect, not so much for themselves, but for their area of knowledge. Knowledge workers expect to make the decisions in their own area.

ACTION POINT: Manage professionals as volunteers by defining for them what the company is trying to do and where it is going. Put them in the right job and offer them educational benefits. Respect them and their areas of expertise. Allow them to make decisions in their own areas.

Managing in the Next Society

Pension-Fund Shareholders

Short-term results and long-term performance are not irreconcilable, but are different, and will have to be balanced.

The new corporation will have to balance short-term performance with the long-term interests of pension-fund shareholders. Maximizing short-term performance will jeopardize the interests of pension-fund stockholders.

Significantly, the claim of the absolute primacy of business gains that made shareholder sovereignty possible has also highlighted the importance of the corporation's social function. The new shareholders whose emergence since 1960 or 1970 produced shareholder sovereignty are not "capitalists" in the traditional sense. They are employees who own a stake in the business through their retirement and pension funds. By 2000, pension funds and mutual funds in the U.S. had come to own the majority of the share capital of America's large companies. This has given shareholders the power to demand short-term rewards. But the need for a secure retirement income will increasingly focus people's minds on the future value of the investment. Corporations, therefore, will have to pay attention both to their short-term business results and to their long-term performance as providers of retirement benefits. The two are not irreconcilable, but they are different, and they will have to be balanced.

ACTION POINT: Manage your company so that it produces *both* short-term results and has strong results over the long term to satisfy the interests of pension-fund shareholders.

Managing in the Next Society
The Next Society (Corpedia Online Program)

Pension-Fund Regulation

The regulation of pension funds, and their protection against looting, will remain a challenge.

For most people over forty-five in developed countries, their stake in a pension fund is one of their largest single assets. During the nineteenth century, the biggest financial need of common people was for life insurance to protect their families in the event of their early death. With life expectancies now almost double those of the nineteenth century, the biggest need of common people today is protection against the threat of living too long. The nineteenth-century "life insurance" was really "death insurance." The pension fund is "old-age" insurance. It is an essential institution in a society in which most people can expect to outlive their working lives by many years.

The regulation of pension funds, and their protection against looting, will remain a challenge to policy makers and lawmakers for years to come. In all likelihood, the challenge will only be met after we have had a few nasty scandals.

ACTION POINT: What are the weaknesses of the current regulations of your pension fund?

Post-Capitalist Society

Pension-Fund Capitalism

Capital market decisions are shifting from the people who are supposed to invest in the future to the people who have to follow the "prudent man rule."

The capital market decisions are effectively shifting from the "entrepreneurs" to the "trustees," from the people who are supposed to invest in the future to the people who have to follow the "prudent man rule," which means, in effect, investing in past performance. Herein lies a danger of starving the new, the young, the small, the growing business. But this is happening at a time when the need for new businesses is particularly urgent, whether they are based on new technology or engaged in converting social and economic needs into business opportunities.

It requires quite different skills and different rules to invest in the old and existing as opposed to the new ventures. The person who is investing in what already exists is, in effect, trying to minimize risk. He invests in established trends and markets, in proven technology and management performance. The entrepreneurial investor must operate on the assumption that out of ten investments, seven will go sour and have to be liquidated with more or less a total loss. There is no way to judge in advance which of the ten investments in the young and the new will turn out failures and which will succeed. The entrepreneurial skill does not lie in "picking investments." It lies in knowing what to abandon because it fails to pan out, and what to push and support with full force because it "looks right" despite some initial setbacks.

ACTION POINT: Consider directing a portion of your pension-fund assets to trustees who have authority to invest in new ventures *and* who have had success doing so in the past.

The Pension Fund Revolution

Test of Pension-Fund Socialism

Penalties on capital formation are a luxury that a society under pension-fund socialism can ill afford.

We have so far given almost no thought in this country to the ways in which capital formation could be increased to offset the actual "dis-saving" resulting from the rise of pension costs, which springs in turn from the growth in the number of older retired people whose consumption has to be financed out of the "pseudo-savings" of employed workers. Only one thing can be said with certainty: obstacles to, and penalties on, capital formation are a luxury that a society under pension-fund socialism—and a society in which a large number of older people have to be supported in retirement—can ill afford. But one can say definitely that capital formation rather than consumption will of necessity become the central problem of domestic economic policy in the years ahead, and the acid test of the economic viability of America's pension-fund socialism.

ACTION POINT: How can capital formation be increased?

The Pension Fund Revolution

18 JUNE

The Business Audit

The rise of pension funds as dominant owners represents one of the most startling shifts in economic history.

Even the largest U.S. pension fund holds much too small a fraction of any one company's capital to control it. Not being businesses, the funds have no access to in-depth commercial or business information. They are not business-focused, nor could they be. They are asset managers. Yet they need in-depth business analysis of the companies they collectively own. And they need an institutional structure in which management accountability is embedded.

I suspect that in the end we shall develop a formal business-audit practice, analogous perhaps to the financial-audit practice of independent professional accounting firms. For while the business audit need not be conducted every year—every three years may be enough in most cases—it needs to be based upon predetermined standards and go through a systematic evaluation of business performance: starting with mission and strategy, through marketing, innovation, productivity, people development, community relations, all the way to profitability.

ACTION POINT: Do you know what pension funds are big shareholders in your organization? What system do they have for getting information about your organization?

Managing for the Future

Inflation Versus Unemployment

Inflation is the greatest threat to retired people on pensions.

Ever since the Great Depression, unemployment has been seen as both the endemic and the most dangerous disease of modern society and economy. Under pension-fund socialism, inflation can be expected to take over both roles instead. Inflation is the greatest threat to the retired people on pensions, and an equally great one to the workers over fifty with an increasing stake in the future purchasing power of their retirement benefits. Together, these two groups constitute a near-majority of the adult population. These two groups, as a result of pension-fund socialism, have a far greater interest in preventing inflation than ever existed before. A substantial constituency of this kind, sharing a common concern, is by definition a major "interest group" in the American political system and a potent political force. At the same time unemployment is far less of a threat, if a threat at all, for the "constituency" of the pension funds, that is, retired people and older workers.

ACTION POINT: Do you agree that inflation is a bigger problem than unemployment?

The Pension Fund Revolution

When Regulation Is Required

It is management's job to get the right regulation enacted.

To make elimination of a detrimental business impact into a business opportunity should always be attempted. But it cannot be done in many cases. More often eliminating an impact means increasing the costs. What was an "externality" for which the general public paid becomes business cost. It therefore becomes a competitive disadvantage unless everybody in the industry accepts the same rule. And this, in most cases, can be done only by regulation—that means by some form of public action.

Whenever an impact cannot be eliminated without an increase in cost, it becomes incumbent upon management to think ahead and work out the regulation that is most likely to solve the problem at the minimum cost and with the greatest benefit to public and business alike. And it is then management's job to work at getting the right regulation enacted. Management—and not only business management—has shunned this responsibility.

ACTION POINT: What detrimental business impact in your industry can you turn into a business opportunity or effective regulation?

Management: Tasks, Responsibilities, Practices

21 JUNE

Work

"The devil finds work for idle hands."

Work, we know, is both a burden and a need, both a curse and a blessing. Unemployment we long ago learned creates severe psychological disturbances, not because of economic deprivation, but primarily because it undermines self-respect. Work is an extension of personality. It is achievement. It is one of the ways in which a person defines himself or herself, measures his worth, and his humanity.

ACTION POINT: Don't let your self-respect be undermined by being unemployed. Remind yourself that there are other ways to define yourself besides work.

Management: Tasks, Responsibilities, Practices

Goal and Vision for Work

"All my life as a musician, I have striven for perfection. It has always eluded me. I surely had an obligation to make one more try."

I have never forgotten these words—they made an indelible impression on me. Verdi, when he was my age, that was eighteen, was of course already a seasoned musician. I had no idea what I would become, except that I knew by that time that I was unlikely to be a success exporting cotton textiles. At eighteen, I was as immature, as callow, as naive as an eighteen-year-old can be. It was not until fifteen years later, when I was in my early thirties, that I really knew what I am good at and where I belong. But I then resolved that, whatever my life's work would be, Verdi's words would be my lodestar. I then resolved that if I ever reached an advanced age, I would not give up, but would keep on. In the meantime, I would strive for perfection even though, as I well knew, it would surely always elude me.

ACTION POINT: Strive for perfection in your work knowing that it will always elude you.

Drucker on Asia

Self-Governing Communities

Managements have tended to reject ideas for the self-governing plant community and for the responsible worker as an "encroachment" on their prerogatives.

Of all my work on management and "the anatomy of industrial order," I consider my ideas for the self-governing plant community and for the responsible worker to be the most important and most original. A self-governing plant community is the assumption of managerial responsibility by the individual employee, the work team, and the employee group alike for the structure of the individual job, for the performance of major tasks, and for the management of such community affairs as shift schedules, vacation schedules, overtime assignments, industrial safety, and, above all, employee benefits.

But managements have tended to reject these ideas as an "encroachment" on their prerogatives. And labor unions have been outright hostile: they are convinced that they need a visible and identifiable "boss," who can be fought as "the enemy." Yet what was achieved in these areas in World War II went way beyond anything that is being trumpeted today as a breakthrough, such as the highly publicized attempt to replace the assembly line at some Swedish automobile companies. This actually goes much less far than the assembly lines that have been standard in American industry, not to mention the responsibility factory-floor work teams have assumed routinely at IBM, hardly a particularly "permissive" company.

ACTION POINT: Delegate responsibility to all employees once you are assured they have been trained to assume this responsibility.

Adventures of a Bystander

Civilizing the City

Only the social sector can create what we now need, communities for citizens.

Civilizing the city will increasingly become top priority in all countries—and particularly in the developed countries such as the United States, the United Kingdom, and Japan. However, neither government nor business can provide the new communities that every major city in the world needs. That is the task of the nongovernmental, nonbusiness, nonprofit organizations. Only the social sector can create what we now need, communities for citizens—and especially for the highly educated knowledge workers who increasingly dominate developed societies. One reason for this is that only nonprofit organizations can provide the enormous diversity of communities we need—from churches to professional associations, from organizations taking care of the homeless to health clubs . . .

The nonprofit organizations are also the only ones that can satisfy the second need for effective community, the need for effective citizenship. The twentieth century saw an explosive growth of both government and business—especially in the developed countries. What the twenty-first century needs above all is equally explosive growth of the nonprofit social sector in building communities in the newly dominant social environment, the city.

ACTION POINT: Reflect on how your favorite nonprofits can help create new communities in cities.

Managing in the Next Society

Human Dignity and Status

It is perhaps the biggest job of the modern corporation—to find a synthesis between justice and dignity, between equality of opportunities and social status and function.

The modern corporation as a child of laissez-faire economics and of the market society is based on a creed whose greatest weakness is the inability to see the need for status and function of the individual in society. In its refusal to concern itself with the unsuccessful majority, the market society was a true child of Calvinism with its refusal to concern itself with the great majority that is not elected to be saved. Following the English philosopher Herbert Spencer, this belief is now expressed usually in the language of Darwinian "survival of the fittest" rather than in theological terms. But this does not alter the fact that the philosophy of the market society only makes sense if the unsuccessful are seen as "rejected by the Lord" with whom to have pity would be as sinful as questioning the decision of the Lord. We can only deny social status and function to the economically unsuccessful if we are convinced that lack of economic success is (a) always a person's own fault, and (b) a reliable indication of his or her worthlessness as a human personality and as a citizen.

ACTION POINT: Provide dignity to everyone you work with simply because they are human beings.

Concept of the Corporation

Enjoying Work

Those who perform love what they're doing.

Those who perform love what they're doing. I'm not saying they like everything they do. That's something quite different. Everybody has to do a lot of the routine; there's an enormous amount of the routine. Every great pianist has to do three hours of playing scales each day. And nobody will tell you they love it. You have to do it. It's not fun, but you enjoy it because even after forty years you still feel the fingers improving. Pianists have a wonderful expression I heard many years ago: "I practice until I have my life in my fingers." And, sure, it's a dull routine, but you enjoy it.

The same is true of people I've seen in business who enjoy the work. Their routine is: *It's got to be done, and I enjoy it because I enjoy the work.* And that is the difference, I believe, not between mediocrity and performing, but between what you call a "learning organization"—one where the whole organization grows and then the process changes—and an organization that maybe does very well but nobody misses it after five o'clock.

ACTION POINT: Practice until you have your life in your fingers.

"Meeting of the Minds," *Across the Board: The Conference Board Magazine*

Legitimacy of Management

It is the purpose of the organization, and the grounds of management authority, to make human strength productive.

It is the task of management to make the institutions of the society of organizations, beginning with the business enterprise, perform for the society and economy, for the community, and for the individual, alike. This requires, first, that managers know their discipline. It requires that they know management. The first task of the manager is indeed to manage the institution for the mission for which it has been designed. The first task of the business manager is, therefore, economic performance. But at the same time she faces the tasks of making the work productive and the worker achieving, and of providing for the quality of life for society and individual. But a leadership group also has to have legitimacy. It has to be accepted by the community as "right." They need to ground their authority in a moral commitment, which at the same time, expresses the purpose and character of organizations. There is only one such principle of morality. It is the purpose of organization, and, therefore, the grounds of management authority, *to make human strength productive.* Organization is the means through which man, as an individual and as a member of the community, finds both contribution and achievement.

ACTION POINT: Use your position of authority to bring out whatever strength there is in the people you are responsible for.

Management: Tasks, Responsibilities, Practices

Economic Progress and Social Ends

Economic expansion and increase are not aims in themselves. They make sense only as means to a social end.

As far as the potential economic future of the capitalist is concerned, Henry Ford—that grand old man of modern capitalism—was undoubtedly right, and the professional gravediggers of capitalism wrong. But Ford, no less than his critics, forgot that economic expansion and increase are not aims in themselves. They make sense only as means to a social end. They are highly desirable as long as they promise to attain this end. But if this promise is proved illusory, the means become of very doubtful value.

Capitalism as a social order and as a creed is the expression of the belief in economic progress as leading toward the freedom and equality of the individual in the free and equal society. All previous creeds had regarded the private profit motive as socially destructive, or at least neutral. Their social orders had intentionally subjected the economic activity of the individual to narrow limitations so as to minimize its harmful effects upon spheres and activities considered socially constructive.

ACTION POINT: Make sure that in the pursuit of economic performance you develop people.

The End of Economic Man

The Social Sector

The bureaucracy cannot admit that the nonprofits succeed where governments fail.

The real answer to the question "Who takes care of the social challenges of the knowledge society?" is neither "the government" nor "the employing organization." It is a separate and new *social sector.* Government has proved incompetent at solving social problems. The nonprofits spend far less for results than governments spend for failures.

Instead of using the federal tax system to encourage donations to nonprofits, we have the IRS making one move after the other to curtail donations to nonprofits. Each of these moves is presented as "closing a tax loophole." The real motivation for such action is the bureaucracy's hostility to the nonprofits—not too different from the bureaucracy's hostility to markets and private enterprise in the former Communist countries. The success of the nonprofits undermines the bureaucracy's power and denies its ideology. Worse, the bureaucracy cannot admit that the nonprofits succeed where governments fail. What is needed therefore is a public policy that establishes the nonprofits as the country's first line of attack on its social problems.

ACTION POINT: Support nonprofits in their efforts to tackle social problems.

Managing in a Time of Great Change

Effective Management of Nonprofits

Nonprofits need management even more than business does.

In the early 1990s, people sentenced to their first prison term in Florida, mostly very poor black or Hispanic youths, were paroled into the Salvation Army's custody—about 25,000 per year, Statistics showed that if these young men and women had gone to jail, the majority would have become habitual criminals. But the Salvation Army was able to rehabilitate 80 percent of them through a strict work program that was run largely by volunteers. And the program cost a fraction of what it would have to keep the offenders behind bars.

Underlying this program and many other effective nonprofit endeavors is a *commitment to management.* Forty years ago, *management* was a dirty word for those involved in nonprofit organizations. It meant business, and nonprofits prided themselves on being free of the taint of commercialism and above such sordid considerations as the bottom line. Now most of them have learned that nonprofits need management even more than business does, precisely because they lack the discipline of the bottom line. The nonprofits are, of course, still dedicated to "doing good." But they also realize that good intentions are no substitute for organization and leadership, for accountability, performance, and results. Those require management and that, in turn, begins with the organization's mission.

ACTION POINT: Commit your nonprofit organization to effective management. Adopt high standards of organization, leadership, accountability, performance, and results.

Managing for the Future

July

1 ◈ Theory of the Business
2 ◈ Reality Test of Business Assumptions
3 ◈ Synergy of Business Assumptions
4 ◈ Communicate and Test Assumptions
5 ◈ The Obsolete Theory
6 ◈ Focus on Excellence
7 ◈ Creating Customer Value
8 ◈ Identifying Core Competencies
9 ◈ Each Organization Must Innovate
10 ◈ Exploiting Success
11 ◈ Organized Improvement
12 ◈ Systematic Innovation
13 ◈ Unexpected Success
14 ◈ Unexpected Failure
15 ◈ Incongruity
16 ◈ Process Need
17 ◈ Industry and Market Structure
18 ◈ Demographics
19 ◈ Changes in Perception
20 ◈ New Knowledge
21 ◈ Innovation in Public-Service Institutions
22 ◈ Service Institutions Need a Defined Mission
23 ◈ Optimal Market Standing
24 ◈ Worship of High Profit Margins
25 ◈ Four Lessons in Marketing
26 ◈ From Selling to Marketing
27 ◈ Cost-Driven Pricing
28 ◈ Cost Control in a Stable Business
29 ◈ Cost Control in a Growth Business
30 ◈ Eliminating Cost Centers
31 ◈ Making Cost-Control Permanent

Theory of the Business

A clear, simple, and penetrating theory of the business, rather than intuition, characterizes the truly successful entrepreneur.

A theory of the business has three parts. First, there are assumptions about the *environment* of the organization: society and its structure, the market, the customer, and technology. The assumptions about the environment define what an organization is paid for. Second, there are assumptions about the *specific mission* of the organization. The assumptions about mission define what an organization considers to be meaningful results—they point to how it envisions itself making a difference in the economy and society at large. Third, there are assumptions about the *core competencies* needed to accomplish the organization's mission. Core competencies define where an organization must excel in order to maintain leadership.

Every one of the great business builders we know of—from the Medici and the founders of the Bank of England down to IBM's Thomas Watson in our day—had a definite idea, had, indeed, *a clear theory of the business* that informed his actions and decisions. A clear, simple, and penetrating theory of the business, rather than intuition, characterizes the truly successful entrepreneur, the person who builds an organization that can endure and grow long after he or she is gone.

ACTION POINT: A company that was a superstar only yesterday finds itself stagnating and in an unmanageable crisis. What does this say about the company's theory of the business?

Management: Tasks, Responsibilities, Practices
Managing in a Time of Great Change

Reality Test of Business Assumptions

Assumptions about environment, mission, and core competencies must fit reality.

The assumptions about environment, mission, and core competencies must fit reality. When four penniless young men from Manchester, England—Simon Marks and his three brothers-in-law—decided in the early 1920s that a humdrum penny bazaar should become an agent of social change, World War I had profoundly shaken their country's class structure. It had also created masses of new buyers for good-quality, stylish, and inexpensive merchandise such as lingerie, blouses, and stockings—Marks and Spencer's first successful product categories. Marks and Spencer then systematically set to work developing brand-new and unheard-of core competencies. Until then, the core competency of a merchant was the ability to buy well. Marks and Spencer decided that it was the merchant, rather than the manufacturer, who knew the customer. Therefore, the merchant, not the manufacturer, should design the products, develop them, and find producers to make the goods to his design, specifications, and costs. This new definition of a merchant took five to eight years to develop and make acceptable to traditional suppliers, who had always seen themselves as "manufacturers," not "subcontractors."

ACTION POINT: What new assumptions about its environment, mission, and core competencies were made by Marks and Spencer?

Managing in a Time of Great Change

Synergy of Business Assumptions

Assumptions in all three areas have to fit one another.

The assumptions about environment, mission, and core competencies must fit one another. Marks and Spencer recognized that World War I had led to a new *environment*—masses of new buyers for good-quality, stylish, and inexpensive merchandise such as lingerie, blouses, and stockings. By the mid-twenties the four brothers-in-law who had built the penny bazaars into a major chain of variety stores might have been satisfied to enjoy their considerable wealth. Instead they decided to rethink the *mission* of their business. The business of Marks and Spencer, they decided, was not retailing. It was social revolution. From having been a successful variety chain, Marks and Spencer purposefully changed its mission into being a highly distinct "specialty" marketer. Finally, it went out and looked for the right manufacturers, whom it often had to help get started—for the existing old-line manufacturers were, for obvious reasons, none too eager to throw in their lot with the brash upstart who tried to tell them how to run their business—thus developing the *core competency* required by the new *environment and mission.*

ACTION POINT: Does the mission of your enterprise fit the environment? Do your core competencies fit the mission?

Management: Tasks, Responsibilities, Practices
Managing in a Time of Great Change

Communicate and Test Assumptions

The theory of the business *is a discipline.*

The theory of the business must be known and understood throughout the organization. This is easy in an organization's early days. But as it becomes successful, an organization tends increasingly to take its theory for granted, becoming less and less conscious of it. Then the organization becomes sloppy. It begins to cut corners. It begins to pursue what is expedient rather than what is right. It stops thinking. It stops questioning. It remembers the answers but has forgotten the questions. The theory of the business becomes "culture." But culture is no substitute for discipline, and the theory of the business is a discipline.

The theory of the business has to be tested constantly. It is not graven on tablets of stone. It is a hypothesis. And it is a hypothesis about things that are in constant flux—society, markets, customers, technology. And so, built into the theory of the business must be the ability to change itself. Some theories are so powerful that they last for a long time. Eventually every theory becomes obsolete and then invalid. It happened to the GMs and the AT&Ts. It happened to IBM. It is also happening to the rapidly unraveling Japanese *keiretsu*.

ACTION POINT: Establish a forum in your organization for communicating, systematically monitoring, and testing your theory of your business.

Managing in a Time of Great Change

The Obsolete Theory

A degenerative disease will not be cured by procrastination. It requires decisive action.

There are, indeed, quite a few CEOs who have successfully changed their theory of the business. The CEO who built Merck into the world's most successful pharmaceutical business did so by focusing solely on the research and development of patented, high-margin breakthrough drugs, then radically changed the company's theory by acquiring a large distributor of generic and nonprescription drugs. He did so without a "crisis" while Merck was ostensibly doing very well.

We can't rely on miracle workers to rejuvenate an obsolete theory of the business. And when one talks to these supposed miracle workers, they deny vehemently that they act by charisma or vision. They start out with diagnosis and analysis. They accept that attaining objectives and rapid growth demand a serious rethinking of the theory of the business. They do not dismiss unexpected failure as the result of a subordinate's incompetence or as an accident but treat it as a symptom of "systems failure." They do not take credit for unexpected success but treat it as a challenge to their assumptions. They accept that a theory's obsolescence is a degenerative and, indeed, life-threatening disease. And they know and accept the surgeon's time-tested principle, the oldest principle of effective decision-making. A degenerative disease will not be cured by procrastination. It requires decisive action.

ACTION POINT: Is your theory of your business obsolete? If so, don't procrastinate. Act decisively to analyze and rethink your assumptions and develop an updated theory.

Managing in a Time of Great Change

6 JULY

Focus on Excellence

What is our specific knowledge?

A valid definition of the specific knowledge of a business sounds simple—deceptively so. It takes practice and regularity to do a knowledge analysis well. The first analysis may come up with embarrassing generalities such as: our business is communications, or transportation, or energy. These general terms may make good slogans for a salesmen's convention; but to convert them to operational meaning—that is, to do anything with them—is impossible. But with repetition, the attempt to define the knowledge of one's own business soon becomes easy and rewarding. Few questions force a management into as objective, as searching, as productive a look at itself as the question: "What is our specific knowledge?" No company can excel in many knowledge areas. A business may be able to excel in more than one area. A successful business has to be at least competent in a good many knowledge areas in addition to being excellent in one. But to have real knowledge of the kind for which the market offers economic reward requires concentration on doing a few things superbly well.

ACTION POINT: What are the few things that your organization does superbly well? Stay focused on them.

Managing for Results

Creating Customer Value

There is no loss to the customer by eliminating activities that do not add value.

Activity-based costing provides the foundation for integrating into one analysis the several procedures required to create customer value. With activity costs as a starting point, the enterprise can separate activities that add value to customers from those that do not, and eliminate the latter. The chain of value-creating activities uncovered during value analysis is the starting point for analyzing the underlying process of value creation. Process analysis seeks to: improve the features of the product or service, restructure the process while reducing costs, and maintain or improve quality.

Process analysis in an automobile company involves designing and redesigning components and subfunctions in order to carry out each function at predetermined cost targets. For instance, the basic function of an automobile is to provide transportation, but secondary functions include comfort, fuel efficiency, and safety. Each of the functions and subfunctions require components or services that create value for the customer. Each also contributes to the quality of the automobile as well as to the cost. A process team is formed from personnel who perform the value-chain activities. This team often includes suppliers and customers. The task of the team is to identify the functions the product or service is to perform and to analyze the components or services that go into each function with the objective of achieving value and quality objectives while meeting cost targets.

ACTION POINT: Eliminate activities that do not create value. Analyze the underlying processes of value-creating activities and redesign the processes if necessary to enhance customer value.

Management Challenges for the 21st Century
From Data to Information Literacy (Corpedia Online Program)

Identifying Core Competencies

Core competencies meld customer value with a special ability of the producer.

Leadership rests on being able to do something others cannot do at all or find difficult to do even poorly. It rests on core competencies that meld market or customer value with a special ability of the producer or supplier. Some examples: the ability of the Japanese to miniaturize electronic components, which is based on their three-hundred-year-old artistic tradition of putting landscape paintings on a tiny lacquered box; or the almost unique ability GM has had for eighty years to make successful acquisitions.

But how does one identify both the core competencies one has already and those the business needs to take and maintain a leadership position? How does one find out whether one's core competence is improving or weakening? Or whether it is still the right core competence and what changes it might need? The first step is to keep careful track of one's own and one's competitors' performance, looking especially for unexpected successes and for unexpected poor performance in areas where one should have done well. The successes demonstrate what the market values and will pay for. They indicate where the business enjoys a leadership advantage. The nonsuccesses should be viewed as the first indication that the market is changing or that the company's competencies are weakening.

ACTION POINT: Identify your organization's core competencies. Determine whether they are improving or getting weaker.

Management Challenges for the 21st Century

Each Organization Must Innovate

Every organization needs one core competence: innovation.

Core competencies are different for every organization; they are, so to speak, part of an organization's personality. But every organization—not just businesses—needs one core competence: innovation. And every organization needs a way to record and appraise its innovative performance. In organizations already doing that—among them, several topflight pharmaceutical manufacturers—the starting point is not the company's own performance. It is a careful record of the innovations in the entire field during a given period. Which of them were truly successful? How many of them were ours? Is our performance commensurate with our objectives? With the direction of the market? With our market standing? With our research spending? Are our successful innovations in the areas of greatest growth and opportunity? How many of the truly important innovation opportunities did we miss? Why? Because we did not see them? Or because we saw them but dismissed them? Or because we botched them? And how well do we do in converting an innovation into a commercial product? A good deal of that, admittedly, is assessment rather than measurement. It raises rather than answers questions, but it raises the right questions.

ACTION POINT: Keep a careful record of innovations in your area and periodically assess your organization's innovation performance.

Management Challenges for the 21st Century

Exploiting Success

Change leaders should starve problems and feed opportunities.

The first—and usually the best—opportunity for successful change is to exploit one's own successes and to build on them. Problems cannot be ignored. And serious problems have to be taken care of. But to be change leaders, enterprises have to focus on opportunities. They have to starve problems and feed opportunities.

This requires a small but fundamental procedural change: an additional "first page" to the monthly report, one that should precede the page that shows the problems. It requires a page that focuses on where results are better than expected, whether in terms of sales, revenues, profits, or volume. As much time then should be spent on this new first page as has traditionally been spent on the problem page. Enterprises that succeed in being change leaders make sure that they staff the opportunities. The way to do this is to list the opportunities on one page and then to list the organization's performing and capable people on another page. Then one allocates the ablest and most performing people to the top opportunities. The best example, perhaps, is the Japanese company Sony. It has built itself into one of the world's leaders in a number of major businesses by systematically exploiting one success after the other—big or small.

ACTION POINT: Every month, prepare a page that lists opportunities, including areas where results were better than expected, whether in terms of sales, revenues, profits, or volume. Follow this with another page that lists the organization's most capable people. Then allocate the best performers to the top opportunities.

Management Challenges for the 21st Century

Organized Improvement

Continuous improvements in any area eventually transform the operation.

The next policy for the change leader is organized improvement. Whatever an enterprise does internally and externally needs to be improved systematically and continuously: product and service production processes, marketing, service, technology, training and development of people, using information. Continuous improvements in any area eventually transform the operation.

However, continuing improvement requires a major decision. What constitutes "performance" in a given area? If performance is to be improved, we need to define clearly what "performance" means. For example, a major commercial bank decided that the way to improve performance in its branches was to offer new and more advanced financial "products." But when the bank introduced the new products in its branches, it rapidly lost customers. Only then did the bank find out that to customers, performance of a bank branch means not having to wait in line for routine transactions. The bank's solution was to concentrate the tellers at the branches on the simple, repetitive, routine services, which require neither skill nor time. The new financial products were assigned to different groups of people who were moved to separate tables, with big signs advertising the products in which each table specialized. As soon as this was done, business went up sharply, both for the traditional and the new services.

ACTION POINT: Make systematic improvement a priority.

Management Challenges for the 21st Century

Systematic Innovation

Successful entrepreneurs do not wait until the "the Muse kisses them" and gives them a bright idea; they go to work.

Systematic innovation means monitoring seven sources for innovative opportunity. The first four sources lie within the enterprise, whether business or public-service institution, or within an industry or service sector. The *unexpected*—the unexpected success, the unexpected failure, the unexpected outside event; the *incongruity*—between reality as it actually is and reality as it is assumed to be or as it "ought to be"; innovation based on *process need; changes in industry structure or market structure* that catch everyone unawares. The second set of sources for innovative opportunity involves changes outside the enterprise or industry: *demographics* (population changes); *changes in perception, mood,* and *meaning; new knowledge,* both scientific and nonscientific.

The lines between these seven source areas of innovative opportunities are blurred, and there is considerable overlap between them. They can be likened to seven windows, each on a different side of the same building. Each window shows some features that can also be seen from the window on either side of it. But the view from the center of each is distinct and different.

ACTION POINT: Monitor the seven windows of innovative opportunity: the unexpected; the incongruity; process need; changes in industry structure or market structure; changes in demographics; changes in perception, mood, and meaning; and new knowledge.

Innovation and Entrepreneurship

Unexpected Success

It takes an effort to perceive unexpected success as one's own best opportunity.

It is precisely because the unexpected jolts us out of our preconceived notions, our assumptions, our certainties, that it is such a fertile source of innovation. In no other area are innovative opportunities less risky and their pursuit less arduous. Yet the unexpected success is almost totally neglected; worse, managements tend actively to reject it. One reason why it is difficult for management to accept unexpected success is that all of us tend to believe that anything that has lasted a fair amount of time must be "normal" and go on "forever."

This explains why one of the major U.S. steel companies, around 1970, rejected the "mini-mill." Management knew that its steelworks were rapidly becoming obsolete and would need billions of dollars of investment to be modernized. A new, smaller "mini-mill" was the solution. Almost by accident, such a "mini-mill" was acquired. It soon began to grow rapidly and to generate cash and profits. Some of the younger people within the steel company proposed that available investment funds be used to acquire additional "mini-mills" and to build new ones. Top management indignantly vetoed the proposal. "The integrated steelmaking process is the only right one," top management argued. "Everything else is cheating—a fad, unhealthy, and unlikely to endure." Needless to say, thirty years later the only parts of the steel industry in America that were still healthy, growing, and reasonably prosperous were "mini-mills."

ACTION POINT: Don't neglect or reject unexpected success. Identify it, absorb it, and learn from it.

Innovation and Entrepreneurship

Unexpected Failure

Failure should always be considered a symptom of an innovative opportunity.

The unexpected failure demands that you go out, look around, and listen. A competitor's unexpected success or failure is equally important. Failure should always be considered a symptom of an innovative opportunity, and taken seriously as such. One does not just "analyze." One goes out to investigate. A good many failures are, of course, nothing but mistakes, the results of greed, stupidity, thoughtless bandwagon-climbing, or incompetence, whether in design or execution. Yet if something fails despite being carefully planned, carefully designed, and conscientiously executed, that failure often bespeaks underlying change and with it, opportunity.

Unexpected failure often informs us of underlying changes in customer values and perceptions. The assumptions upon which a product or service, its design or market strategy, were based can quickly become outdated. Perhaps customers have changed their value proposition—they may be buying the same thing, but they are actually purchasing a very different value. For example, after the failure of the Edsel, Ford decided that income segmentation no longer applied to the automobile industry. Rather, it was lifestyle segmentation that mattered to consumers.

ACTION POINT: Identify an important unexpected failure, yours or a competitor's. Identify plausible explanations for the failure. Apply these lessons to your current business.

Innovation and Entrepreneurship
Driving Change (Corpedia Online Program)

Incongruity

The incongruity bespeaks an underlying "fault."

There is often a discrepancy between "what is" and what management thinks "ought to be" that represents an incongruity within an industry, a market, and a process. The incongruity may be clearly visible to the people within or close to the industry, market, or process. Insiders may notice it but think, "this is the way it has always been," as a reason for not initiating a change. Change leaders exploit these incongruities to the organization's advantage.

Take, for example, the unequal information in the hands of buyers and sellers of automobiles. There are a few things about buying vehicles most of us dislike. These include haggling over price, misleading ads, spending hours at a dealership while the salesperson goes back and forth between the sales manager and us, and so on. Several online organizations have created one-stop shopping for used and new automobiles with complete and accurate information about vehicles of all types, including warranties, financing, and insurance. They have leveled the playing field for consumers.

ACTION POINT: Are there any incongruities within a process or within your market that may be exploited to your advantage?

Innovation and Entrepreneurship
Driving Change (Corpedia Online Program)

Process Need

"Necessity is the mother of invention."

The first two possibilities for innovation are *opportunity driven*. But the third is anchored in the old proverb, "Necessity is the mother of invention." Here need is the source of innovation. I call it *process need.* Everybody in the organization always knows that the process need exists. Yet usually no one does anything about it. However, when the innovation appears, it is immediately accepted as "obvious" and soon becomes "standard."

Process innovation starts with the job to be done and requires the presence of five basic criteria: a self-contained process, a weak or missing link, a clear definition of the objectives, clearly defined specifications for the solution, and widespread realization that there ought to be a better way. Take for example, O. M. Scott and Company, a leader among American producers of lawn-care products. It gained its leadership position based upon a simple gadget called the spreader that users can set to evenly distribute proper quantities of lawn-care chemicals. Without such a tool there was an internal incongruity in the existing process and this incongruity frustrated consumers who were unable to evenly distribute chemicals. There are now many such spreaders.

ACTION POINT: Define a process in your organization that has a missing link. Describe the process, the objectives of the process, the level of awareness of the existence of a missing link, the missing link, and the specifications for a solution.

Innovation and Entrepreneurship
Driving Change (Corpedia Online Program)

Industry and Market Structure

Market and industry structures are quite brittle.
One small scratch and they disintegrate, often fast.

Industry and market structures appear so solid that the people in an industry are likely to consider them foreordained, part of the order of nature, and certain to endure forever. A change in market or industry structure is a major opportunity for innovation. In industry structure, a change requires entrepreneurship from every member of the industry. It requires that each one ask anew: "What is our business?" And each of the members will have to give a different, but above all a new, answer to that question. Large, dominant producers and suppliers, having been successful and unchallenged for many years, tend to be arrogant. At first they dismiss the newcomer as insignificant and, indeed, amateurish. But even when the newcomer takes a larger and larger share of their business, they find it hard to mobilize themselves for counteraction.

For example, the U.S. Post Office did not react when UPS and FedEx took away larger and larger shares of its business. What had made the Post Office so vulnerable was rapid growth in the demand for urgent delivery of time-sensitive documents and packages.

ACTION POINT: Never stop asking yourself, "What is our business?"

Innovation and Entrepreneurship
Driving Change (Corpedia Online Program)

Demographics

Changing demographics is both a highly productive and a highly dependable innovative opportunity.

Of all external changes, demographics—defined as changes in population, its size, age structure, composition, employment, educational status, and income—are the clearest. They are unambiguous. They have the most predictable consequences. They have a major impact on what will be bought, by whom, and in what quantities.

Demographic shifts may be inherently unpredictable, yet they do have long lead times before impact, and lead times, moreover, that are predictable. Particularly important are age distribution and with the highest predictive value changes in the center of population gravity, that is, in the age group that at any given time constitutes both the largest and the fastest-growing age cohort in the population. In the U.S. in the 1960s, this was a shift to teenagers as the fastest-growing group. With these shifts came a change in what would be considered "representative" behavior. The teenagers of course continued to behave like teenagers. But that was widely dismissed as the way teenagers behave rather than seen as a change in the constitutive values of behavior of society. Statistics are only the starting point. For those genuinely willing to go out into the field, to look and to listen, changing demographics is both a highly productive and a highly dependable innovative opportunity.

ACTION POINT: What are the demographic factors that affect the market for your products or services? Project these factors five to ten years into the future. What opportunities do they create?

Innovation and Entrepreneurship

Changes in Perception

If general perception changes from seeing the glass as "half-full" to seeing the glass as "half-empty," there are major innovative opportunities.

In mathematics there is no difference between "the glass is half full" and "the glass is half empty." But the meanings of these two statements are totally different, and so are their consequences. If general perception changes from seeing the glass as "half full" to seeing it as "half empty," there are major innovative opportunities.

Unexpected success or unexpected failure is often an indication of change in perception and meaning for the consumer. When a change in perception takes place, the facts do not change. Their meaning does. For example, American health hypochondria represents a change in American values, such as worship of youth, more than a reaction to the health statistics. Forty years ago even minor improvements in the nation's health were seen as major steps forward. Now dramatic improvements are barely paid attention to. This change in perception has created a vast market for new health-care magazines, alternative sources of medicine, physical fitness centers, and other "wellness" goods and services.

ACTION POINT: Define a major change in perception influencing your industry. Exploit this change.

Innovation and Entrepreneurship
Driving Change (Corpedia Online Program)

New Knowledge

In the theory and practice of innovation and entrepreneurship, the bright-idea innovation belongs in the appendix.

New knowledge is not the most reliable or most predictable source of successful innovations. For all the visibility, glamour, and importance of science-based innovation, it is actually the least reliable and least predictable one. Knowledge-based innovation has the longest lead-time of any innovation. First, there is a long time span between the emergence of new knowledge, and it's becoming applicable to technology. And then there is another long period before the new technology turns into products, processes, or services in the marketplace.

The introduction of innovation creates excitement and attracts a host of competitors, meaning that innovators have to be right the first time. They are unlikely to get a second chance. Here, even successful innovators almost immediately have far more company than they want and must prepare themselves to weather the storm that lies ahead. For example, Apple Computer invented the personal computer. IBM was able to wrest market leadership from Apple through creative imitation. Apple failed to maintain its leadership position and became a niche player because it failed to predict and respond to the competition it would face. In the theory and practice of innovation and entrepreneurship, the bright-idea innovation belongs in the appendix. But it should be appreciated and rewarded. It represents qualities that society needs: initiative, ambition, and ingenuity.

ACTION POINT: Are you and your organization inventors or imitators? If the former, remember to predict the competition that your successful invention might inspire, and plan on responding to that competition.

Innovation and Entrepreneurship
Driving Change (Corpedia Online Program)

Innovation in Public-Service Institutions

Most innovations in public-service institutions are imposed on them either by outsiders or by catastrophe.

Institutions such as government agencies, labor unions, churches, universities and schools, hospitals, community and charitable organizations, professional and trade associations, and the like need to be entrepreneurial and innovative fully as much as any business does. Indeed, they may need it more.

The rapid changes in today's society, technology, and economy are simultaneously an even greater threat to them and an even greater opportunity. Yet public-service institutions find it far more difficult to innovate than even the most "bureaucratic" company. The "existing" seems to be even more of an obstacle. To be sure, every service institution likes to get bigger. In the absence of a profit test, size is the one criterion of success for a service institution, and growth a goal in itself. And then, of course, there is always so much more that needs to be done. But stopping what has "always been done" and doing something new are equally anathema to service institutions, or at least excruciatingly painful to them. Most innovations in public-service institutions are imposed on them either by outsiders or by catastrophe. For example, the modern American university in the mid-nineteenth century came into being when the country's traditional colleges and universities were dying and could no longer attract students.

ACTION POINT: Fight the bureaucrats at your nonprofit institution who just do what has "always been done." Do something new that addresses the rapid social, technological, or economic changes buffeting your institution.

Innovation and Entrepreneurship

Service Institutions Need a Defined Mission

We have attained what we were trying to do.

First, the public-service institution needs a *clear definition of its mission.* What is it trying to do? Why does it exist? It needs to focus on objectives rather than on programs and projects. Programs and projects are means to an end. They should always be considered as temporary and, in fact, short-lived. Second, the public-service institution needs *a realistic statement of goals.* It should say, "Our job is to assuage famine," rather than, "Our job is to eliminate hunger." It needs something that is genuinely attainable and therefore a commitment to a realistic goal, so that it can say eventually, "Our job is finished." Most objectives can and should be phrased in optimal rather than in maximal terms. Then it is possible to say, "We have attained what we were trying to do." Third, failure to achieve objectives should be considered an indication that the *objective is wrong or at least defined wrongly.* If an objective has not been attained after repeated tries, one has to assume that it is the wrong one. Failure to attain objectives is a prima facie reason to question the validity of the objective—the exact opposite of what most public-service institutions believe.

ACTION POINT: Write down your nonprofit institution's mission. Is it attainable or is it an open-ended, wishful statement? If it's the latter, replace it with a realistic and genuinely attainable statement of goals.

Innovation and Entrepreneurship

23 JULY

Optimal Market Standing

Market domination produces tremendous internal resistance against any innovation.

A major decision underlying marketing objectives is market standing. One common approach is to say, "We want to be the leader." The other one is to say, "We don't care what share of the market we have as long as sales go up." Both sound plausible, but both are wrong. It does not do much good for a company's sales to go up if it loses market share, that is, if the market expands much faster than the company's sales do. A company with a small share of the market will eventually become marginal in the marketplace, and thereby exceedingly vulnerable. There is also a maximum market standing above which it may be unwise to go—even if there were no antitrust laws. Market domination tends to lull the leader to sleep; monopolists flounder on their own complacency rather than on public opposition. Market domination produces tremendous internal resistance against any innovation and thus makes adaptation to change dangerously difficult. There is also well-founded resistance in the marketplace to dependence on one dominant supplier. No one likes to be at the mercy of the monopoly supplier.

The market standing to aim at is not the maximum but the *optimum*. This requires careful analysis of customers, of products or services, of market segments, and of distribution channels. It requires a market strategy, and it requires a decision of high risk.

ACTION POINT: Define your institution's optimal market share by carefully analyzing your customers, competitors, market segments, and distribution channels. Base your market strategy on your optimal market share, not on simply dominating the market or increasing market share.

Management: Tasks, Responsibilities, Practices

Worship of High Profit Margins

High profit margin holds an umbrella over the competitor.

Most businesspeople are aware that *profit* is not the same as *profit margin*. Profit is profit margin multiplied by the turnover of capital. Maximum profitability and maximum profit flow are thus obtained by the profit margin that produces the *optimum market standing* and with it the *optimum* turnover *of capital*.

Why is the worship of high profit margin likely to damage—if not destroy—the business? It not only holds an umbrella over the competitor; it also makes competing practically risk-free and virtually guarantees that the competitor will take over the market. Xerox invented the copier, and in all of business history very few products have been as successful as the Xerox copy machine. But then Xerox began to chase profit margin. It put more and more gimmicks on the machine, each developed primarily to increase the profit margin. But each of these new accessories also increased the price of the machine, and what was probably even more important, each made it more difficult to service the machine. And the great majority of users didn't need these additional features. And so a Japanese company, Canon, developed what was not much more than a replica of the original Xerox machine. The Canon model was simple and cheap, and easy to service, and it captured the U.S. market in less than one year.

ACTION POINT: Is your organization guilty of worshiping high profit margins?

Managing in a Time of Great Change
The Five Deadly Business Sins (Corpedia Online Program)

Four Lessons in Marketing

Henry Ford is supposed to have said: "We can sell the Model T at such a low price only because it earns such a nice profit."

Of the top marketing lessons for the highly competitive twenty-first century, the most crucial one is that *buying customers doesn't work.* The collapse of the Hyundai Excel was a spectacular marketing failure. There was nothing wrong with the car. But the company had greatly underpriced it. As a result, it had no profits to plow back into promotion, service, dealers, or improvements to the car itself.

How to define the market is the second lesson—the lesson of what was both a marketing success and a major marketing fiasco: the conquest of the American market by the fax machine. The Japanese did not ask, "What is the market for this *machine?*" Instead they asked, "*What is the market for what it does?*" And they immediately saw, when looking at the growth of courier services such as Federal Express, that the market for the fax machine had already been established. The next lesson is that marketing starts with *all customers* in the market rather than with *our* customers. The final lesson is that of the success of the new "pastoral" churches by *exploiting demographic changes as a marketing opportunity.*

ACTION POINT: Apply these four marketing lessons to your business: Don't try to buy customers. Ask, "What is the market for what the product does?" Consider all customers in the market. Exploit demographic changes.

Managing for the Future

From Selling to Marketing

Consumerism is the "shame of marketing."

Despite the emphasis on marketing and the marketing approach, marketing is still rhetoric rather than reality in far too many businesses. "Consumerism" proves this. For what consumerism demands of business is that it actually market. It demands that business start out with the needs, the realities, the values of the customer. It demands that business define its goal as the satisfaction of customer needs. It demands that business base its reward on its contribution to the customer. That after years of marketing rhetoric consumerism could become a powerful popular movement proves that not much marketing has been practiced. Consumerism is the "shame of marketing." Indeed, selling and marketing are antithetical rather than synonymous or even complementary.

There will always, one can assume, be a need for some selling. But the aim of marketing is to make selling superfluous. The aim of marketing is to know and understand the customer so well that the product or service fits her and sells itself. Ideally, marketing should result in a customer who is ready to buy. We may be a long way from this ideal. But consumerism is a clear indication that the right motto for business management should increasingly be, "From selling to marketing."

ACTION POINT: Are your institution's products and services meeting the actual needs of your customers? If not, does this explain your marketing difficulties?

Management: Tasks, Responsibilities, Practices

Cost-Driven Pricing

Customers do not see it as their job to ensure that manufacturers make a profit.

Most American and European companies set their prices by adding up costs and then putting a profit margin on top. And then, as soon as they have introduced the product or service, they have to start cutting the price, have to redesign the product at enormous expense, have to take losses—and, often, have to drop a perfectly good product or service because it is priced incorrectly. Their argument? "We have to recover our costs and make a profit." But the only sound way to price is to start out with what the market is willing to pay and design to that price specification. To start out with price and then whittle down costs is certainly more work initially. But in the end it is much less work than to start out wrong and then spend loss-making years bringing costs into line.

Price-led costing is an American invention and over one hundred years old. It gave the General Electric company world leadership in electric generating stations way back in the early years of the twentieth century. That's when GE began to design turbines and transformers to the price the customers, the electric power companies, could pay. They were designed from the price the customer could pay and was willing to pay; and so the customer could and did buy them.

ACTION POINT: Investigate your pricing practices. Set prices according to customer realities and then form a team to help achieve a cost structure that will allow you to make the necessary profit at a preset price.

Managing in a Time of Great Change
The Five Deadly Business Sins (Corpedia Online Program)

Cost Control in a Stable Business

In cost control an ounce of prevention is worth a pound of cure.

All of us have learned that it is much harder to get rid of five extra pounds than it is not to put them on in the first place. In no other area is it as true as it is in cost control that an ounce of prevention is worth a pound of cure. An absolute necessity is to watch like a hawk to make sure that costs do not go up as fast as revenues; and, conversely, that they fall at least as fast as revenues if there is a recession and revenues go down.

One example of a follower of this rule is one of the world's largest pharmaceutical companies, a company that grew almost eightfold, adjusted for inflation, between 1965 and 1995. During those thirty years, it held cost increases to a fixed percentage of its increase in revenues; a maximum 6 percent rise in costs for every 10 percent rise in revenues. After five or six years of trying, it also learned how to make sure that costs go down in the same proportion as revenues go down in a down period. It took quite a few years to make this work; now it's almost second nature in that company.

ACTION POINT: Hold increases in operating costs to a fixed percentage of increases in operating revenues. Make sure operating costs go down by the percentage decrease in operating revenues.

Permanent Cost Control (Corpedia Online Program)
Managing for Results

Cost Control in a Growth Business

How much business can we expect in this new company if we are successful? And how much front-end investment is then justified?

To grow a business one has to put in front-end money. That money is invested in tomorrow's profit makers, so those front-end investments will only be costs and no returns, and sometimes for a long time. How does one manage those to maintain cost control? The first thing is to *budget* these activities separately. I call it the *opportunities budget.* The second rule, therefore, is to think through *what results we expect* from these investments in the future and within *what time period.*

The best example I know is how Citibank became the world's only successful transnational bank in the heady 1970s and 1980s. The reason was that Citi first thought through how much front-end investment in a new branch could be justified. It thought through what the minimum results in the new territory could and should be. Citibank asked: "How much business can we expect in this new country if we are successful and become a market leader? And how much front-end investment is then justified assuming that the front-end investment must not exceed a certain percentage of the potential results?" And then Citi knew from its own experience how long it should take before this new branch should reach break-even, that is, before it should begin to produce profits.

ACTION POINT: Budget development projects separately. Develop most likely estimates of expected results. Monitor results and adjust expectations accordingly.

Permanent Cost Control (Corpedia Online Program)
Innovation and Entrepreneurship

Eliminating Cost Centers

Would the roof cave in if we stopped doing this work altogether?

No matter how well a business prevents cost inflation, it will still have to *cut costs.* This is because businesses are like people, and people often get sick no matter how carefully they exercise, control their diet, and avoid substance abuse. There is thus always the need for *cost cutting.* To start cost cutting, management usually asks: "How can we make this operation more efficient?" It is the wrong question. The question should be: "Would the roof cave in if we stopped doing this work altogether?" And if the answer is "probably not," one eliminates the operation. It is always amazing how many of the things we do will never be missed. But businesses that actually succeed in cutting costs don't wait until they have to cut costs. They build cost-cutting into normal operations. They build into their routine operations *organized abandonment.* Otherwise, eliminating activities and operations runs into extreme political resistance.

ACTION POINT: Set up a systematic process of reviewing all products, processes, and services. Abandon those that no longer contribute to customer value.

Permanent Cost Control (Corpedia Online Program)

Making Cost-Control Permanent

Cost control is not a matter of cost cutting but of cost prevention.

What matters is not really the method. It is the realization that the cost-effectiveness of an activity depends on the way it is being structured. It depends heavily on accepting the premise that *cost control is not a matter of cost cutting but of cost prevention.* And costs never drift down, so cost prevention is a never-ending task. No matter how well structured the organization, its cost-effectiveness needs to be looked at again and again. No matter how carefully it controls its costs, its activities and processes need to be put on trial for their lives every few years.

This process also ensures that the entire workforce embraces and accepts cost control. It should actually see it as an opportunity and not a threat. If cost control is seen as cost cutting, the workforce will see it as a job threat and will refuse to support it. But if cost control is seen and practiced as cost prevention, then the workforce will actually see it as an opportunity, or at the very least it will support the cost control for the sake of better and more secure jobs.

ACTION POINT: Put all the activities in your organization on trial every two or three years.

Permanent Cost Control (Corpedia Online Program)

August

Diversification

"Shoemaker, stick to your last!"

The old cliché is still sound advice. The less diverse a business, the more manageable it is. Simplicity makes for clarity. People can understand their own job and see its relationship to results and to the performance of the whole. Efforts will tend to be concentrated. Expectations can be defined, and results can easily be appraised and measured. The less complex a business is, the fewer things can go wrong. And the more complex a business is, the more difficult it is to figure out what went wrong and to take the right remedial action. Complexity creates problems of communications. The more complex a business, the more layers of management, the more forms and procedures, the more meetings, and the more delays in making decisions.

There are only two ways in which diversity can be harmonized into unity. A business can be highly diversified and yet have fundamental unity if its businesses and technologies, its products and product lines, and its activities are embraced within the unity of a common *market*. And a business can be highly diversified and have fundamental unity if its businesses, its markets, its products and product lines, and its activities are held together in a common *technology*.

ACTION POINT: Examine your business. Is it focused or diffused? If diffused, develop a plan to bring unity out of the diversity using *market* or *technology* as the basis for unity.

Management: Tasks, Responsibilities, Practices

Being the Wrong Size

A business that is the wrong size is a business that does not have the right niche to survive and prosper.

Being the wrong size is a chronic, debilitating, wasting—and a very common—disease. Being the wrong size is curable in the majority of cases. But the cure is neither easy nor pleasant. The symptoms are clear and are always the same. In a business that is the wrong size, there is always one area, activity, function, or effort—or at most a very few—that is out of all proportion and hypertrophied. This area has to be so big, requires so much effort, and imposes so much cost on the business as to make economic performance and results impossible. The old American Motors furnishes the example. American Motors announced successive plans to aggressively recruit new and strong dealers and push up its sales. In order to obtain the sales volume that would have given the business a viable size, the expenses that made the business nonviable had to be increased. And this is precisely what the business could not afford.

The most rewarding strategy to come to grips with the problem is to attempt to *change the character of the business*. A business that is the wrong size is a business that does not have the right niche to survive and prosper. A comparison between American Motors and Volkswagen shows the difference between being the wrong size as a result of lack of distinction, and being the right size by occupying a distinct niche.

ACTION POINT: Analyze your business. Are you too small to compete in the business? If so, develop a profitable niche within which you can compete effectively.

Management: Tasks, Responsibilities, Practices

Growth

Growth that results only in volume and does not produce higher overall productivities is fat—it should be sweated.

Management needs to think through the minimum of growth that its company requires. What is the minimum of growth without which the company would actually lose strength, vigor, and ability to perform, if not to survive? A company needs a viable market standing. Otherwise it soon becomes marginal. It soon becomes, in effect, the wrong size. And if the market expands, whether domestically or worldwide, a company has to grow with the market to maintain its viability. At times a company therefore needs a very high minimum growth rate.

A business needs to distinguish between the wrong kind of growth and the right kind of growth, between muscle, fat, and cancer. The rules are simple: Any growth that, within a short period of time, results in an overall increase in the total productivities of the enterprise's resources is healthy growth. It should be fed and supported. But growth that results only in volume and does not, within a fairly short period of time, produce higher overall productivities is fat. Any increase in volume that does not lead to higher overall productivity should be sweated off again. Finally, any increase in volume that leads to reduced productivities should be eliminated by radical surgery—fast.

ACTION POINT: Determine the minimum growth rate for maintaining your organization's market standing.

Managing in Turbulent Times
Management: Tasks, Responsibilities, Practices

Managing the New Venture

Every new project is an infant and infants belong in the nursery.

Innovative efforts, especially those aimed at developing new businesses, products, or services, should normally report directly to the "executive in charge of innovation." They should never report to line managers charged with responsibility for ongoing operations. Unfortunately, this is a common error.

The new project is an infant and will remain one for the foreseeable future, and infants belong in the nursery. The "adults," that is, the executives in charge of existing businesses or products, will have neither time nor understanding for the infant project. The best-known practitioners of this approach are three American companies: Procter & Gamble, the soap, detergent, edible oil, and food producer; Johnson & Johnson, the hygiene and health-care supplier; and 3M, a major manufacturer of industrial and consumer products. These three companies differ in the details of practice, but essentially all three have the same policy. They set up the new venture as a separate business from the beginning and put a project manager in charge.

ACTION POINT: Keep infant businesses in the nursery. Separate "infants" from "adults."

Innovation and Entrepreneurship

Calculated Obsolescence

Being the one who makes your product, process, or service obsolete is the only way to prevent your competitor from doing so.

Innovating organizations spend neither time nor resources on defending yesterday. Systematic abandonment of yesterday alone can free the resources, and especially the scarcest resource of them all, capable people, for work on the new.

Your being the one who makes your product, process, or service obsolete is the only way to prevent your competitor from doing so. One major American company that has long understood and accepted this is DuPont. When nylon came out in 1938, DuPont immediately put chemists to work to invent new synthetic fibers to compete with nylon. It also began to cut nylon's price—thus making it less attractive for would-be competitors to find a way around DuPont's patents. This explains why DuPont is still the world's leading synthetic-fiber maker, and why DuPont's nylon is still in the market, and profitably so.

ACTION POINT: Cannibalize your own products before your competitor does.

Managing for the Future

Tunnel-Vision Innovation

Often a prescription drug designed for a specific ailment sometimes ends up being used for some other quite different ailment.

When a new venture does succeed, more often than not it is in a market other than the one it was originally intended to serve, with products or services not quite those with which it had set out, bought in large part by customers it did not even think of when it started, and used for a host of purposes besides the ones for which the products were first designed. If a new venture does not anticipate this, organizing itself to take advantage of the unexpected and unseen markets; if it is not totally market-focused, if not market-driven, then it will succeed only in creating an opportunity for a competitor.

The new venture therefore needs to start out with the assumption that its product or service may find customers in markets no one thought of, for uses no one envisaged when the product or service was designed, and that it will be bought by customers outside its field of vision and even unknown to the new venture. If the new venture does not have such a market focus from the very beginning, all it is likely to create is the market for a competitor.

ACTION POINT: When innovating, go with the market response, not with your preconceived ideas. Don't marry your pet ideas about a new venture.

Innovation and Entrepreneurship

Social Innovation: The Research Lab

Management is increasingly becoming the agent of social innovation.

The research lab dates back to 1905. It was conceived and built for the General Electric Company in Schenectady, New York, by one of the earliest "research managers," the German-American physicist Charles Proteus Steinmetz. Steinmetz had two clear objectives from the start: to organize science and scientific work for purposeful technological invention and to build continuous self-renewal through innovation into that new social phenomenon—the big corporation.

Steinmetz's lab radically redefined the relationship between science and technology in research. In setting the goals of his project, Steinmetz identified the new theoretical science needed to accomplish the desired technological results and then organized the appropriate "pure" research to obtain the needed new knowledge. Steinmetz himself was originally a theoretical physicist. But every one of his "contributions" was the result of research he had planned and specified as part of a project to design and to develop a new product line, for example, fractional horsepower motors. Technology, traditional wisdom held and still widely holds, is "applied science." In Steinmetz's lab, science—including the purest of "pure research"—is technology-driven, that is, a means to a technological end.

ACTION POINT: Follow the example of Steinmetz and do market-driven research and development.

The Ecological Vision

Social Innovation: The Lab Without Walls

Steinmetz's technology-driven science is anathema to many academic scientists.

Steinmetz's innovation also led to the "lab without walls," which is America's specific, and major, contribution to very large scientific and technological programs. The first of these, conceived and managed by President Franklin D. Roosevelt's former law partner, Basil O'Connor, was the National Foundation for Infantile Paralysis (March of Dimes), which tackled polio in the early 1930s. This project continued for more than twenty-five years and brought together in a planned, step-by-step effort a large number of scientists from half a dozen disciplines, in a dozen different locations across the country, each working on his own project but within a central strategy and under overall direction.

This then established the pattern for the great World War II projects: the RADAR lab, the Lincoln Laboratory, and, most massive of them all, the Manhattan Project for atomic energy. Similarly, NASA organized a "research lab without walls" when this country decided, after Sputnik, to put a man on the moon. Steinmetz's technology-driven science is still highly controversial. Still, it is the organization we immediately reach for whenever a new scientific problem emerges, for example, when AIDS suddenly became a major medical problem in 1984–85.

ACTION POINT: Terrorism is a major social problem confronting the civilized world. How can this problem be turned into a "Manhattan" type R and D project?

The Ecological Vision

Research Laboratory: Obsolete?

Technologies crisscross industries and travel incredibly fast.

What accounts for the decline in the number of major corporate research labs? The company-owned research laboratory was one of the nineteenth century's most successful inventions. Now many research directors, as well as high-tech industrialists, tend to believe that such labs are becoming obsolete. Why? Technologies crisscross industries and travel incredibly fast, making few of them unique anymore. And increasingly, the knowledge needed in a given industry comes out of some totally different technology with which, very often, the people in the industry are quite unfamiliar. As a result the big research labs of the past are becoming obsolete.

The research laboratory of the big telephone companies, the famous Bell Laboratories of the U.S., was for many decades the source of all major innovations in the telephone industry. But no one in that industry worked on fiberglass cables or had ever heard of them. They were developed by a glass company, Corning. Yet they have revolutionized communications worldwide.

ACTION POINT: Scan the environment for a technology developed in another industry that can help you now.

Managing in the Next Society
The Next Society (Corpedia Online Program)

The Infant New Venture

Businesses are not paid to reform customers.

Above all, the people who are running a new venture need to spend time outside: in the marketplace, with customers, and with their own sales force, looking and listening. The new venture needs to build in systematic practices to remind itself that a "product" or a "service" is defined by the customer, not by the producer. It needs to work continuously on challenging itself in respect to the utility and value that its products or services contribute to customers. The greatest danger for the new venture is to "know better" than the customer what the product or service is or should be, how it should be bought, and what it should be used for. Above all, the new venture needs willingness to see the unexpected success as an opportunity rather than as an affront to its expertise. And it needs to accept that elementary axiom of marketing: Businesses are not paid to reform customers. They are paid to satisfy customers. Lack of market focus is typically a disease of the "neonatal," the infant new venture. It is the most serious affliction of the new venture in its early stages—and one that can permanently stunt even those that survive.

ACTION POINT: See the unexpected success of a new venture as an opportunity not as a problem.

Innovation and Entrepreneurship

The Rapidly Growing New Venture

The more successful a new venture is, the more dangerous the lack of financial foresight.

The lack of adequate financial focus and the right financial policies is the greatest threat to the new venture in the next stage of its growth. It is, above all, a threat to the rapidly growing new venture. Suppose that a new venture has successfully launched its product or service and is growing fast. It reports "rapidly increasing profits" and issues rosy forecasts. The stock market then "discovers" the new venture, especially if it is high-tech or in a field otherwise currently fashionable. Predictions abound that the new venture's sales will reach a billion dollars within five years.

Eighteen months later, the new venture collapses. It is suddenly awash in red ink, lays off 180 of its 275 employees, fires the president, or is sold at a bargain price to a big company. The causes are always the same: lack of cash; inability to raise the capital needed for expansion; and loss of control, with expenses, inventories, and receivables in disarray. These three financial afflictions often hit together at the same time. Yet any one of them by itself endangers the health, if not the life, of the new venture. Once this financial crisis has erupted, it can be cured only with great difficulty and considerable suffering.

ACTION POINT: Develop sound financial plans and controls for your new venture. Don't look at your accounting and finance people as "bean counters."

Innovation and Entrepreneurship

Managing Cash in the New Venture

There is an old banker's rule of thumb according to which one assumes that bills will have to be paid sixty days earlier than expected and receivables will come in sixty days later.

Entrepreneurs starting new ventures are rarely unmindful of money; on the contrary, they tend to be greedy. They therefore focus on profits. But this is the wrong focus for a new venture, or rather, it comes last rather than first. Cash flow, capital, and controls come much earlier. Without them, the profit figures are fiction—good for twelve to eighteen months, perhaps, after which they evaporate. Growth has to be fed. In financial terms this means that growth in a new venture demands adding financial resources rather than taking them out. The healthier a new venture and the faster it grows, the more financial feeding it requires.

The new venture needs cash-flow analysis, cash-flow forecasts, and cash management. The fact that America's new ventures of the last few years (with the significant exception of high-tech companies) have been doing so much better than new ventures used to do is largely because the new entrepreneurs in the United States have learned that entrepreneurship demands financial management. Cash management is fairly easy if there are reliable cash-flow forecasts, with "reliable" meaning "worst case" assumptions rather than hopes. If the forecast is overly conservative, the worst that can happen is a temporary cash surplus.

ACTION POINT: Develop "worst case" estimates of cash flow and cash forecasts for new ventures. Monitor receivables and inventory levels closely.

Innovation and Entrepreneurship

Management Team for the New Venture

Key activities are not to be found in books.
They emerge from analysis of the specific enterprise.

Whenever the objective economic indicators of a new venture indicate that the business may double within three or five years, then it is the duty of the founder or founders to build the management team the new venture will soon require. First of all the founders, together with other key people in the firm, will have to think through the key activities of their business. What are the specific areas upon which the survival and success of this particular business depend? Every activity that any member of the group thinks belongs there should go down on the list.

The next step is, then, for each member of the group, beginning with the founder, to ask: "What are the activities that I am doing well? And what are the activities that each of my key associates in this business is actually doing well?" Next one asks: "Which of the key activities should each of us, therefore, take on as his or her first and major responsibility because they fit the individual's strengths? Which individual fits which key activity?" Then the work on building a team can begin. But all key activities need to be covered by someone who has proven ability in performance.

ACTION POINT: Examine a successful new venture either inside or outside of your enterprise. Was the innovator successful in defining key activities and assigning those to people of proven competence?

Innovation and Entrepreneurship

Unrealized Business Potential

"Opportunity is where you find it," not where it finds you.

Luck, chance, and catastrophe affect business as they do all human endeavors. But luck never built a business. Prosperity and growth come only to the business that systematically finds and exploits its potential. No matter how successfully a business organizes itself for the challenges and opportunities of the present, it will still be far below its optimum performance. Its potential is always greater than its realized actuality.

Dangers and weaknesses indicate where to look for business potential. To convert them from problems into opportunities brings extraordinary returns. Opportunities have to be reflected against the experience of a company and against its past successes and failures. Sometimes all that is needed to accomplish this transformation is a change in the attitude of the executives. Three questions will bring out the hidden potential of a business:

- What are the restraints and limitations that make the business vulnerable?
- What are the imbalances of the business?
- What are we afraid of, what do we see as a threat to this business—and how can we use it as an opportunity?

ACTION POINT: Answer these three questions for your enterprise and move closer to optimum performance.

Managing for Results

Finding Opportunities in Vulnerabilities

Finding and realizing the potential of a business is psychologically difficult.

Finding and realizing the potential of a business is psychologically difficult. It will always be opposed from within because it means breaking with old, established habits. It often means giving up the very skill people are proudest of. To fight the threat, to manage an imbalance, and above all to make a process efficient despite its inherent weaknesses, requires great effort.

Searching for the potential of opportunity in a company's vulnerabilities, limitations, and weaknesses is therefore likely to be resented by its most accomplished people as a direct attack on their position, pride, and power. This is the reason why the opportunities are often not realized by the industry leaders but by people on or near the outside. That this area is difficult, both objectively and psychologically, only means that businesses have to work hard at it and that managements have to stress it heavily.

ACTION POINT: Convert the vulnerabilities of your enterprise into opportunities.

Managing for Results

Exploiting Innovative Ideas

Creativity is sexy, but the real problem is the shockingly high mortality rate of healthy new products or services.

There usually are more good ideas in even the stodgiest organization than can possibly be exploited. The real problem is the shockingly high mortality rate of healthy new products or services. And like yesterday's infant mortality rate, the mortality rate of new products and services is totally unnecessary. It can be reduced fairly fast and without spending a great deal of money. Much of it is simply the result of ignorance of the *entrepreneurial strategies*. The right entrepreneurial strategy has a very high chance of success.

There are four specifically entrepreneurial strategies aiming at *market leadership*: being "Fustest with the Mostest"; "Hitting Them Where They Ain't"; finding and occupying a specialized "ecological niche"; and changing the economic characteristics of a product, a market, or an industry. These four strategies are not mutually exclusive. One and the same entrepreneur often combines two, sometimes even elements of three, in one strategy. Still, each of these four has its prerequisites. Each fits certain kinds of innovation and does not fit others. Each requires specific behavior on the part of the entrepreneur. Finally, each has its own limitations and carries its own risks.

ACTION POINT: Be systematic in exploiting innovative ideas, remembering these four strategies for success.

Innovation and Entrepreneurship
Entrepreneurial Strategies (Corpedia Online Program)

First with the Most

"Being Fustest with the Mostest."

"First with the most" was the expression used by a Confederate general to describe his cavalry unit's consistent victories in the Civil War. In business, it describes the strategy in which an innovator looks to attain leadership, if not outright dominance. This is the entrepreneurial strategy with the potentially highest rewards; but it's also the most risky one. There can be no mistakes or second chances. The outcome is either market and industry leadership or nothing at all. Entrepreneurs must be right the first time; otherwise, they fail. For every innovator that succeeds with this strategy, dozens fail. Yet if the "first with the most" strategy succeeds, the innovator reaps tremendous rewards. It's the strategy that underlies the success and market leadership of such giants as 3M, Procter & Gamble, Intel, and Microsoft.

Yet there is a special risk to this strategy: to achieve initial success, then to be outflanked by someone practicing the next entrepreneurial strategy, "hitting them where they aren't." For example, the two young engineers who started the Apple computer company in the proverbial garage, without financial backers or previous business experience, aimed from the beginning at creating an industry and dominating it. But they were soon outflanked by IBM.

ACTION POINT: When you develop a new product, process, or service, remember, protect your flank.

Innovation and Entrepreneurship
Entrepreneurial Strategies (Corpedia Online Program)

Hitting Them Where They Aren't

"Hitting them where they aren't" outflanks the leader by creative imitation.

Here, the innovator doesn't create a major new product or service. Instead, it takes something just created by somebody else and improves upon it. This is imitation. But it is creative imitation because the innovator reworks the new product or service to better satisfy customers' wants and needs. Once the innovator succeeds in creating what customers want, it can achieve leadership and take control of the market.

The perfect example is how IBM became the leading producer of PCs in the 1970s. Apple invented the PC. When the Apple appeared, it was an instant sensation. IBM set to work to outflank the Apple. It asked, "What are Apple's shortcomings?" Within eighteen months IBM had on the market a PC that did everything the PC customers needed and wanted but had what the Apple lacked: software. And within another year IBM's PC had become the market leader worldwide; it held that position for more than ten years. And Apple had become marginal. It almost went under and only turned itself around into a respectable niche player twenty-odd years later, in the late 1990s.

ACTION POINT: Look for a successful innovation of a competitor's and improve upon it, thus outflanking your competitor.

Innovation and Entrepreneurship
Entrepreneurial Strategies (Corpedia Online Program)

Entrepreneurial Judo

Entrepreneurial Judo turns what the market leaders consider their strengths into the very weaknesses that defeat them.

The Japanese judo master looks for the strength that is his opponent's pride and joy. He assumes, and does so with high probability, that the opponent bases his strategy on this strength in every fight. And then the judo master figures out where this continuing reliance on a particular strength leaves the opponent vulnerable and undefended. Then he turns his opponent's strength into the opponent's fatal weakness that defeats the opponent.

Businesses, like judo fighters, tend to become set in their behaviors. And then Entrepreneurial Judo turns what the market leaders consider their strengths into the very weaknesses that defeat them. For example, the Japanese became the leaders in one American market after the other: first in copiers, then in machine tools, then in consumer electronics, then in automobiles, and then in fax machines. The strategy was always the same. They turned what the Americans considered their strength into a weakness that defeated the American companies. The Americans saw high profitability as their greatest strength. And thus they focused on the high end of the market and left the mass market undersupplied and underserviced. The Japanese moved in with low-cost products with minimum features. The Americans didn't even try to fight them. But when the Japanese had taken over the mass market they had the cash flow to move in on the high-end market, too. And they soon came to dominate both the mass market and the high-end market.

ACTION POINT: Be agile, recognize the strengths of your competitors, and look for opportunities in parts of the market that they have ignored.

Innovation and Entrepreneurship
Entrepreneurial Strategies (Corpedia Online Program)

Changing Economic Characteristics

Successful innovators price according to what the customer pays for.

Under the other entrepreneurial strategies, the innovator has to come up with an innovative product or service; here the *strategy itself* is the innovation. The innovative strategy converts an existing product or service into something new by changing its utility, its value, and its economic characteristics. There is new economic value and new customers, but no new product or service. Often the most successful way to change the economic characteristics of a product or service is to change its pricing. In the end the producer gets at least the same amount of money, if not a good deal more. But the way pricing is structured reflects the customer's reality rather than the reality of the producer.

Here is an example. The Internet was designed as an *information network*. And most providers charged for access to it, such as for hosting an e-mail address. But Yahoo and other companies give away Internet access. It gets paid for by advertisers whose ads the customers have to see when they go online. Yahoo asked: "*Who* is the customer?" Its answer: "It's a supplier who wants access to a potential customer." This changed the characteristics of the industry. It gave the Internet a new dimension.

ACTION POINT: Determine what your customers really buy. Serve them in a way that better meets their needs and also creates enhanced economic results for your organization.

Innovation and Entrepreneurship
Entrepreneurial Strategies (Corpedia Online Program)

Ecological Niche: Tollbooth Strategy

If the innovator succeeds, it will have a nearly impenetrable position.

The fourth major entrepreneurial strategy, occupying an ecological niche, allows an innovator to establish a virtual monopoly in a small niche market. The first niche strategy is the *tollbooth strategy.* Under the tollbooth strategy, the innovator creates a product or service that is an indispensable part of a larger process. Then the cost of using the product becomes eventually irrelevant. Here the market must be so limited that whoever occupies the niche first is able to effectively bar anyone else from entering it.

Here is an example: Alcon, a company started in the late 1950s by a salesman for a major pharmaceutical company. He had known all along that there was a major incongruity in the operation for senile cataracts in the eyes. There was one dangerous procedure in the surgery where the surgeon had to sever a piece of muscle tissue with a slight risk of bleeding that would destroy the eye. The innovator read up on what was known about this muscle and found almost immediately that an enzyme dissolved it without bleeding or cutting. But there had been no way to prevent this enzyme from disintegrating and to give it shelf life. Then the innovator found that since 1890 a number of substances had been developed to give enzymes stability and shelf life. He patented the application of one of these substances to the enzyme, and within eighteen months he had the world market for the stuff.

ACTION POINT: Exploit an incongruity in an internal process using the tollbooth strategy.

Innovation and Entrepreneurship
Entrepreneurial Strategies (Corpedia Online Program)

Ecological Niche: Specialty-Skill Strategy

If the specialty skill is properly maintained the innovator is usually protected against competition.

The second ecological niche is the specialty-skill strategy. Here the niche an innovator occupies is just as unique as in the tollbooth strategy, but it tends to be somewhat larger. For example, everyone can name the major U.S. automobile manufacturers. But how many people know the companies that make the brake pads or electrical circuits or headlamps that go into these cars? Those largely unknown companies occupy a specialty-skill position in an ecological niche. Developing high skill at a very early time in a new industry or market captures this position. Once the market begins to grow, the innovator has a significant head start over potential competitors and has already become the standard industry supplier.

The best example is that of America's leading twentieth-century inventor, Charles Kettering. Kettering aimed in all his inventions at creating a vastly profitable *niche* business. And his first, and probably the world's most profitable invention, was aimed at creating a specialty-skill niche market. It was the self-starter. Until then, automobiles had to be started by cranking by hand, which was very hard and also quite dangerous. But for fifteen years or so, during the period of the most rapid growth in the automobile industry, every carmaker had to buy Kettering's self-starter. It added very little to the cost of the car, maybe 1 or 2 percent. But Kettering's profit margins were known to be around 500 percent *or more.*

ACTION POINT: Exploit rapidly growing segments in your industry by providing a specialty skill for that industry that improves upon existing operations.

Innovation and Entrepreneurship
Entrepreneurial Strategies (Corpedia Online Program)

Ecological Niche: Specialty Market

With the specialty-market strategy the innovator must create a small but profitable new market.

The final niche strategy is to establish a specialty-market niche big enough to be profitable but small enough not to make it worthwhile for potential competitors to invade it. For example, the most profitable financial product for twenty or more years, from 1919 until World War II and even a decade beyond, was the American Express Travelers Cheque—a specialty-market niche. The Travelers Cheque was much safer than carrying a lot of cash and usable everywhere—they were accepted, for instance, by every European hotel. Banks sold the Cheques and got a small fee for each transaction. This not only kept American Express from needing to market the Cheques, but it also discouraged the banks from launching a competing service. And American Express made oodles of money because Cheque owners would hold the Cheques for months, or even years, before cashing them, during which time American Express had the "float," that is, the interest-free use of the money the Cheque holders had paid. Everyone in the financial industry knew how profitable the Travelers Cheques were. But the market then was so small that there was no point in any major bank trying to muscle its way into it.

ACTION POINT: Describe your own examples of the three ecological-niche innovation strategies: Tollbooth, Specialty Skill, and Specialty Market. Exploit one or more of these ecological strategies.

Innovation and Entrepreneurship
Entrepreneurial Strategies (Corpedia Online Program)

Threats to Niche Strategies

While it lasts, the niche strategy is the most profitable entrepreneurial strategy.

What all niche strategies have in common is that they are unlikely to endure forever. One threat is for the niche to be outflanked, and especially by technological change. That happened to Alcon. Fifteen years after it became a worldwide near-monopoly, somebody in Czechoslovakia invented a new cataract operation, the implant lens, in which eye muscle has to be maintained rather than dissolved. And Alcon's solvent became history.

Another threat is if a niche becomes the main mass market. That's what happened to the Travelers Cheque. Before World War II, a European trip for Americans was still the rare exception. Now the transatlantic jets carry more passengers in two days between Europe and the U.S. than all the steamships carried in an entire year before World War II. And the new mass traveler uses a credit card. And when the automobile market became a mass market, in the U.S. during World War I and in Europe and Japan after World War II, the intense pressure to cut costs meant that to be the niche supplier depending on a specialty skill ceased to yield niche profits. These players were the ones, and still are, on which the automobile companies put the greatest pressure to cut prices. And they had no choice but to yield.

ACTION POINT: Evaluate the threats of obsolescence to any of your products, processes, and services. Maintain a systematic program of innovation to offset inevitable threats to the products and services of your enterprise.

Innovation and Entrepreneurship
Entrepreneurial Strategies (Corpedia Online Program)

Three Case Studies on Innovation Strategy

Three pharmaceutical companies—*Able, Baker,* and *Charlie*—are among the most successful pharmaceutical businesses in the world. *Able* and *Baker* are very large. *Charlie* is medium-sized, but growing fast. All three companies spend about the same percentage of their revenues on research. There the similarity ends. Each of them approaches research quite differently.

Able Company: Research Strategy

Able's aim is to gain early leadership in a major area, acquire dominance in it, and then maintain this leadership position.

Able Company—spends a great deal of research money on one carefully selected area at a time. It picks this area when pure research in the universities first indicates a genuine breakthrough. Then, long before commercial products are available, it hires the very best people in the field, and puts them to work. Outside of these areas, however, the company spends no research money and is perfectly willing not to be a factor at all. The company takes big positions in big fields at a very early stage, at great risk, but also at great reward.

ACTION POINT: Able Company is pursuing the______entrepreneurial strategy (see *August 16*) and the______window of opportunity (see *July 12*).

Management Cases

Baker Company: Research Strategy

Baker's aim is to come up with a small number of drugs in each field that are clearly superior and offer significant advances to medical practice.

The strategy of *Baker* Company is completely different. Its research lab, perhaps the most famous in the pharmaceutical industry, works in an enormous number of fields. It does not, however, enter a field until the basic scientific theoretical work has been done. Then it goes to work. Of every ten products that come out of its own laboratory, the company itself markets no more than two or three. When it becomes reasonably clear that an effective drug will result from a line of research, the company carefully scrutinizes the product and, indeed, the entire field. First, is the new product likely to be medically so superior as to become the new "standard"? Second, is it likely to have major impact throughout the field of health care and medical practice rather than be confined to one specialty area, even a large one? And finally, is it likely to remain the "standard" for a good many years, rather than to be overtaken by competitive products?

If the answer to any of these three questions is "No," the company will license or sell the development, rather than convert it into a product of its own. This has been highly profitable in two ways. It has generated licensing income almost equal to the profits the company makes on the drugs it makes and sells under its own name. And it has assured that each of the company's products is considered the "leader" by the medical profession.

ACTION POINT: Test your organization's innovative strategy against that of Baker Company.

Management Cases

Charlie Company: Research Strategy

Charlie Company does no research. It looks for areas where a fairly simple development can give it a near-monopoly position in a small but important area.

Charlie Company does no research. All it does is develop. It will not tackle any of the products Able or Baker companies consider attractive. It looks for areas in medical and surgical practice where existing products are not doing a good job, and where a fairly simple change can greatly improve the doctor's or surgeon's performance. And it looks for fields that are so small that once there is a truly superior product, there is no incentive for anyone else to go in and compete.

Its first product was a simple enzyme—actually known for forty years—to make cataract operations virtually bloodless and greatly ease the eye surgeon's job. All the work that had to be done was to find a way to extend the shelf life of the enzyme. The next product was a very simple ointment to put on the umbilical cord of infants to prevent infection and speed up healing. It has become standard in every maternity hospital throughout the world. The company later brought out a product to replace the toxic solution with which newborn babies used to be washed to prevent infection—again, primarily a matter of compounding rather than discovering. In each area, the world market is so limited—maybe to $20 million—that a single supplier, provided it offers a truly superior product, can occupy a near-monopoly position with a minimum of competition and practically no pressure on price.

ACTION POINT: Test your organization's innovative strategy against that of Charlie Company.

Management Cases

Success Always Creates New Realities

Only the fairy story ends "They lived happily ever after."

Success always obsoletes the very behavior that achieved it. It always creates new realities. It always creates, above all, its own and different problems. It is not easy for the management of a successful company to ask, "What is our business?" Everybody in the company thinks that the answer is so obvious as not to deserve discussion. It is never popular to argue with success, never popular to rock the boat. But the management that does not ask "What is our business?" when the company is successful is, in effect, smug, lazy, and arrogant. It will not be long before success will turn into failure.

The two most successful American industries of the 1920s were anthracite coal mines and railroads. Both believed that God had given them an unshakable monopoly forever. Both believed that the definition of their business was so obvious as to eliminate all need for thought, let alone for action. Neither need have tumbled from its leadership position—the anthracite industry into total oblivion—had their managements not taken success for granted. Above all: when a management attains the company's objectives, it should always ask seriously, "What is our business?" This requires self-discipline and responsibility. The alternative is decline.

ACTION POINT: Pick a product or service of your organization. How is the market share computed? What is your share of the market? Broaden your definition of the market (for example, from railroad to transportation). What is your share of the broader market?

Management: Tasks, Responsibilities, Practices

The Opportunity-Focused Organization

Performing organizations enjoy what they're doing.

Organizations have a gravity, the weight is constantly being pushed into being problem-focused, and one has to fight it all the time. Not very many organizations are good at what I call "exploitation of success." Look at what is today the world's largest consumer-electronics entertainment company: Sony. Basically, all Sony has ever done is run with the tape recorder and build on its success. But if you build that into the organization and demand it from everybody, then you create a receptivity for being opportunity-focused rather than problem-focused. And above all, you create enjoyment. I know this is not the academically respectable thing to say, but performing organizations enjoy what they're doing. I'm always asked how I know what kind of an organization to accept as a client. When you walk through the door, you know in two minutes whether they enjoy it. And if they don't enjoy it, then I'd rather not work for them. But if they like it and they feel that tomorrow is going to be better—that creates a totally different climate.

ACTION POINT: Do what you enjoy.

"Meeting of the Minds," *Across the Board: The Conference Board Magazine*

Finding Opportunity in Surprises

One survives problems by making them irrelevant because of success.

Every surprise is something to be taken seriously. The entire reporting system kind of encourages the neglect of opportunities and surprises, but also it's fairly easy to change. Fifty years ago, a friend and mentor of mine invented a system used in a big company that's become very successful as a result. Every manager, down to the first-line supervisor, sits down every month and writes a letter with one subject: the unexpected. Not what went right or what went wrong, but the unexpected. And then they have a meeting and look at these things with the question: Does this tell us something? Now, the great majority don't, the great majority are just anecdotes, but there are usually three or four that are relevant. And out of this, the company—a pharmaceutical company—has grown from a fairly unimportant commodity producer to one of the world's leaders. And it's come out of surprises, clinical surprises, like when a physician uses a medication for what it was not developed for and has amazing results. You have to focus on success, especially unexpected success, and run with it.

ACTION POINT: Write a letter to your boss each month identifying unexpected events. Pick out unexpected successes and pursue them.

"Meeting of the Minds," *Across the Board: The Conference Board Magazine*

Maintaining Dynamic Equilibrium

Management has to maintain the dynamic equilibrium between change and continuity.

My publisher in Japan, Diamond, recently published selected essays of mine, written over the last fifty years, under the title *The Future Which Already Happened* (*The Ecological Vision*, 1993). For this book, I wrote a kind of intellectual autobiography, which constitutes the last chapter of the book. In it, I record the beginning of my work more than sixty years ago, which was concerned with the balance between change and continuity. It was this concern that, ten years later, led me to the study of management. For I see in management, the specific organ of society that has to maintain the dynamic equilibrium between change and continuity, without which societies, organizations, and individuals perish.

ACTION POINT: Institute a systematic process of innovation to lead change.

Drucker on Asia

September

Know Thy Time

Effective executives start with their time.

"Know thyself," the old prescription for wisdom, is almost impossibly difficult for mortal men. But everyone can follow the injunction "Know thy time" if one wants to, and be well on the road toward contribution and effectiveness.

Most discussions of the executive's task start with the advice to plan one's work. This sounds eminently plausible. The only thing wrong with it is that it rarely works. The plans always remain on paper, always remain good intentions. They seldom turn into achievement. Effective executives, in my observation, do not start with their tasks. They start with their time. And they do not start out with planning. They start by finding out where their time actually goes. Then they attempt to manage their time and to cut back unproductive demands on their time. Finally they consolidate their "discretionary" time into the largest possible continuing units. This three-step process

- recording time
- managing time
- consolidating time

is the foundation of executive effectiveness.

ACTION POINT: Find out where your time goes by recording, managing, and consolidating your time.

The Effective Executive

Record Time and Eliminate Time Wasters

All one has to do is to learn to say "no" if an activity contributes nothing.

The first step toward executive effectiveness is to record actual time-use. There are executives who keep such a time log themselves. Others have their secretaries do it for them. The important thing is that it gets done, and that the record is made in "real" time. A good many effective executives keep such a log continuously and look at it regularly every month. After each such sample, they rethink and rework their schedule. First one tries to identify and eliminate the things that need not be done at all, the things that are purely a waste of time without any results whatever. To find these time wasters, one asks of all activities in the time records: "What would happen if this were not done at all?" And if the answer is, "Nothing would happen," then obviously the conclusion is to stop doing it.

ACTION POINT: Create a time log of your activities. Eliminate those activities that are time wasters.

The Effective Executive

Consolidate Time

Effective executives know that one rarely overprunes.

The final step in time management is to consolidate the time that record and analysis show as normally available and under the executive's control. To be effective every executive needs to be able to dispose of time in fairly large chunks. This is particularly true with respect to time spent working with people, which is, of course, a central task in the work of the executive. The manager who thinks that she can discuss the plans, direction, and performance of one of her subordinates in fifteen minutes is just deceiving herself.

There are a good many ways to consolidate time. Some people work at home one or more days a week. Other executives schedule all the operating work—the meetings, reviews, problem-sessions, and so on—for two days a week and set aside the mornings of the remaining days for consistent, continuing work on major issues. But the method by which one consolidates one's discretionary time is far less important than the approach. Effective executives start out by estimating how much discretionary time they can realistically call their own. And if they find later that other matters encroach on this reserve, they scrutinize their record again and get rid of some more time demands from less-than-fully-productive activities.

ACTION POINT: Consolidate your time and set aside large blocks of time to complete major tasks.

The Effective Executive

Practices of Effective Executives

All that effective executives have in common is the ability to get the right things done.

The effective executives I have seen differ widely in their temperaments and abilities, in what they do and how they do it, in their personalities, their knowledge, their interests—in fact, in almost everything that distinguishes human beings. But all effective executives I've known perform only necessary tasks and eliminate unnecessary ones.

Five practices have to be acquired to be effective. Effective executives know *where their time goes.* They work systematically at managing the little of their time that can be brought under their control. Effective executives focus on *outward contributions.* Effective executives *build on strengths*—theirs and others. They do not build on weaknesses. Effective executives *concentrate on superior performance* where superior performance will produce outstanding results. They force themselves to stay within priorities. Effective executives make *effective decisions.* They know that this is a system—the right steps in the right sequence. They know that to make decisions fast is to make the wrong decisions. Whenever I have found a person who—no matter how great in intelligence, industry, imagination, or knowledge—fails to observe these practices, I have also found an executive deficient in effectiveness.

ACTION POINT: Commit these five tasks to memory and practice them: know where your time goes; focus on outward contributions; build on strengths; concentrate on superior performance; and make effective decisions.

The Effective Executive

Focus on Contribution

The question "What should I contribute?" *gives freedom because it gives responsibility.*

The great majority of executives tend to focus downward. They are occupied with efforts rather than with results. They worry over what the organization and their superiors "owe" them and should do for them. And they are conscious above all of the authority they "should have." As a result, they render themselves ineffectual. The effective executive focuses on contribution. He looks up from his work and outward toward goals. He asks: "What can I contribute that will significantly affect the performance and the results of the institution I serve?" His stress is on responsibility.

The focus on contribution is the key to effectiveness: in a person's own work—its content, its level, its standards, and its impacts; in his relations with others—his superiors, his associates, his subordinates; in his use of the tools of the executive such as meetings or reports. The focus on contribution turns the executive's attention away from his own specialty, his own narrow skills, his own department, and toward the performance of the whole. It turns his attention to the outside, the only place where there are results.

ACTION POINT: Maintain a constant focus on the *contribution* you can and should make to your organization.

The Effective Executive
Management Challenges for the 21st Century

Performance Appraisals

Appraisals—and the philosophy behind them—are far too much concerned with "potential."

Effective executives usually work out their own unique form of performance appraisal. It starts out with a statement of the major contributions expected from a person in his past and present positions and a record of his performance against these goals. Then it asks four questions:

1. What has he [or she] done well?
2. What, therefore, is he likely to be able to do well?
3. What does he have to learn or to acquire to be able to get the full benefit from his strength?
4. If I had a son or daughter, would I be willing to have him or her work under this person?
    a. If yes, why?
    b. If no, why?

This appraisal actually takes a much more critical look at a person than the usual procedure does. But it focuses on strengths. Weaknesses are seen as limitations to the full use of strengths and to one's own achievement, effectiveness, and accomplishment. The last question (b.) is the only one that is not primarily concerned with strengths. Subordinates, especially bright, young, and ambitious ones, tend to mold themselves after a forceful boss. There is, therefore, nothing more corrupting and more destructive in an organization than a forceful but basically corrupt executive. Here, therefore, is the one area where weakness is a disqualification by itself rather than a limitation on performance capacity and strength.

ACTION POINT: Adhere to the four questions in this reading when conducting performance appraisals.

The Effective Executive

How to Develop People

Any organization develops people; it either forms them or deforms them.

Any organization develops people; it has no choice. It either helps them grow or it stunts them. What do we know about developing people? Quite a bit. We certainly know what *not* to do, and those don'ts are easier to spell out than the dos. First, one does not try to build upon people's weakness. One can expect adults to develop manners and behavior and to learn skills and knowledge. But one has to use people's personalities the way they are, not the way we would like them to be. A second don't is to take a narrow and shortsighted view of the development of people. One has to learn specific skills for a specific job. But development is more than that: it has to be for a career and for a life. The specific job must fit into this longer-term goal. Another thing we know is not to establish crown princes. Look always at performance, not at promise. With the focus on performance and not potential, the executive can make high demands. One can always relax standards, but one can never raise them. Next, the executive must learn to place people's strengths.

In developing people the lesson is to focus on strengths. Then make really stringent demands, and take the time and trouble (it's hard work) to review performance. Sit down with people and say: "This is what you and I committed ourselves to a year ago. How have you done? What have you done well?"

ACTION POINT: Develop your people. Focus first on their strengths. Then make high demands based on a person's strengths. Finally, periodically review their performance.

Managing the Non-Profit Organization

Knowledge Worker as Effective Executive

The executive who works at making strengths productive—his own as well as those of others—works at making organizational performance compatible with personal achievement.

Self-development of the executive toward effectiveness is the only available answer to satisfy both the objective needs of society for performance by the organization, and the needs of the person for achievement and fulfillment. It is the only way in which organization goals and individual needs can come together. Executives who work at making strengths productive—his own as well as those of others—work at making organizational performance compatible with personal achievement. They work at making their knowledge area become organizational opportunity. And by focusing on contribution, they make their own values become organization results.

Knowledge workers demand economic rewards too. Their absence is a deterrent. But their presence is not enough. They need opportunity; they need achievement; they need fulfillment; they need values. Only by making themselves into effective executives can knowledge workers obtain these satisfactions. Only executive effectiveness can enable society to harmonize its two needs: the needs of the organization to obtain from the individual the contribution it needs, and the need of the individuals to have the organization serve as their tool for the accomplishment of their purposes.

ACTION POINT: Know your strengths. Apply them to areas in your organization where you can make a contribution. Make sure your values and the values of the organization are compatible.

The Effective Executive

Take Responsibility for Your Career

The stepladder is gone, and there's not even the implied structure of an industry's rope ladder. It's more like vines, and you bring your own machete.

If a young man in a gray flannel suit represented the lifelong corporate type, what's today's image? Taking individual responsibility and not depending on any particular company. Equally important is managing your own career. You don't know what you'll be doing next, or whether you'll work in a private office or one big amphitheater or even out of your home. You have to take responsibility for knowing yourself, so you can find the right jobs as you develop and as your family becomes a factor in your values and choices.

Remarkably few Americans are prepared to select jobs for themselves. When you ask, "Do you know what you are good at? Do you know your limitations?" they look you in the eye with a blank stare. Or they often respond in terms of subject knowledge, which is the wrong answer. When they prepare their résumés, they try to list positions like steps up a ladder. It is time to give up thinking of jobs or career paths as we once did and think in terms of taking on one assignment after another. We have to leap right over the search for objective criteria and get into the subjective—what I call *competencies.*

ACTION POINT: Take responsibility for your own career. List your strengths and limitations. What assignments are you prepared to take on next? Prepare to take on these assignments either inside of or outside of your current organization.

Managing in a Time of Great Change

Defining One's Performance

Performance is not hitting the bull's-eye with every shot—that is a circus act.

The first requirement of organizational health is a high demand on performance. Indeed, one of the major reasons for demanding that management be by objectives and that it focus on the objective requirements of the task is the need to have managers set high standards of performance for themselves. This requires that performance be understood properly. Performance is not hitting the bull's-eye with every shot. Performance is rather the consistent ability to produce results over prolonged periods of time and in a variety of assignments. A performance record must include mistakes. It must include failures. It must reveal a person's limitations as well as his strengths.

The one person to distrust is the one who never makes a mistake, never commits a blunder, never fails in what he tries to do. Either he is a phony, or he stays with the safe, the tried, and the trivial. The better a person is, the more mistakes he will make—for the more new things he will try.

ACTION POINT: Define performance as a "batting average." Create an atmosphere where people are permitted to make mistakes. Evaluate a person's performance as "the consistent ability to produce results over a relatively long period of time."

Management: Tasks, Responsibilities, Practices

Results That Make a Difference

What results have to be achieved to make a difference?

One question has to be asked to decide "What should I contribute?" "*Where and how can I have results that make a difference?*" The answer to this question has to balance a number of things. Results should be hard to achieve. They should require "stretching," to use the present buzzword. But they should be within reach. To aim at results that cannot be achieved—or can be achieved only under the most unlikely circumstances—is not being "ambitious." It is being foolish. At the same time, results should be meaningful. They should make a difference. And they should be visible and, if at all possible, measurable.

The decision about "What should my contribution be?" balances three elements. First comes the question: "What does the situation require?" Then comes the question: "How could I make the greatest contribution, with my strengths, my way of performing, my values, to what needs to be done?" Finally, there is the question: "What results have to be achieved to make a difference?" This then leads to the *action conclusions:* what to do, where to start, how to start, what goals and deadlines to set.

ACTION POINT: Define results for your position that will make a difference. How can you make the greatest contribution based upon your strengths? Establish goals and set deadlines for them.

Management Challenges for the 21st Century

Managing Oneself: Identify Strengths

It takes far less energy to move from first-rate performance to excellence than it does to move from incompetence to mediocrity.

You can learn to identify your strengths by using *feedback analysis*. This is a simple process in which you write down every one of your key decisions and key actions along with the results that you expect them to achieve. Nine to twelve months later, check the actual results against expectations. After two to three years of use, you will know your strengths by tracking those decisions and actions where actual results fell in line with or exceeded expectations. Once you have identified your strengths through feedback analysis, you can use this knowledge to improve performance and results. You can make this happen in five ways.

First, concentrate on your strengths. Second, work on improving strengths. You may need to learn new knowledge or to update old. Third, recognize disabling habits. The worst, and most common, one is arrogance. Oftentimes poor performance results from an unwillingness to pursue knowledge outside one's own narrow specialty. Fourth, remedy bad habits and bad manners. All too often, a bad habit such as procrastination or bad manners makes cooperation and teamwork all but impossible. And fifth, figure out what you should not do.

ACTION POINT: Use feedback analysis to identify your strengths. Then go to work on improving your strengths. Identify and eliminate bad habits that hinder the full development of your strengths. Figure out what you should do and do it. Finally, decide what you should not do.

Management Challenges for the 21st Century
Managing Oneself (Corpedia Online Program)

Managing Oneself: How Do I Perform?

Performance that violates your values corrupts,
and it will ultimately sap and destroy your strengths.

Just as different people have different strengths and weaknesses, they also work and perform in different ways. For example, some people learn by reading, others by listening. And few readers can become successful listeners or vice versa. Learning style is just one of several factors that go into making up a person's work style. There are other questions that must be answered. Do you work best when cooperating with others, or do you achieve results when working alone? If you work best with others, is it usually as a subordinate, peer, or supervisor? Do you need a predictable, structured work environment? Do you thrive under pressure?

You also have to consider your personal values: are they comparable to or at least compatible with your strengths? If there is any conflict between your values and strengths, always choose values. Performance that violates your values corrupts, and it will ultimately sap and destroy your strengths. These are just some of the questions that must be answered. What is important is to figure out your unique work style.

ACTION POINT: Think through your work style by answering the questions in this reading. Think through your values. Do not apply your strengths to a position that will destroy your values. Find a position that is compatible with your values.

Management Challenges for the 21st Century
Managing Oneself (Corpedia Online Program)

Managing Oneself: What to Contribute?

Successful careers are not the products of luck or planning; they are built by people who are able to seize those opportunities that match their own strengths.

Now that you have identified your strengths and work style you can begin to look for the right opportunities. These are the assignments that will enable you to use your strength, match your work style, and fit within your personal value system. They are also the assignments that help you to make the right contribution. But you first have to decide what your contribution should be.

Figuring out the right contribution helps you move from knowledge to action. What do you think you should contribute? In other words, how can you make a difference within your organization? Answering these questions helps you to analyze opportunities in search for the right few. When such opportunities do come along, it's best to accept them if they suit you and how you work. It requires you to think through the requirements of a specific situation, your greatest potential contribution, and the results that must be achieved. It is through such processes that successful careers are built. They are not the products of luck or planning; they are built by people who are able to seize those opportunities that match their own strengths, work styles, and values.

ACTION POINT: Seek the opportunities that allow you to apply your strengths and match your work style and values.

Management Challenges for the 21st Century
Managing Oneself (Corpedia Online Program)

Managing Oneself: Work Relationships

Organizations are built on trust, and trust is built on communication and mutual understanding.

Just as it is important for you to know your own strengths, work styles, and values, it is also important that you learn the strengths, work styles, and values of the people around you. Each person is an individual, and there are likely to be great differences between yourself and others. But such differences do not matter. What does matter is whether everyone performs. Consistent group performance can be achieved only if each person within the group is able to perform as an individual. And to help make this happen, you must build on other people's strengths, other people's work styles, and other people's values.

Once you have identified your strengths, work style, and values, as well as what your contribution should be, you must then consider who else needs to know about it. Everyone who depends on you and on whom you depend needs to know this information about how you work. Since communication is a two-way process, you should feel comfortable asking your coworkers to think through and define their own strengths, work styles, and values.

ACTION POINT: List the people who depend upon your contributions and the specific contribution each person requires. List those people on whom you depend and the contributions you require from each person. Inform both groups and be sure each person is served properly, including you.

Management Challenges for the 21st Century
Managing Oneself (Corpedia Online Program)

Managing the Boss

There is nothing quite as conducive to success as a successful and rapidly promoted superior.

Almost everybody has at least one boss. And the trend is for knowledge workers to have an increasing number of bosses, an increasing number of people on whose approval and appraisal they depend, and whose support they need.

There are keys to success in managing bosses. First, put down on a piece of paper a "boss list," everyone to whom you are accountable, everyone who appraises you and your work, everyone on whom you depend to make effective your work and that of your people. Next, go to each of the people on the boss list at least once a year and ask, "What do I do and what do my people do that *helps you* do your job?" And, "What do we do that *hampers you* and makes life more difficult for you?" It is your job to enable *each of your bosses to perform as unique individuals* according to their working styles. Your bosses should feel comfortable that you are *playing to their strengths* and *safeguarding them from their limitations and weaknesses.*

ACTION POINT: Make a "boss list." Ask the questions listed in this reading to each person on your boss list.

The Effective Executive
Managing the Boss (Corpedia Online Program)

Managing Oneself: The Second Half

What to do with the second half of one's life?

Knowledge workers are able physically to keep on working into old age, and well beyond any traditional retirement age. But they run a new risk: they may become mentally finished. What's commonly called "burnout," the most common affliction of the fortysomething knowledge worker, is very rarely the result of stress. Its common, all too common, cause is boredom on the job.

In one big and highly successful company top management said to me: "Our engineers are slacking off. Can you try to find out why?" And so I talked to about a dozen very competent, very successful, very well paid people in engineering. And they all said: "My job is important to the success of the company. I like it. I have done it now for about ten years and I am very good at it and I am very proud of it. But I can do it now in my sleep. It no longer challenges me. I am just plain bored. I no longer look forward to coming into the office every morning." Yet the obvious answer, that is to rotate people, would have been the wrong answer. These people are topflight specialists. What they needed was to regain some true interest. And once they had that—one of them, for instance, started to tutor high school students in math and science—suddenly their work, too, became again satisfying.

ACTION POINT: Set goals outside of your current work. Begin to pursue these goals now.

Management Challenges for the 21st Century
Managing Oneself (Corpedia Online Program)

Managing Oneself: Revolution in Society

Managing oneself is based on these realities: Workers are likely to outlive organizations, and the knowledge worker has mobility.

M*anaging oneself* is a REVOLUTION in human affairs. It requires new and unprecedented things from the individual, and especially from the knowledge worker. For, in effect, it demands that each knowledge worker think and behave as a chief executive officer. It also requires an almost 180-degree change in the knowledge workers' thoughts and actions from what most of us still take for granted as the way to think and the way to act.

The shift from manual workers who do as they are being told—either by the task or by the boss—to knowledge workers who have to manage themselves profoundly challenges social structure. For every existing society, even the most "individualist" one, takes two things for granted, if only subconsciously: Organizations outlive workers, and most people stay put. Managing oneself is based on the very opposite realities. In the United States MOBILITY is accepted. But even in the United States, workers outliving organizations—and with it the need to be prepared for a *second and different half of one's life*—is a revolution for which practically no one is prepared. Nor is any existing institution, for example, the present retirement system.

ACTION POINT: Begin thinking of a second career you find fulfilling. List areas of work that interest you, including that of a volunteer in a nonprofit organization.

Management Challenges for the 21st Century

A Noncompetitive Life

No one can expect to live very long without experiencing a serious setback in one's life or in one's work.

Given the competitive struggle, a growing number of highly successful knowledge workers of both sexes—business managers, university teachers, museum directors, doctors—plateau in their forties. They know they have achieved all they will achieve. If their work is all they have, they are in trouble. Knowledge workers therefore need to develop, preferably while they are still quite young, a noncompetitive life and community of their own, and some serious outside interest. This outside interest will give them the opportunity for personal contribution and achievement beyond the workplace.

No one can expect to live very long without experiencing a serious setback in one's life or in one's work. There is the competent engineer who at age forty-two is being passed over for promotion in the company. The engineer now knows that he has not been very successful in his job. But in his outside activity—for example, as treasurer in his local church—he has achieved success and continues to have success. And, one's own family may break up, but in that outside activity, there is still a community.

ACTION POINT: Develop an interest that does not subject you to the competitive pressures you face at work. Try to find a community in this area of outside interest.

Management Challenges for the 21st Century
The Next Society (Corpedia Online Program)

Staffing Decisions

Where there are peaks, there are valleys.

The people decision is a big gamble—by basing it on what a person can do, it at least becomes a rational gamble. Effective executives make strength productive. They fill positions and promote based upon what a person can do—not to minimize weakness but to maximize strength. Strong people always have strong weaknesses. Where there are peaks there are valleys. There is no such thing as a "good person"; "good for what?" is the question. Look for excellence in one major area, and not for performance that gets by all around. Human excellence can only be achieved in one area, or at the most, in very few. Always start out with what a person should be able to do well and then demand that he or she really do it.

There is one area where weakness in itself is of importance and relevance. By themselves *character* and *integrity* do not accomplish anything. But their absence faults everything else. Here is the one area where weakness is an absolute disqualification.

ACTION POINT: When making people decisions, make sure you know the assignment. Then choose a candidate who has proven strengths in skill-areas required by the new assignment.

The Effective Executive

"Widow-Maker" Positions

A widow-maker position is a job that defeats two competent people in a row.

"Widow-maker" is the term that nineteenth-century New England shipbuilders used to describe a well-built new ship that still managed to have two fatal accidents in a row. Instead of attempting to fix the problems with the ship, they immediately broke it up to prevent another accident from occurring. In organizations, a widow-maker is a job that defeats two competent people in a row. It will almost certainly defeat a third one, no matter how competent. The only thing to do is to abolish the widow-maker position and restructure the work. Widow-makers typically appear when an organization experiences rapid growth or rapid change. I have since seen this phenomenon in a lot of organizations—for example, in a university that within ten years had moved from being primarily an undergraduate teaching institution to becoming a major research university. That killed off two excellent people who took on the presidency as it had been structured the old way, and by the way, any number of deans—again, these positions could be filled successfully only after the university had restructured itself thoroughly.

The "widow-maker" job is usually the result of accident. One person who somehow combined temperamental characteristics that are not usually found in one person created the job and acquitted himself or herself well. In other words, what looked like a logical job was an accident of personality rather than the result of a genuine function. But one cannot replace personality.

ACTION POINT: Is there a "widow-maker" position in your organization? Either restructure the position or eliminate it.

People Decisions (Corpedia Online Program)
Management: Tasks, Responsibilities, Practices

Overage Executives

Stay out of decisions if one won't be around to help bail out the organization.

An employer should have in place a policy for the over-sixties in managerial and professional ranks. The basic rule, and one that should be clearly established and firmly enforced, is that people beyond their early sixties should ease out of major managerial responsibilities. It is a sensible rule for anyone, and not only for the executive, to stay out of decisions if one won't be around to help bail out the company when the decisions cause trouble a few years down the road—as most of them do. The older executive should move into work one performs on one's own rather than be the "boss." This way, he or she specializes and concentrates on one major contribution, advises, teaches, sets standards, and resolves conflicts, rather than works as a "manager." The Japanese have "counselors," and they work very effectively, sometimes well into their eighties.

ACTION POINT: Develop a retirement policy for senior executives. Make sure these executives are not the sole decision-makers in decisions whose outcomes will occur beyond the tenure of these executives.

The Frontiers of Management

Controls, Control, and Management

The probability of an event's being meaningful is a much more important datum than the event itself.

We are rapidly acquiring great capacity to design controls in business and in other social institutions, based on a great improvement in techniques, especially the ability to process and analyze large masses of data very fast. What does this mean for "control"? Especially, what are the requirements for these greatly improved controls to give better control to management? For, in the task of a manager, controls are purely a means to an end; the end is control. If we deal with a human being in a social institution, controls must become personal motivation that leads to control. A translation is required before the information yielded by the controls can become grounds for action—the translation of one kind of information into another, which we call *perception*. In the social institution there is a second complexity, a second "uncertainty principle." It is almost impossible to prefigure the responses appropriate to a certain event in a social situation.

But a control-reading "profits are falling" does not indicate, with any degree of probability, the response "raise prices," let alone by how much; the control-reading "sales are falling" does not indicate the response "cut prices," and so on. The event itself may not even be meaningful. But even if it is, it is by no means certain what it means.

ACTION POINT: Review each of the performance measures you use to manage your organization. Eliminate each of those measures that is not meaningful to the results of the organization.

Management: Tasks, Responsibilities, Practices

Controls: Neither Objective nor Neutral

The act of measurement changes both the event and the observer.

In any social situation of the kind we deal with in enterprise, the act of measurement is neither objective nor neutral. It is subjective and of necessity biased. It changes both the event and the observer. Events in the social situation acquire value by the fact that they are being singled out for the attention of being measured. The fact that this or that set of phenomena is singled out for being "controlled" signals that it is considered to be important. *Controls in a social institution such as a business are goal-setting and value-setting.* They are not "objective." They are of necessity moral. Controls create vision. They change both the events measured and the observer. They endow events not only with meaning but with value. And this means that the basic question is not "How do we control?" but "What do we measure in our control system?"

ACTION POINT: Remember, "What you measure is what you get." Ensure that every measure of performance is pertinent to the achievement of a goal or value of your organization. Otherwise, you risk misdirecting your organization.

Management: Tasks, Responsibilities, Practices

Controls Should Focus on Results

What today's organization needs are synthetic sense organs for the outside.

Every social institution exists to contribute to society, economy, and individual. In consequence *results* exist only on the outside—in economy, in society, and with the customer. It is the customer only who creates a profit. Everything inside a business creates only costs, is only a "cost center." But results are entrepreneurial. Yet we do not have adequate, let alone reliable, information regarding the "outside." The century of patient analysis of managerial, inside phenomena, events and data, the century of patient, skillful work on the individual operations and tasks within the business, has no counterpart with respect to the entrepreneurial job. We can easily record and therefore quantify efficiency, that is, efforts. It is of little value to have the most efficient engineering department if it designs the wrong product. And it mattered little, I daresay, during the period of IBM's great expansion in the fifties and sixties how "efficient" its operations were; its basic entrepreneurial idea was the right, the effective one.

The outside, the area of results, is much less accessible than the inside. The central problem of executives in the large organization is their insulation from the outside. What today's organization therefore needs are synthetic sense organs for the outside. If modern controls are to make a contribution, it would be, above all, here.

ACTION POINT: Develop a systematic method of collecting critical information on the environment. The information should include knowledge of customer satisfaction, noncustomer buying habits, technological developments, competitors, and relevant government policies.

Management: Tasks, Responsibilities, Practices

Controls for Nonmeasurable Events

A balance between the measurable and the nonmeasurable is a central and constant problem of management.

Business, like any other institution, has important results that are incapable of being measured. Any experienced executive knows companies or industries that are bound for extinction because they cannot attract or hold able people. This, every experienced executive also knows, is a more important fact about a company or an industry than last year's profit statement. Yet the statement cannot be defined clearly let alone "quantified." It is anything but "intangible"; it is very "tangible" indeed. It is just nonmeasurable. And measurable results will not show up for a decade.

A balance between the measurable and the nonmeasurable is therefore a central and constant problem of management and a true decision area. Measurements that do not spell out the assumptions with respect to the nonmeasurable statements that are being made—misdirect, therefore. They actually misinform. Yet the more we can quantify the truly measurable areas, the greater the temptation to put all-out emphasis on those—the greater, therefore, the danger that what looks like better controls will actually mean less control if not a business out of control altogether.

ACTION POINT: List both nonmeasurable and measurable variables that are important to the achievement of the goals of your organization. Develop quantitative assessments for those variables that can be so measured and qualitative assessments for those critical variables that are qualitative.

Management: Tasks, Responsibilities, Practices

The Ultimate Control of Organizations

People act as they are being rewarded or punished.

There is a fundamental, incurable, basic limitation to controls in a social institution. A social institution is comprised of persons, each with his own purpose, his own ambitions, his own ideas, his own needs. No matter how authoritarian the institution, it has to satisfy the ambitions and needs of its members, and do so in their capacity as individuals through *institutional* rewards and punishments, incentives, and deterrents. The expression of this may be quantifiable—such as a raise in salary. But the system itself is not quantitative in character and cannot be quantified.

Yet here is the real control of the institution. People act as they are being rewarded or punished. For this, to them, rightly, is the true expression of the values of the institution and of its true, as against its professed, purpose and role. A system of controls that is not in conformity with this ultimate control of the organization, which lies in its people decisions, will therefore at best be ineffectual. At worst it will cause never-ending conflict and will push the organization out of control. In designing controls for an organization, one has to understand and analyze the actual control of the business, its people decisions. One has to realize that even the most powerful "instrument board" complete with computers is secondary to the invisible, qualitative control of any human organization, its systems of rewards and punishments, of values and taboos.

ACTION POINT: Specify the system of rewards and punishments in your organization, including the procedure used for making promotion decisions. Evaluate the performance measures in place in your organization. Make sure that good performance on the performance measures leads to rewards, promotions, and punishments.

Management: Tasks, Responsibilities, Practices

Harmonize the Immediate and Long-range Future

A manager must, so to speak, keep his nose to the grindstone while lifting his eyes to the hills—quite an acrobatic feat.

A manager has two specific tasks. The first is creation of a true whole that is larger than the sum of its parts, a productive entity that turns out more than the sum of the resources put into it. The second specific task of the manager is to harmonize in every decision and action the requirements of the immediate and of the long-range future. A manager cannot sacrifice either without endangering the enterprise.

If a manager does not take care of the next hundred days, there will be no next hundred years. Whatever the manager does should be sound in expediency as well as in basic long-range objective and principle. And where he cannot harmonize the two time dimensions, he must at least balance them. He must calculate the sacrifice he imposes on the long-range future of the enterprise to protect its immediate interests, or the sacrifice he makes today for the sake of tomorrow. He must limit either sacrifice as much as possible. And he must repair as soon as possible the damage it inflicts. He lives and acts in two time dimensions, and is responsible for the performance of the whole enterprise and of his own component in it.

ACTION POINT: Develop a system of performance measures that will lead to maximizing the total wealth-producing capacity of your organization. Include both short-term measures and long-term measures, as well as quantitative and qualitative measures.

Management: Tasks, Responsibilities, Practices

Misdirection by Specialization

"I am building a cathedral."

An old story tells of three stonecutters who were asked what they were doing. The first replied, "I am making a living." The second kept on hammering while he said, "I am doing the best job of stonecutting in the entire country." The third one looked up with a visionary gleam in his eyes and said, "I am building a cathedral." The third man is, of course, the true manager. The first man knows what he wants to get out of the work and manages to do so. He is likely to give a "fair day's work for a fair day's pay." But he is not a manager and will never be one. It is the second man who is a problem. Workmanship is essential: in fact, an organization demoralizes if it does not demand of its members the highest workmanship they are capable of. But there is always a danger that the true workman, the true professional, will believe that he is accomplishing something when in effect he is just polishing stones or collecting footnotes. Workmanship must be encouraged in the business enterprise. But it must always be related to the needs of the whole.

ACTION POINT: Develop a process whereby each person in the organization understands his or her contribution to producing the products and services of the enterprise.

Management: Tasks, Responsibilities, Practices

Compensation Structure

Compensation must always try to balance recognition of the individual with stability and maintenance of the group.

People have to be paid, but every compensation system is liable to misdirect. Compensation always expresses status, both within the enterprise and in society. It entails judgments on a person's worth as much as on performance. It is emotionally tied to all our ideas of fairness, justice, and equity. Money is, of course, quantitative. But the money in any compensation system expresses the most intangible, but also the most sensitive, values and qualities. No attempt at a "scientific formula" for compensation can therefore be completely successful.

The best possible compensation plan is of necessity a compromise among the various functions and meanings of compensation, for the individual as well as for the group. Even the best plan will still disorganize as well as organize, misdirect as well as direct, and encourage the wrong as well as the right behavior. The preference should be for simple compensation systems rather than for complex ones. It should be for compensation systems that allow judgment to be used and that enable pay to be fitted to the job of the individual rather than impose one formula on everybody. All one can do is to watch lest the compensation system reward the wrong behavior, emphasize the wrong results, and direct people away from performance for the common good.

ACTION POINT: Develop a compensation system that rewards individual performance while balancing individual rewards with rewards that help maintain the continuity of the entire organization as a whole.

Management: Tasks, Responsibilities, Practices

October

1 OCTOBER

Pursuing Perfection

"The Gods can see them."

The greatest sculptor of ancient Greece, Phidias, around 440 BC made the statues that to this day, 2,400 years later, still stand on the roof of the Parthenon in Athens. When Phidias submitted his bill, the city accountant of Athens refused to pay it. "These statues stand on the roof of the temple, and on the highest hill in Athens. Nobody can see anything but their fronts. Yet, you have charged us for sculpturing them in the round, that is, for doing their backsides, which nobody can see." "You are wrong," Phidias retorted. "The Gods can see them."

Whenever people ask me which of my books I consider the best, I smile and say, "The next." I do not, however, mean it as a joke. I mean it the way Verdi meant it when he talked of writing an opera at eighty in the pursuit of a perfection that had always eluded him. Though I am older now than Verdi was when he wrote *Falstaff*, I am still thinking and working on two additional books, each of which, I hope, will be better than any of my earlier ones, will be more important, and will come a little closer to excellence.

ACTION POINT: Pursue perfection in your work, however elusive.

Drucker on Asia

Decision Objectives

A decision, to be effective, needs to satisfy the boundary conditions.

A decision process requires clear specifications as to what the decision has to accomplish. What are the objectives the decision has to reach? In science these are known as "boundary conditions." A decision, to be effective, needs to be adequate to its purpose. The more concisely and clearly boundary conditions are stated, the greater the likelihood that the decision will indeed be an effective one and will accomplish what it set out to do. Conversely, any serious shortfall in defining these boundary conditions is almost certain to make a decision ineffectual, no matter how brilliant it may seem.

"What is the minimum needed to resolve this problem?" is the form in which the boundary conditions are usually probed. "Can our needs be satisfied," Alfred P. Sloan presumably asked himself when he took command of General Motors in 1922, "by removing the autonomy of the division heads?" His answer was clearly in the negative. The boundary conditions of his problem demanded strength and responsibility in the chief operating positions. This was needed as much as control at the center and unity. The boundary conditions demanded a solution to a problem of structure, rather than an accommodation among personalities. And this, in turn, made his solution last.

ACTION POINT: Take a decision you are facing today. Clearly specify what purpose or need you want to fulfill by making the decision.

The Effective Executive

3 OCTOBER

Decision Making

Start with what is right rather than what is acceptable.

One has to start out with what is right rather than what is acceptable precisely because one always has to compromise in the end. But if one does not know what is right, one cannot distinguish between the right compromise and the wrong compromise—and will end up by making the wrong compromise. I was taught this when I started in 1944 on my first big consulting assignment, a study of the management structure and management policies of the General Motors Corporation. Alfred P. Sloan, Jr., who was then chairman and chief executive officer of the company, called me to his office at the start of my study and said: "I shall not tell you what to study, what to write, or what conclusions to come to. My only instruction to you is to put down what you think is right as you see it. Don't you worry about our reaction. And don't you, above all, concern yourself with the compromises that might be needed to make your recommendations acceptable. There is not one executive in this company who does not know how to make a compromise without any help from you. But he can't make the right compromise unless you first tell him what 'right' is."

The executive thinking through a decision might put this in front of him- or herself in neon lights.

ACTION POINT: Define an outcome for the decision in the previous reading that would perfectly satisfy your requirements.

The Effective Executive

The Right Compromise

"Half a loaf is better than no bread."

One has to start out with what is right rather than what is acceptable (let alone who is right) precisely because one always has to compromise in the end. But if one does not know what is right to satisfy the specifications and boundary conditions, one cannot distinguish between the right compromise and the wrong compromise—and will end up by making the wrong compromise.

There are two different kinds of compromise. One kind is expressed in the old proverb, "Half a loaf is better than no bread." The other kind is expressed in the story of the Judgment of Solomon, which was clearly based on the realization that "half a baby is worse than no baby at all." In the first instance, the boundary conditions are still being satisfied. The purpose of bread is to provide food, and half a loaf is still food. Half a baby, however, does not satisfy the boundary conditions. For half a baby is not half of a living and growing child. It is a corpse in two pieces.

ACTION POINT: Now think through the problem you specified in the two previous readings. Make a decision that represents a compromise, half a loaf, but goes in the right direction toward the ideal solution. Then think of a compromise that is "no bread at all."

The Effective Executive

Building Action into the Decision

A decision is only a hope until carrying it out has become somebody's work assignment and responsibility, with a deadline.

A decision is a commitment to action. Until the right thing happens, there has been no decision. And one thing can be taken for granted: the people who have to take the action are rarely the people who have made the decision. No decision has, in fact, been made until carrying it out has become somebody's work assignment and responsibility—and with a deadline. Until then, it's still only a hope.

A decision will not become effective unless needed actions have been built into it from the start. Converting a decision into action requires answering several questions:

- Who has to know of this decision?
- What action has to be taken?
- Who is to take it?
- What does the action have to be so that the people who have to do it can do it?

The action must be appropriate to the capacities of the people who have to carry it out. This is especially important if people have to change their behavior, habits, or attitudes for the decision to become effective.

ACTION POINT: Think through a decision you have made. Who has to know of the decision? What action has to be taken? Who has to take the action? Make sure the people who have to take the action are able to do so.

The Effective Executive
The Elements of Decision Making (Corpedia Online Program)

Organize Dissent

The effective decision-maker organizes dissent.

Decisions of the kind the executive has to make are not made well by acclamation. They are made well only if based on the clash of conflicting views, the dialogue between different points of view, the choice between different judgments. The first rule in decision making is that one does not make a decision unless there is disagreement.

Alfred P. Sloan, Jr., is reported to have said at a meeting of one of the GM top committees, "Gentlemen, I take it we are all in complete agreement on the decision here." Everyone around the table nodded assent. "Then," continued Mr. Sloan, "I propose we postpone further discussion of this matter until our next meeting to give ourselves time to develop disagreement and perhaps gain some understanding of what the decision is all about." There are three reasons why dissent is needed. It first safeguards the decision maker against becoming the prisoner of the organization. Everybody is a special pleader, trying—often in perfectly good faith—to obtain the decision he favors. Second, disagreement alone can provide alternatives to a decision. And a decision without an alternative is a desperate gambler's throw, no matter how carefully thought through it might be. Above all, disagreement is needed to stimulate the imagination.

ACTION POINT: Organize dissent for a particular decision by bringing people with diverse points of view into the decision process. Choose on the basis of "what is right," not "who is right."

Management: Tasks, Responsibilities, Practices

Elements of the Decision Process

Ignore a single element in the process and the decision will tumble down like a badly built wall in an earthquake.

Good decision makers know that decision making has its own process and its own clearly defined elements and steps. Every decision is risky: it is a commitment of present resources to an uncertain and unknown future. But if the process is faithfully observed and if the necessary steps are taken, the risk will be minimized and the decision will have a good chance of turning out successful. Good decision makers

- Know when a decision is necessary
- Know that the most important part of decision making is to make sure that the decision is about the right problem
- Know how to define the problem
- Don't even think about what is acceptable until they have thought through what the right decision is
- Know that, in all likelihood, they will have to make compromises in the end
- Know that they haven't made a decision until they build its implementation and effectiveness into it

ACTION POINT: Take a predicament you are facing right now. What is the problem? Do not take any steps toward making a decision until you are sure that you have diagnosed the problem completely and correctly.

The Effective Executive
The Elements of Decision Making (Corpedia Online Program)

Is a Decision Necessary?

One does not make unnecessary decisions any more than a good surgeon does unnecessary surgery.

Unnecessary decisions not only waste time and resources, but they also threaten to make all decisions ineffectual. Therefore, it is important that you be able to distinguish between necessary and unnecessary decisions. Surgeons provide perhaps the best example of effective decision-making, as they have had to make risk-taking decisions on a daily basis for thousands of years now. Since there is no such thing as risk-free surgery, unnecessary operations must be avoided. The rules used by surgeons to make decisions are:

Rule one: In a condition that is likely to cure itself or to stabilize itself without risk or danger or great pain to the patient, you put it on watch and check regularly. But you don't cut. To do surgery in such a condition is an unnecessary decision.

Rule two: If the condition is degenerative or life-threatening and there is something you can do, you do it—fast and radically. It is a necessary decision despite the risk.

Rule three: This is the problem in between, and it's probably the largest single category—the condition that is not degenerative and not life-threatening but still not self-correcting and quite serious. This is where the surgeon has to weigh opportunity against risk. And it is this decision that distinguishes the first-rate surgeon from the also-ran.

ACTION POINT: List three problems you are facing right now. Classify these problems as falling under rules 1, 2, or 3. Do not make unnecessary decisions.

The Effective Executive
The Elements of Decision Making (Corpedia Online Program)

Classifying the Problem

By far the most common mistake is to treat a generic situation as if it were a series of unique events.

Executives face four basic types of problems:

1. Generic events that are common within the organization and throughout the industry
2. Generic events that are unique for the organization but common throughout the industry
3. Truly unique events
4. Events that appear to be unique but are really the first appearance of a new generic problem

All but the truly unique event requires a generic solution. Generic problems can be answered with standard rules and practices. Once the right principle has been developed, all manifestations of the same generic event can be handled by applying the standard principle. All the executive must do is adapt the principle to the concrete circumstances of the specific problem. Unique events, however, require a unique solution and must be treated individually. Truly unique events are quite rare; someone else has solved virtually every problem an organization faces already. Applying a standard rule or principle can solve most types of problems.

ACTION POINT: Cite an example of a problem you are facing that has a generic solution to it. What is that solution? Cite a problem you are facing that requires a unique solution. Develop the unique solution by following the rules for effective decision-making.

The Effective Executive
The Elements of Decision Making (Corpedia Online Program)

Defining the Problem: An Example

The right answer to the wrong problem is very difficult to fix.

Defining the problem may be the most important element in making effective decisions—and the one executives pay the least attention to. A wrong answer to the right problem can, as a rule, be repaired and salvaged. But the right answer to the wrong problem, that's very difficult to fix, if only because it's so difficult to diagnose.

The management of one of America's largest manufacturing companies prided itself on its safety record. The company had the lowest number of accidents per one thousand employees of any company in its industry and one of the very lowest of any manufacturing place in the world. Yet its labor union constantly berated it for its horrendous accident rate, and so did OSHA. The company thought this a public-relations problem and spent large sums of money advertising its near-perfect safety record. And yet the union attacks continued. By aggregating all accidents and showing them as accidents per thousand workers, the company did not see the places where there was a very high accident rate. Once the company segregated its accidents and reported them in a number of categories it found, almost immediately, that there was a very small number of places, about 3 percent of all units, that had above-average accident rates. And an even smaller number of places had very high accident rates. But they were the places the union got its complaints from, the places whose accidents got into the papers and into OSHA reports.

ACTION POINT: The manufacturing company described above defined the problem of its accidents as a public-relations problem. What "facts" did this problem definition ignore, making it the wrong definition?

The Effective Executive
The Elements of Decision Making (Corpedia Online Program)

Defining the Problem: The Principles

Until the definition of a problem explains and encompasses all observable facts, the definition is incomplete or wrong.

How do effective decision makers determine what the right problem is? Effective decision makers ask:

- What is this all about?
- What is pertinent here?
- What is key to this situation?

Questions such as these are not new, yet they are of critical importance in defining the problem. The problem must be considered from all angles to ensure that the right problem is being tackled. The one way to make sure that the problem is correctly defined is to check it against the observable facts. Until problem definition explains and encompasses all observable facts, the definition is either still incomplete or, more likely, the wrong definition. But once the problem has been correctly defined, the decision itself is usually pretty easy.

ACTION POINT: Describe an occasion where you or someone else in your organization implemented the right answer to the wrong problem. What could you have done differently to ensure that the right problem was being tackled?

The Effective Executive
The Elements of Decision Making (Corpedia Online Program)

Getting Others to Buy *The Decision*

If you wait until you have made the decision and then start to "sell" it, it's unlikely to ever become effective.

Unless the organization has "bought" the decision, it will remain ineffectual; it will remain a good intention. And for a decision to be effective, being bought has to be built into it from the start of the decision-making process. This is one lesson to learn from Japanese management. As soon as it starts the decision-making process, and long before the final decision is made, Japanese management sells the decision.

Everyone who is likely to be affected by a decision—say, to go into a joint venture with a Western company or to acquire a minority stake in a potential U.S. distributor—is asked to write down how such a decision would affect his work, job, and unit. He is expressly forbidden to have an opinion and to recommend or to object to the possible move. But he is expected to think it through. And top management, in turn, then knows where each of these people stands. Then top management makes the decision from the top down. There isn't much "participatory management" in Japanese organizations. But everyone who will be affected by the decision knows what it is all about—whether he likes it or not—and is prepared for it. There is no need to sell it—it's been sold.

ACTION POINT: Involve everyone who will have to carry out a decision in the process of making the decision. Then, based upon their contributions, decide who is most likely to carry out the decision effectively.

Management: Tasks, Responsibilities, Practices
The Elements of Decision Making (Corpedia Online Program)

Testing the Decision Against Results

"Poor Ike. . . . Now . . . he'll give an order and not a damn thing is going to happen."

Feedback has to be built into the decision to provide a continuous testing, against actual events, of the expectations that underlie the decision. Decisions are made by people. People are fallible; at their best, their works do not last long. Even the best decision has a high probability of being wrong. Even the most effective one eventually becomes obsolete.

When General Dwight D. Eisenhower was elected president, his predecessor, Harry S. Truman, said: "Poor Ike; when he was a general, he gave an order and it was carried out. Now he is going to sit in that big office and he'll give an order and not a damn thing is going to happen." The reason why "not a damn thing is going to happen" is, however, not that generals have more authority than presidents. It is that military organizations learned long ago that futility is the lot of most orders and organized the feedback to check on the execution of the order. They learned long ago that to go oneself and look is the only reliable feedback. Reports—all a president is normally able to mobilize—are not much help.

ACTION POINT: Make sure you go out and "kick the tires" and get on-site feedback. Find out if decisions have accomplished their intended results.

The Effective Executive

Continuous Learning in Decision Making

Feedback from the results of a decision compared against the expectations when it was being made makes even moderately endowed executives into competent decision makers.

In no area is it more important than in decision making to build continuous learning into the executive's work. And the way to do this is to feed back from results of the decision to the expectations when it was being made. Whenever executives make an important decision, they put down in writing what results are expected and when. And then the executive, nine months or a year later, begins to feed back from the actual results to the expected ones and keeps on doing this as long as the decision is in force. So in an acquisition, for example, an executive compares the actual results to the expected ones for the two to five years it takes fully to integrate an acquisition.

It's amazing how much we learn by doing this and how fast. And physicians have been taught since Hippocrates in Greece 2,400 years ago to write down what course they expect a patient's condition to take as a result of the treatment the physician prescribes, that is, as a result of the physician's decision. And that, as every experienced physician will tell you, is what makes even moderately endowed doctors into competent practitioners within a few years.

ACTION POINT: When you make an important decision, make sure to write down the expected "prognosis." Then at a time appropriate for the particular decision, go out and look at what results have transpired. Compare results to your prognosis. Use what you learn in subsequent decision situations.

The Effective Executive
The Elements of Decision Making (Corpedia Online Program)

Placing Decision Responsibility

Executives should be high enough to have the authority needed to make the decisions and low enough to have the detailed knowledge.

There are four basic characteristics that determine the nature of any business decision. First, there is the degree of *futurity* in the decision. For how long into the future does it commit the company? The second criterion is the *impact* a decision has on other functions, on other areas, or on the business as a whole. The character of a decision is also determined by the number of *qualitative factors* that enter into it: basic principles of conduct, ethical values, social and political beliefs, and so on. Finally, decisions can be classified according to whether they are periodically *recurrent* or *rare*, if not unique, decisions.

A decision should always be made at the lowest possible level and as close to the scene of action as possible. However, a decision should always be made at a level ensuring that all activities and objectives affected are fully considered. The first rule tells us how far down a decision *should* be made. The second how far down it *can* be made, as well as which managers must share in the decision and which must be informed of it. The two together tell us where certain activities should be placed.

ACTION POINT: Push decision making down to as close to the action as possible. But remember: The longer a decision commits the organization, the wider its impact upon other functions, the greater the number of qualitative factors involved and finally, the rarer the decision, the higher in the organization the decision should be made.

Management: Tasks, Responsibilities, Practices

Legitimate Power in Society

No society can function as a society unless the decisive social power is legitimate.

Legitimate power stems from the same basic belief of society regarding man's nature and fulfillment on which the individual's social status and function rest. Indeed legitimate power can be defined as rulership that finds its justification in the basic ethos of society. In every society there are many powers that have nothing to do with such a principle, and institutions that in no way are either designed or devoted to its fulfillment. In other words, there are always a great many "unfree" institutions in a free society, a great many inequalities in an equal society, and a great many sinners among the saints. But as long as the decisive social power that we call rulership is based upon the claim of freedom, equality, or saintliness, and is exercised through institutions that are designed toward the fulfillment of these ideal purposes, society can function as a free, equal, or saintly society. For its institutional structure is one of legitimate power.

ACTION POINT: Think about the problem of creating legitimate power in Iraq after the fall of Saddam Hussein. What "unfree" institutions are likely to remain? What inequalities are likely to persist once legitimate power is established?

The Future of Industrial Man

The Conscience of Society

Religion cannot accept any society without abandoning its true Kingdom.

The End of Economic Man reached the conclusion that the churches could not, after all, furnish the basis for European society and European politics. They had to fail, though not for the reasons for which the contemporaries tended to ignore them. Religion could indeed offer an answer to the despair of the individual and to his existential agony. But, it could not offer an answer to the despair of the masses. I am afraid that this conclusion still holds today. Western Man—indeed today Man altogether—is not ready to renounce this world. Indeed he still looks for secular salvation, if he expects salvation at all. And churches, especially Christian churches, can (and should) preach a "social gospel." But they cannot (and should not) substitute politics for Grace, and social science for Redemption. Religion, the critic of any society, cannot accept any society or even any social program, without abandoning its true Kingdom, that of a Soul alone with its God. Therein lies both the strength of the churches as the conscience of society and their incurable weakness as political and social forces of society.

ACTION POINT: Religion should serve as a critic of society and not as a political force. How does this principle compare with the role of religion in the U.S. at the present time?

The End of Economic Man

Capitalism Justified

Capitalism as a social order and as a creed is the expression of the belief in economic progress as leading toward the freedom and equality of the individual in the free and equal society.

Capitalism expects the free and equal society to result from the enthronement of private profit as supreme ruler of social behavior. Capitalism did not, of course, invent the "profit motive." Profit has always been one of the main motivating forces of the individual and will always be—regardless of the social order in which one lives. But the capitalist creed was the first and only social creed that valued the profit motive positively as the means by which the ideal free and equal society would be automatically realized. All previous creeds had regarded the profit motive as socially destructive, or at least neutral.

Capitalism has, therefore, to endow the economic sphere with independence and autonomy, which means that economic activities must not be subjected to noneconomic considerations, but must rank higher. All social energies have to be concentrated upon the promotion of economic ends, because economic progress carries the promise of the social millennium. This is capitalism: and without this social end it has neither sense nor justification.

ACTION POINT: Think through to what extent your own economic activity or that of your organization contributes to social ends.

The End of Economic Man

Moving Beyond Capitalism

I believe it is socially and morally unforgivable when managers reap huge profits for themselves but fire workers.

I am for the free market. Even though it doesn't work too well, nothing else works at all. But I have serious reservations about capitalism as a system because it idolizes economics as the be-all and end-all of life. It is one-dimensional. For example, I have often advised managers that a 20–1 salary ratio between senior executives and rank-and-file white-collar workers is the limit beyond which they cannot go if they don't want resentment and falling morale to hit their companies.

Today, I believe it is socially and morally unforgivable when managers reap huge profits for themselves but fire workers. As societies, we will pay a heavy price for the contempt this generates among middle managers and workers. In short, whole dimensions of what it means to be a human being and treated as one are not incorporated into the economic calculus of capitalism. For such a myopic system to dominate other aspects of life is not good for any society.

ACTION POINT: Have executives in your organization reaped huge profits for themselves while laying off significant numbers of workers? Enumerate the ways these policies have led to contempt and falling morale.

Managing in the Next Society

The Efficiency of the Profit Motive

The profit motive alone gives fulfillment through power over things.

The only relevant and meaningful question is whether the profit motive is the socially most efficient one of the available directions in which the drive for power can be channeled. But we can say that of the channels available and known to us, the profit motive has a very high, if not the highest, social efficiency. All the other known forms in which the lust for power can be expressed offer satisfaction by giving the ambitious man direct power and domination over his fellow men. The profit motive alone gives fulfillment through power over things.

ACTION POINT: Take a position: power over things is less dangerous socially than power over people.

Concept of the Corporation

The Megastate

Government ceased to be the rule setter, the facilitator, the insurer, the disbursement agent. It became the doer and the manager.

While the nation-state was the sole political reality in the centuries of empires and superstates, it has transformed itself profoundly in the last hundred years. It mutated into the Megastate. The shift from the national state to the Megastate began in the last decades of the nineteenth century. The first small step toward the Megastate was German chancellor Bismarck's invention in the 1880s of the Welfare State. The other major social program of the period immediately after World War II, the British National Health Service, was the first one (outside of the totalitarian countries) to take government beyond the role of insurer or provider. Hospitals and hospital care under the National Health Service were taken over by government. The people working in hospitals became government employees; and government actually manages the hospitals.

By 1960, it had become accepted doctrine in all developed Western countries that government is the appropriate agent for all social problems and all social tasks. And this held until the 1990s.

ACTION POINT: Use the Internet to check out the service level provided by the British National Health Service. Based upon this example and others which you are aware of, form an opinion as to the effectiveness of government as a provider of health services versus nonprofit and for-profit entities.

Post-Capitalist Society

Purpose of Government

Every government is a "government of forms."

Government is a poor manager. It is, of necessity, concerned with procedure, and it is also, of necessity, large and cumbersome. Government is also properly conscious of the fact that it administers public funds and must account for every penny. It has no choice but to be "bureaucratic." Whether government is a "government of laws" or a "government of men" is debatable. But every government is, by definition, a "government of forms." This means inevitably high costs.

But, the purpose of government is to make fundamental decisions, and to make them effectively. The purpose of government is to focus the political energies of society. It is to dramatize issues. It is to present fundamental choices. The purpose of government, in other words, is to govern. This, as we have learned, in other institutions, is incompatible with "doing." Any attempt to combine governing with "doing" on a large scale, paralyzes the decision-making capacity. Business has had to face, on a much smaller scale, the problem that modern government now faces: the incompatibility between "governing" and "doing." Business management learned that the two have to be separated, and that the top organ, the decision maker, has to be detached from "doing." Otherwise he does not make decisions, and the "doing" does not get done either. In business this goes by the name of "decentralization."

ACTION POINT: What are some clear examples of nonprofit organizations that are doing a better job addressing a social problem than a government agency?

The Age of Discontinuity

Government Decentralization

Reprivatization will restore strength and performance capacity to sick and incapacitated government.

"Decentralization" applied to government would not be just another form of "federalism" in which local rather than central government discharges the "doing" tasks. It would rather be a systematic policy of using the other, the nongovernmental institutions of the society of organizations, for the actual "doing," that is, for performance, operations, execution.

Government would start out by asking the question: "How do these institutions work and what can they do?" It would then ask: "How can political and social objectives be formulated and organized in such a manner as to become opportunities for performance for these institutions?" It would then ask: "And what opportunities for accomplishment of political objectives do the abilities and capacities of these institutions offer to government?" Reprivatization will not weaken government. Indeed, its main purpose is to restore strength and performance capacity to sick and incapacitated government. We cannot go much further along the road on which government has been traveling. All we can get this way is more bureaucracy and not more performance.

ACTION POINT: Draft a proposal to turn a social program into an opportunity for your organization or one you might start.

The Age of Discontinuity

24 OCTOBER

Strong Government

Government would be the "conductor" who tries to think through what each instrument is best designed to do.

We do not face a "withering away of the state," as Karl Marx promised. On the contrary, we need a vigorous, a strong, and a very active government. But we do face a choice between big and impotent government and a government that is strong because it confines itself to decision and direction and leaves the "doing" to others. We do not face a "return of laissez-faire" in which the economy is left alone. In all major areas we have a new choice in this pluralist society of organizations: an organic diversity in which institutions are used to do what they are best equipped to do.

Government would figure out how to structure a given political objective so as to make it attractive to one of the autonomous institutions. And just as we praise a composer for his ability to write "playable" music, which best uses the specific performance characteristic of French horn, violin, or flute, we may come to praise the lawmaker who best structures a particular task so as to make it most congenial for this or that of the autonomous, self-governing, private institutions of pluralist society.

ACTION POINT: Write a letter to an editor praising a lawmaker who structures government programs to be managed by nongovernmental institutions and to have the ability to solve social problems where government programs are deficient.

The Age of Discontinuity

25 OCTOBER

Government in the International Sphere

Environmental protection might well be the most productive purpose of foreign aid.

We need strong, effective governments in the international sphere so that we can make the sacrifices of sovereignty needed to give us working supranational institutions for the world society and world economy.

Protection of the environment today requires international ecological laws. We might "quarantine" polluters and forbid shipment in international commerce of goods produced under conditions that seriously pollute or damage the human habitat—for example, by polluting the oceans, by raising the temperature of the atmosphere, or by depleting its ozone. This will be decried as "interference with sovereign nations"—and so it is. It will probably require that the developed rich countries compensate the developing poor ones for the high costs of environmental protection, such as sewage treatment plants. In fact, environmental protection might well be the most productive purpose of foreign aid and far more successful than development aid.

ACTION POINT: Support the use of foreign aid to protect the environment.

The Age of Discontinuity
The New Realities

Needed: Strong Labor Unions

To become again a dynamic, effective, legitimate organ, the labor union will have to transform itself.

The true strength of the labor movement in developed countries has been moral: its claim to be the political conscience of a modern secular society.

Management—no matter who "owns" and no matter whether the institution is a business, a government agency, or a hospital—has to have considerable power and authority—power and authority grounded in the needs of the enterprise and based on competence. And power, as the drafters of the American Constitution knew, needs to be limited by countervailing power. Modern society, a society of organizations each requiring strong management, needs an organ such as the labor union. In the last few years events have amply proved this. But to become again a dynamic, effective, legitimate organ, the labor union will have to transform itself drastically. Otherwise the union will become irrelevant.

ACTION POINT: Reflect on constructive ways labor unions can check the power of businesses, governments, and hospitals.

The Frontiers of Management

Political Integration of Knowledge Workers

Knowledge workers are, to coin a term, "uniclass."

The new majority, the "knowledge worker," does not fit any interest-group definition. Knowledge workers are neither farmers nor labor nor business; they are employees of organizations. Yet they are not "proletarians" and do not feel "exploited" as a class. Collectively, they are "capitalists" through their pension funds. Many of them are themselves bosses and have "subordinates." Yet they also have a boss themselves. They are not middle-class, either. They are, to coin a term, "uniclass"—though some of them make more money than others. It makes absolutely no difference to their social position whether they work for a business, a hospital, or a university. Knowledge workers who move from accounting work in a business to accounting work in a hospital are not changing social or economic position. They are changing a job.

This status implies no specific economic or social culture. So far there is no political concept, no political integration that fits them.

ACTION POINT: Knowledge workers are capitalists in both the old and new senses. Do you see any political party addressing the interests of these new capitalists?

The New Realities

The Corporation as a Political Institution

In dealing with constituencies outside the primary task, managers have to think politically.

When it comes to the performance of the primary task of an institution—whether economic goods and services in the case of the business, health care in that of a hospital, or scholarship and higher education in that of the university—the rule is to optimize. There, managers have to base their decisions on what is right rather than on what is acceptable. But in dealing with the constituencies outside and beyond this narrow definition of the primary task, managers have to think politically—in terms of the minimum needed to placate and appease and keep quiet constituent groups that otherwise might use their power of veto. Managers cannot be politicians. They cannot confine themselves to "satisficing" decisions. But they also cannot be concerned only with optimization in the central area of performance of their institution. They have to balance both approaches in one continuous decision-making progress. The corporation is an economic institution. But it is also a political institution.

Managers have to think through what the constituencies are that can effectively veto and block decisions, and what their minimum expectations and needs should be.

ACTION POINT: List the constituents of your enterprise. Next, list how you plan to optimize the needs of your customers and meet at least the minimum expectations of each of the other constituents.

A Functioning Society

Converting Good Intentions into Results

"It's much easier to sell the Brooklyn Bridge than to give it away."

The nonprofit institution is not merely delivering a service. It wants the end user to be not a user but a *doer.* It uses a service to bring about a change in human beings. It attempts to become a part of the recipient rather than merely a supplier.

Nonprofit institutions used to think they didn't need marketing. But, as a famous old saying by a great nineteenth-century con man has it, "It's much easier to sell the Brooklyn Bridge than to give it away." Nobody trusts you if you offer something for free. You need to market even the most beneficial service. But the marketing you do in the nonprofit sector is quite different from selling. It's more a matter of looking at your service from the recipient's point of view. You have to know what to sell, to whom to sell, and when to sell.

ACTION POINT: The mission of the Salvation Army is to make citizens out of the rejected. How does that service look from the recipient's point of view? How should the Salvation Army market that service?

Managing the Non-Profit Organization

Fund Development in the Nonprofit

Fund-raising is going around with a begging bowl.

The nonprofit institution needs a fund-development strategy. The source of its money is probably the greatest single difference between the nonprofit sector and business and government. A business raises money by selling to its customers; the government taxes. The nonprofit institution has to raise money from donors. It raises money, or at least a large portion of it—from people who want to participate in the cause but who are not beneficiaries.

A nonprofit institution that becomes a prisoner of money-raising is in serious trouble and in a serious identity crisis. The purpose of a strategy for raising money is precisely to enable the nonprofit institution to carry out its mission without subordinating that mission to fund-raising. This is why nonprofit people have now changed the term they use from "fund raising" to "fund development." Fund development is creating a constituency that supports the organization because it *deserves* it. It means developing a membership that participates through giving.

ACTION POINT: A nonprofit institution that becomes a prisoner of money-raising has a serious identity crisis. Have you seen examples of this in your associations with nonprofits?

Managing the Non-Profit Organization

Effective Nonprofit Boards of Directors

Membership on this board is not power; it is responsibility.

To be effective, a nonprofit needs a strong board, but a board that does the board's work. The board not only helps think through the institution's mission, it is the guardian of that mission and makes sure the organization lives up to its basic mission. The board has the responsibility of making sure the nonprofit has competent management—and the *right* management. The board's role is to appraise the performance of the organization. The board is also the premier fund-raising organ of a nonprofit organization.

Over the door to the nonprofit's boardroom there should be an inscription in big letters that says: MEMBERSHIP ON THIS BOARD IS NOT POWER; IT IS RESPONSIBILITY. Board membership means responsibility not just to the organization but to the board itself, to, the staff, and to the institution's mission. A common problem is the badly split board. Every time an issue comes up, the board members fight out their basic policy rift. This is much more likely in nonprofit institutions precisely because the mission is, and should be, so important. The role of the board then becomes both more important and more controversial. At that point, teamwork between the chairperson and chief executive officer becomes absolutely vital.

ACTION POINT: Have you served on one or more nonprofit organization boards? Have these boards helped fulfill the nonprofit's mission or frustrated the mission?

Managing the Non-Profit Organization

November

Organizational Agility

Fleas can jump many times their own height, but not elephants.

Large organizations cannot be versatile. A large organization is effective through its mass rather than through its agility. Mass enables the organization to put to work a great many more kinds of knowledge and skill than could possibly be combined in any one person or small group. But mass is also a limitation. An organization, no matter what it would like to do, can only do a small number of tasks at any one time. This is not something that better organization or "effective communications" can cure. The law of organization is concentration.

Yet modern organization must be capable of change. Indeed it must be capable of initiating change, that is innovation. It must be able to move scarce and expensive resources of knowledge from areas of low productivity and nonresults to opportunities for achievement and contribution. This, however, requires the ability to stop doing what wastes resources.

ACTION POINT: What is the small number of tasks that your large organization is doing? Are they the right ones? If not, discontinue them and focus on others.

The Age of Discontinuity

Business Intelligence Systems

Erroneous assumptions can be disastrous.

A *business intelligence system* is a systematic process of organizing information about the business environment. It involves gathering and organizing outside information and then integrating this information into decisions. Organized information about the environment needs to include information about actual and potential competitors worldwide. However, not all outside information is available. But, even when information is available, many businesses are oblivious to it. Half of new technologies that transform an industry come from outside the industry, and information about these new technologies is available. Molecular biology and genetic engineering were not developed by the giant pharmaceutical industry, yet they are transforming the entire health-care industry. Information on these developments is available and companies in the pharmaceutical industry must keep abreast of these developments.

ACTION POINT: Identify three technologies that are transforming your business that have come from outside of your industry. Set up an intelligence system to gather information about these and other emerging technologies and capitalize on them before your competitors do.

Management Challenges for the 21st Century
From Data to Information Literacy (Corpedia Online Program)

Gathering and Using Intelligence

Information has to be organized to test a company's assumptions about its theory of its business.

Information has to be organized to challenge a company's strategy. It has to test the company's assumptions about its theory of its business. This includes testing the company's assumptions about its environment—society and its structure, the market, the customer, and technology. And information on the environment, where the major threats and opportunities are likely to arise, has become increasingly urgent. Then there are assumptions about the specific mission of the company. Third, there are assumptions about an organization's core competencies needed to accomplish its mission. Software may be designed to provide this information tailored to a specific group such as hospitals, universities, or casualty insurance companies.

Companies can produce some of the information they need themselves, such as information about customers and noncustomers. But even big companies will have to hire outside experts to help them acquire and organize the information they need. The sources are simply too diverse. Most of what the enterprise needs to know about the environment is available only from outside sources—from all kinds of data banks and data services, from journals in many languages, from trade associations, from government publications, from World Bank reports, from scientific papers, or from specialized studies.

ACTION POINT: Do you have the information you need to challenge your company's strategy and assumptions?

Management Challenges for the 21st Century
From Data to Information Literacy (Corpedia Online Program)

The Test of Intelligence Information

The ultimate test of an information system is that there are no surprises.

The ultimate test of an information system is that there are no surprises. Before events become significant, executives have already adjusted to them, analyzed them, understood them, and taken appropriate action. One example is the very few American financial institutions that, in the late 1990s, were not surprised by the collapse of mainland Asia. They had thought through what "information" means in respect to Asian economies and Asian currencies. They had gradually eliminated all the information they got from within their own subsidiaries and affiliates in these countries—these, they had begun to realize, were just "data." Instead, they had begun to organize their information about such things as the ratio between short-term borrowing and the country's balance of payments and information about funds available to service foreign short-term debt. Long before these ratios turned so unfavorable as to make a panic in mainland Asia inevitable, these executives had realized that it was coming. They realized that they had to decide whether to pull out of these countries, or to stay for the very long term. They had, in other words, realized what economic data are meaningful in respect to emerging countries, had organized them, had analyzed them, and had interpreted them. They had turned the data into information—and had decided what action to take long before that action became necessary.

ACTION POINT: Identify key variables in your environment. Make sure you have intelligence information about each of these variables to minimize surprises.

Management Challenges for the 21st Century

The Future Budget

The budget for the future remains stable throughout good times and bad.

In most enterprises—and again not just in business—there is only one budget, and it is adjusted to the business cycle. In good times expenditures are increased across the board. In bad times expenditures are cut across the board. This, however, practically guarantees missing out on the future. The change leader's *first* budget is an operating budget that shows operating and capital outlays to maintain the present business. That budget should always be approached with the question: "What is the minimum we need to spend to keep operations going?" And in poor times it should, indeed, be adjusted downward.

And then the change leader has a *second*, separate budget for the future. The future budget should be approached with the question: "What is the maximum funding these new activities require to produce optimal results." That amount should be maintained in good times or bad—unless times are so catastrophic that maintaining expenditures threatens the survival of the enterprise.

ACTION POINT: Prepare a "development budget" that contains funds to exploit opportunities. Make sure the budget provides stability of funding in good times and bad.

Management Challenges for the 21st Century

Winning Strategies

"One prays for miracles but works for results," *Saint Augustine said.*

There is an old saying that good intentions don't move mountains, bulldozers do. In nonprofit management, the mission and the plan—if that is all there is—are the good intentions. Strategies are the bulldozers. They convert what you want to do into accomplishment. They are particularly important in nonprofit organizations. Strategies lead you to work for results. They convert what you want to do into accomplishment. They also tell you what you need to have by way of resources and people to get the results.

I was once opposed to the term "strategy." I thought it smacked too much of the military. But I have slowly become a convert. That is because in many businesses and nonprofit organizations, planning is an intellectual exercise. You put it in a nicely bound volume on your shelf and leave it there. Everybody feels virtuous; we have done the planning. But until it becomes actual work, you have done nothing. Strategies, on the other hand, are action-focused. So I have reluctantly accepted the word because it's clear that strategies are not something you *hope* for; strategies are something you *work* for.

ACTION POINT: Have a strategy in place.

Managing the Non-Profit Organization

The Failed Strategy

Most of the people who persist in the wilderness leave nothing behind but bleached bones.

When a strategy or an action doesn't seem to be working, the rule is, "If at first you don't succeed, try once more. Then do something else." The first time around, a new strategy very often doesn't work. Then one must sit down and ask what has been learned. Maybe the service isn't quite right. Try to improve it, to change it, and make another major effort. Maybe, though I am reluctant to encourage this, you might make a third effort. After that, go to work where the results are. There is only so much time and so many resources, and there is so much work to be done.

There are exceptions. You can see some great achievements where people labored in the wilderness for twenty-five years. But these examples are very rare. Most of the people who persist in the wilderness leave nothing behind but bleached bones. There are also true believers who are dedicated to a cause where success, failure, and results are irrelevant, and we need such people. They are our conscience. But very few of them achieve. Maybe their rewards are in Heaven. But that's not sure either. "There is no joy in Heaven over empty churches," Saint Augustine wrote sixteen hundred years ago to one of his monks who busily built churches all over the desert. So, if you have no results, try a second time. Then look at it carefully and move on to something else.

ACTION POINT: If at first you don't succeed, sit down and ask what you have learned. Improve your approach and try once more. Maybe make a third effort. Then do something else.

Managing the Non-Profit Organization

Strategic Planning

Strategic planning deals with the futurity of present decisions.

Traditional planning asks: "What is most likely to happen?" Planning for uncertainty asks, instead: "What has already happened that will create the future?"

Strategic planning *is not a box of tricks, a bundle of techniques.* It is analytical thinking and commitment of resources to action. It is the continuous process of making present entrepreneurial *decisions* systematically and with the greatest knowledge of their futurity, organizing systematically the *efforts* needed to carry out these decisions, and measuring the results of these decisions against the expectations through organized, *systematic feedback.* The question that faces the strategic decision-maker is not what his organization should do tomorrow. It is: "What do we have to do today to be ready for an uncertain tomorrow?" The question is not what will happen in the future. It is: "What futurity do we have to build into our present thinking and doing, what time spans do we have to consider, and how do we use this information to make a rational decision now?"

ACTION POINT: Develop a strategic planning process that focuses present decisions on the future welfare of your organization. Establish responsibilities for the implementation and monitoring of these strategic decisions. Perform audits of the results of each strategic decision in order to improve your effectiveness in making strategic decisions.

Managing in a Time of Great Change
Management: Tasks, Responsibilities, Practices

Long-Range Planning

The future will not just happen if one wishes hard enough.

The future requires decisions—now. It imposes risk—now. It requires action—now. It demands allocation of resources, and above all, of human resources—now. It requires work—now.

The idea of long-range planning—and much of its reality—rests on a number of misunderstandings. The long range is largely made by short-run decisions. Unless the long range is built into, and based on, short-range plans and decisions, the most elaborate long-range plan will be an exercise in futility. And conversely, unless the short-range plans—that is, the decisions on the here *and* now—are integrated into one unified plan of action, they will be expedient, guess, and misdirection. "Short range" and "long range" are not determined by any given time span. A decision is not short range because it takes only a few months to carry it out. What matters is the time span over which it is effective. Long-range planning should prevent managers from uncritically extending present trends into the future, from assuming that today's products, services, markets, and technologies will be the products, services, markets, and technologies of tomorrow, and, above all, from dedicating their resources and energies to the defense of yesterday. Everything that is "planned" becomes immediate work and commitment.

ACTION POINT: Focus your long-range planning on decisions based on such questions as these: "Which of our *present* businesses should we abandon? Which should we play down? Which should we push and supply new resources to?"

Management: Tasks, Responsibilities, Practices

How to Abandon

Abandonment must be practiced systematically.

"To abandon what?" and "To abandon how?" have to be practiced systematically. Otherwise they will always be "postponed," for they are never "popular" policies.

In one fairly big company offering outsourcing services in most developed countries, the first Monday of every month is set aside for an abandonment meeting at every management level from top management to the supervisors in each area. Each of these sessions examines one part of the business—one of the services one Monday, one of the regions in which the company does business a month later, the way this or that service is organized the Monday morning of the third month, and so on. Within the year, the company this way examines itself completely, including its personnel policies, for instance. In the course of a year, three to four major decisions are likely to be made on the "what" of the company's services and perhaps twice as many decisions to change the "how." But also each year, three to five ideas for new things to do come out of these sessions. These decisions to change anything—whether to abandon something, whether to abandon the way something is being done, or whether to do something new—are reported each month to all members of management. And twice a year all management levels report on what has actually happened as a result of their sessions, what action has been taken and with what results.

ACTION POINT: Implement a process of systematic abandonment, such as setting aside the first Monday of every month for an abandonment meeting.

Management Challenges for the 21st Century

Divestment

In looking for a husband for your daughter, says an old proverb, don't ask: "Who'll make the best husband for her?" Ask instead: "For which kind of a man would she make a good wife?"

Divestment is a "marketing" rather than a "selling" problem. The question is not: "What do we want to sell and for how much?" It is: "For whom is this venture 'value' and under what conditions?" The salient point is finding the potential buyer for whom what is misfit to the seller is a perfect fit, the buyer to whom the venture to be sold offers the best opportunity or solves the worst problem. This is then also the buyer who will pay the most.

A major printing company decided that a mass-circulation magazine it owned was at best a partial fit and should be sold. The magazine had been bought originally to hold its printing contract. They asked, "What is value to a magazine publishing company?" "If it is a growing magazine company," they answered, "its greatest need is cash. For a growing magazine requires heavy cash investments in building circulation for several years. "How can we supply this need of the potential buyer to our own advantage?" was the next question. And the answer was, "By giving him ninety days rather than the customary thirty days to pay his print and paper bill to our printing plants." The printing company then rapidly found a publishing group that filled their requirements.

ACTION POINT: Identify a "partial fit" business of yours. For whom is this misfit a perfect fit?

Management: Tasks, Responsibilities, Practices

The Work of the Manager

Managers can improve their performance by improving their performance of these constituent activities.

There are five basic operations in the work of the manager.

- Managers, in the first place, set objectives. They determine what the objectives should be. They determine what the goals in each area of objectives should be. They decide what has to be done to reach these objectives. They make the objectives effective by communicating them to the people whose performance is needed to attain them.
- Second, managers organize. They analyze the activities, decisions, and relations needed. They classify the work. They divide it into manageable activities and further divide the activities into manageable jobs. They group these units and jobs into an organization structure. They select people for the management of these units and for the jobs to be done.
- Next, managers motivate and communicate. They make a team out of the people who are responsible for various jobs.
- The fourth basic element in the work of the manager is measurement. The manager establishes yardsticks—and few factors are as important to the performance of the organization and of every person in it.
- Finally, managers develop people, including themselves.

ACTION POINT: Manage by setting objectives and organizing, motivating, communicating with, measuring, and developing people, including yourself.

Management: Tasks, Responsibilities, Practices

Management by Objectives and Self-Control

"Control" is an ambiguous word.

The greatest advantage of management by objectives is perhaps that it makes it possible for a manager to control his own performance. Self-control means stronger motivation: a desire to do the best rather than just enough to get by. It means higher performance goals and broader vision. Even if management by objectives were not necessary to give the enterprise the unity of direction and effort of a management team, it would be necessary to make possible management by self-control.

"Control" means the ability to direct oneself and one's work. It can also mean domination of one person by another. Objectives are the basis of "control" in the first sense; but they must never become the basis of "control" in the second, for this would defeat their purpose. Indeed, one of the major contributions of management by objectives is that it enables us to substitute management by self-control for management by domination. It should be clearly understood what behavior and methods the company bars as unethical, unprofessional, or unsound. But within these limits every manager must be free to decide what he or she has to do.

ACTION POINT: Management by objectives has enjoyed widespread use, but not self-control. Why is this?

The Practice of Management

How to Use Objectives

Objectives are not fate; they are direction.

If objectives are only good intentions, they are worthless. They must degenerate into work. And work is always specific, always has—or should have—clear, unambiguous, measurable results, a deadline, and a specific assignment of accountability. But objectives that become a straitjacket do harm. Objectives are always based on expectations. And expectations are, at best, informed guesses. The world does not stand still.

The proper way to use objectives is the way an airline uses schedules and flight plans. The schedule provides for the 9 AM flight from Los Angeles to get to Boston by 5 PM. But if there is a blizzard in Boston that day, the plane will land in Pittsburgh instead and wait out the storm. The flight plan provides for flying at thirty thousand feet and for flying over Denver and Chicago. But if the pilot encounters turbulence or strong headwinds, he will ask flight control for permission to go up another five thousand feet and to take the Minneapolis–Montreal route. Yet no flight is ever operated without a schedule and flight plan. Any change is immediately fed back to produce a new schedule and flight plan. Objectives are not fate; they are direction. They are not commands; they are commitments. They do not determine the future; they are a means to mobilize the resources and energies of the business for the making of the future.

ACTION POINT: Set and use objectives the way an airline uses schedules and flight plans.

Management: Tasks, Responsibilities, Practices

The Management Letter

Managing managers requires special efforts not only to establish common direction, but to eliminate misdirection.

Setting objectives is so important that some of the most effective managers I know have each of their subordinates write a "manager's letter" twice a year. In this *letter* to his superior, each manager first defines the objectives of his superior's job and of his own job as he sees them. He then sets down the performance standards that he believes are being applied to him. Next, he lists the things he must do to attain these goals—and the things within his own unit he considers the major obstacles. He lists the things his superior and the company do that help him and the things that hamper him. Finally, he outlines what he proposes to do during the next year to reach his goals. If his superior accepts this statement, the "manager's letter" becomes the charter under which the manager operates.

Mutual understanding can never be attained by "communications down," can never be created by talking. It can result only from "communications up." It requires both the superior's willingness to listen and a tool especially designed to make lower managers heard.

ACTION POINT: Write a management letter to your superior twice a year.

The Practice of Management
Management: Tasks, Responsibilities, Practices

The Right Organization

The only things that evolve by themselves in an organization are disorder, friction, malperformance.

The pioneers of management a century ago were right: *organizational structure* is needed. The modern enterprise needs organization. But the pioneers were wrong in their assumption that there is—or should be—one right organization. Instead of searching for the right organization, management needs to learn to look for, to develop, to test, *the organization that fits the task.*

There are some "principles" of organization. One is that organization has to be transparent. People have to know and have to understand the organization structure they are supposed to work in. Someone in the organization must have the authority to make the final decision in a given area. It also is a sound principle that authority be commensurate with responsibility. It is a sound principle that any one person in an organization should have only one "master." These principles are not too different from the ones that inform an architect's work. They do not tell him what kind of building to build. They tell him what the restraints are. And this is pretty much what the various principles of organization structure do.

ACTION POINT: Reflect on whether your organization is transparent, if decision-making authority is clear, whether authority is commensurate with responsibility, and whether each person has only one master.

Management Challenges for the 21st Century
Management: Tasks, Responsibilities, Practices

Limits of Quantification

Quantification for most of the phenomena in a social ecology is misleading or at best useless.

The most important reason why I am not a quantifier is that in social affairs, events that matter cannot be quantified. For example, Henry Ford's ignorance in 1900 or 1903 of the prevailing economic wisdom that the way to maximize profit was to be a monopolist—that is, to keep production low and prices high—led him to assume that the way to make money was to keep prices low and production high. This, the invention of "mass production," totally changed industrial economics. It would have been impossible, however, to quantify the impact even as late as 1918 or 1920, years after Ford's success had made him the richest industrialist in the United States, and probably in the world. He had revolutionized industrial production, the automobile industry, and the economy in general, and had, above all, completely changed our perception of industry.

The unique event that changes the universe is an event "at the margin." By the time it becomes statistically significant, it is no longer "future"; it is, indeed, no longer even "present." It is already "past."

ACTION POINT: Identify a unique event with an impact that is unquantifiable now, but is likely to transform your organization in the next decade. Be out in front and take advantage of the opportunities it will afford.

The Ecological Vision

Hierarchy and Equality

One hears a great deal today about "the end of hierarchy." That is blatant nonsense.

To attack industrial society, as would the sentimental equalitarian, because it is based on subordination instead of on formal equality is a misunderstanding of the nature of both industry and society. Like every other institution that coordinates human efforts to a social end, the corporation must be organized on hierarchical lines. But, also, everybody from the boss to the sweeper must be seen as equally necessary to the success of the common enterprise. At the same time, the large corporation must offer equal opportunities for advancement. This is simply the traditional demand for justice, a consequence of the Christian concept of human dignity.

The demand for equal opportunities is not, as is often mistakenly assumed, a demand for absolute equality of rewards. On the contrary, equal opportunities automatically assume an inequality of rewards. For the very concept of justice implies rewards graduated according to unequal performance and unequal responsibility.

ACTION POINT: Does your organization value the contribution of the boss and the sweeper, or just the boss?

Concept of the Corporation
Management Challenges for the 21st Century
A Functioning Society

Characteristics of Organizations

Organization is a tool. As with any tool, the more specialized its given task, the greater its performance capacity.

Organizations are special-purpose institutions. They are effective because they concentrate on one task. If you were to go to the American Lung Association and say, "Ninety percent of all adult Americans suffer from ingrown toenails; we need your expertise in research, health education, and prevention to stamp out this dreadful scourge," you'd get the answer: "We are interested only in what lies between the hips and the shoulders." That explains why the American Lung Association or the American Heart Association or any of the other organizations in the health field get results.

Society, community, family, have to deal with whatever problem arises. To do so in an organization is "diversification." And in an organization, diversification means splintering. It destroys the performance capacity of any organization—whether business, labor union, school, hospital, community service, or church. Because the organization is composed of specialists, each with his or her own narrow knowledge area, its mission must be crystal clear. The organization must be single-minded, otherwise its members become confused. They will follow their specialty rather than applying it to the common task. They will each define "results" in terms of that specialty, imposing their own values on the organization. Only a clear, focused, and common mission can hold the organization together and enable it to produce results.

ACTION POINT: Make sure your organization has a clear focus, a mission that everyone can identify with, and that it concentrates on producing results.

Post-Capitalist Society

The Federal Principle

Federalism relieves top management from operating duties and sets it free to devote itself to its proper functions.

What the enterprise needs is a principle that gives both the center and the parts genuine managerial functions and powers. This principle is *federalism,* in which the whole of the enterprise is conceived as made up of autonomous units. The federal enterprise and all its units are in the same business. The same economic factors determine the future of the whole as well as of all units; the same basic decisions have to be made for all of them; the same kind and type of executive is needed. Hence the whole requires a unified management in charge of the basic functions: the decision what business the enterprise is in, the organization of the human resources, and the selection, training, and testing of future leaders.

At the same time, each unit is a business by itself. It produces its own products for a distinct market. Each unit must, therefore, have wide autonomy within limits set by the general decisions of the management of the whole. Each unit has to have its own management. The local management will be primarily an operating management; it will be concerned mainly with the present and immediate future rather than with basic policy. But within a limited scope it will have also to discharge real top-management functions.

ACTION POINT: Make maximum use of the federal principle.

The New Society

Federal Decentralization: Strengths

The greatest strength of the federal principle is that it alone of all known principles of organization prepares and tests people for top-management responsibility at an early stage.

In "federal decentralization" a company is organized into a number of autonomous businesses. Each unit has responsibility for its own performance, its own results, and its own contribution to the total company. Each unit has its own management which, in effect, runs its own "autonomous business."

In a federally organized structure, each manager is close enough to business performance and business results to focus on them. The federal principle therefore enables us to divide large and complex organizations into a number of businesses that are small and simple enough that managers know what they are doing and can direct themselves toward the performance of the whole instead of becoming prisoners of their own work, effort, and skill. Because *management by objectives* and *self-control* become effective, the number of people or units under one manager is no longer limited by the span of control; it is limited only by the much wider span of managerial responsibility. The greatest strength of the federal principle is, however, with respect to *manager development.* This by itself makes it the principle to be used in preference to any other.

ACTION POINT: Give people maximum responsibility by organizing according to the federal principle. Become an organization that develops numerous people.

Management: Tasks, Responsibilities, Practices

Federal Decentralization: Requirements

As a minimum the unit must contribute a profit to the company rather than merely contribute to the profit of the company.

Federal decentralization has stringent requirements. Federal decentralization is applicable only where a company can truly be organized into a number of genuine "businesses." This is its basic limitation. As a minimum the unit must contribute a profit to the company. And it must be a genuine profit determined by the objective judgment of the marketplace.

Federal decentralization will work only if the top-management job is clearly defined and thought through. Federalization, if properly applied, makes top management capable of doing its own job precisely because it does not have to worry about operations, but can concentrate on direction, strategy, objectives, and key decisions for the future. The federal principle demands great responsibility from the operating units, the autonomous businesses. They are given the maximum of autonomy; and this requires that they assume the maximum of responsibility. Federal decentralization requires centralized controls and common measurements. Both the managers of the autonomous businesses and top management must know what is expected of each business, what is meant by "performance," and what developments are important. To be able to give autonomy one must have confidence. And this requires controls that make opinions unnecessary. A federal unit of a company is autonomous, but it is not independent and should not be. Its autonomy is a means toward better performance for the entire company.

ACTION POINT: Ensure that executives of your autonomous units have maximum autonomy and maximum responsibility. Implement this by establishing a system of controls that makes performance or the lack of performance very evident.

Management: Tasks, Responsibilities, Practices

Reservation of Authority

There must be a kind of "supremacy clause" reserving to central management the decisions that affect the business as a whole and its long-range future welfare.

Top management in a decentralized company must think through carefully what decisions it reserves for itself. For there are decisions that have to do with the entire company, its integrity, and its future. These decisions can be made only by somebody who sees the whole and is responsible for the whole. Specifically, there must be *three reserved areas* if the business is to remain a whole rather than splinter into fragments. Top management, and top management alone, can make the decision on what technologies, markets, and products to go into, what businesses to start and what businesses to abandon, and also what the basic values, beliefs, and principles of the company are. Second, top management must reserve to itself the control of the allocation of the key resource of capital. Both the supply of capital and its investment are top-management responsibilities that cannot be turned over to the autonomous units of a federal organization.

Third, the other key resource is people. The people in a federally organized company, and especially managers and key professionals, are a resource of the entire company rather than of any one unit. The company's policies with respect to people and decisions on key appointments in the decentralized autonomous businesses are top-management decisions—though of course, autonomous business managers need to take an active part in them.

ACTION POINT: Reserve certain key decisions for top management, especially those having to do with the mission, values, and direction of the organization; the allocation of capital; and the selection of key people.

Management: Tasks, Responsibilities, Practices

Simulated Decentralization

The main rule is to look upon simulated decentralization as a last resort *only.*

Whenever a unit can be set up as a business, no design principle can match federal decentralization. We have learned, however, that a great many large companies cannot be divided into genuine businesses. Yet they have clearly outgrown the limits of size and complexity of the functional or of the team structure. These are the companies that are increasingly turning to "simulated decentralization" as the answer to their organization problem. Simulated decentralization forms structural units that are not businesses but which are still set up as if they were businesses, with maximum possible autonomy, with their own management, and with at least a "simulation" of profit-and-loss responsibility. They buy from and sell to each other using "transfer prices" determined internally rather than by an outside market. Or their "profits" are arrived at by internal allocation of costs to which then, often, a "standard fee," such as 20 percent of costs, is added.

ACTION POINT: Produce internal competition by using "micro" profit-centers when feasible. Attribute revenue to each unit and match revenue with its cost.

Management: Tasks, Responsibilities, Practices

Building Blocks of Organization

Contribution determines ranking and placement.

"What activities belong together and what activities belong apart?" A searching analysis is needed that groups activities by the *kind of contribution* they make. There are four major groups of activities, if distinguished by their contribution. First, *result-producing activities*—that is, activities that produce measurable results that can be related, directly or indirectly, to the results and performance of the entire enterprise. Second, *support activities* that, while needed and even essential, do not by themselves produce results but have results only through the use made of their "output" by other components within the business. Third, activities that have no direct or indirect relationship to the results of the business, activities that are truly ancillary. They are *hygiene and housekeeping activities.* Finally, is the *top-management activity.* Among the result-producing activities, there are some that directly bring in *revenues* (or in service institutions, directly produce "patient care" or "learning"). Here belong innovating activities, selling and all the work needed to do a systematic and organized selling job. Here also belongs the treasury function, that is, the supply and management of money in the business.

Key activities should never be subordinated to nonkey activities. Revenue-producing activities should never be subordinated to nonrevenue-producing activities. And support activities should never be mixed with revenue-producing and result-contributory activities.

ACTION POINT: Give result-producing activities high visibility in your organization. Make sure support activities are subordinated to result-producing activities. Consider delegating employee welfare activities to employee teams.

Management: Tasks, Responsibilities, Practices

Fundamentals of Communications

To improve communications, work not on the utterer but the recipient.

It is the recipient who communicates. Unless there is someone who hears, there is no communication. There is only noise. One can *perceive* only what one is capable of perceiving. One can communicate only in the recipients' language or in their terms. And the terms have to be experience-based. We perceive, as a rule, what we *expect* to perceive. We see largely what we expect to see, and we hear largely what we expect to hear. The unexpected is usually not received at all. Communication always makes *demands*. It always demands that the recipient become somebody, do something, believe something. It always appeals to motivation. If it goes against her aspirations, her values, her motivations, it is likely not to be received at all or, at best, to be resisted.

Where communication is *perception*, information is *logic*. As such, information is purely formal and has no meaning. Information is always encoded. To be received, let alone to be used, the code must be known and understood by the recipient. This requires prior agreement, that is, some communication.

ACTION POINT: Take steps to improve communications by asking recipients to initiate an information exchange. Formulate questions such as, "What objectives do you believe are appropriate for your area of responsibility next quarter?"

Management: Tasks, Responsibilities, Practices

Rules for Staff Work

Staff work is not done to advance knowledge; its only justification is the improvement of the performance of operating people and of the entire organization.

First, staff should *concentrate on tasks of major importance* that will continue for many years. A task of major importance that will not last forever—for example, the reorganization of a company's management—is better handled as a one-time assignment. Staff work should be *limited to a few tasks of high priority*. Proliferation of staff services deprives them of effectiveness. Worse, it destroys the effectiveness of the people who produce results, the operating people. Unless the number of staff tasks is closely controlled, staff will gobble up more and more of operating people's scarcest resource: time.

Effective staff work requires *specific goals and objectives, clear targets,* and *deadlines.* "We expect to cut absenteeism in half within three years" or "Two years from now we expect to understand the segmentation of our markets sufficiently to reduce the number of product lines by at least one third." Objectives like these make for productive staff work. Vague goals such as "getting a handle on employee behavior" or "a study of customer motivation" do not. Every three years or so, it is important to sit down with every staff unit and ask, "*What have you contributed these last three years that makes a real difference to this company?*"

ACTION POINT: Keep support staff small and few. Establish specific goals and deadlines for all staff work. Make sure goals are linked directly to one or more organizational goals.

The Frontiers of Management

Rules for Staff People

Unless staff people have proved themselves in operations, they will lack credibility among operating people and will be dismissed as "theoreticians."

Rules for staff people are just as important as rules for staff work. Don't ever put anyone into a staff job *unless he or she has successfully held a number of operating jobs*, preferably in more than one functional area. For if staff people lack operating experience, they will be arrogant about operations, which always look so simple to the "planner." But today, in government even more than in business, we put young people fresh out of business or law school into fairly senior staff jobs as analysts or planners or staff counsel. Their arrogance and their rejection by the operating organization practically guarantee that they will be totally unproductive.

With rare exceptions, *staff work should not be a person's "career"* but only be a part of his or her career. After five to seven years on a staff job, people ought to go back into operating work and not return to a staff assignment for five years or so. Otherwise, they will soon become behind-the-scene wire pullers, "gray eminences," "kingmakers," "brilliant mischief-makers."

ACTION POINT: Rotate staff people in and out of operating work.

The Frontiers of Management

Role of Public Relations

"Public Relations" has acquired a connotation of ballyhoo, propaganda, and whitewashing.

To the general public, "public relations" means publicity—essentially an extension of advertising from advertising a product to advertising its producer. But, the emphasis should be on acquainting the broad public with the problems of the enterprise rather than on convincing it of the company's virtues and achievements. This leads to the realization that to reach the public with its problems, the enterprise must understand the public's problems first.

Every major decision of a great corporation affects the public somehow, as workers, consumers, citizens; hence the public will react consciously or subconsciously to every move the company makes. On this reaction depends, however, the effectiveness of the company's decision—simply another way of saying that any corporation lives in society. Hence the effectiveness of the executive's decision depends not only on his understanding the problems of his business but also on his understanding the public attitude toward his problems. Hence the program of public relations is to give both central-office and divisional executives a knowledge of public attitudes and beliefs, and an understanding of the reasons behind them.

ACTION POINT: Understand public reaction to company decisions. Understand public attitudes toward the firm, and evaluate these attitudes. Recognize that an enterprise exists at the will of the public.

Concept of the Corporation

Control Middle Management

Start middle-management weight control.

Now is the time to start middle-management weight control. One means is *attrition.* As a job becomes vacant through retirement, death, or resignation, don't automatically fill it. Leave jobs open for six or eight months and see what happens; unless there is an overwhelming clamor for filling the job, then abolish it. The few companies that have tried this report that about half the "vacancies" disappeared after six months. A second way to reduce middle-management bulk is to substitute job-enlargement for promotion. The one and only way to provide satisfaction and achievement for young managers and executives—and for the even younger people working under them—is to make jobs bigger, more challenging, more demanding, and more autonomous, while increasingly using lateral transfers to different assignments, rather than promotions, as a reward for outstanding performance.

Forty years ago we built into the performance review of managerial people the question, "Are they ready for promotion?" Now we need to replace that question with "Are they ready for a bigger, more demanding challenge and for the addition of new responsibilities to their existing job?"

ACTION POINT: Create a flat organization. Use information processing—its structure, its content, and its direction—to ensure that your organization is agile and effective.

The Frontiers of Management

December

The Work of the Social Ecologist

If this change is relevant and meaningful, what opportunities does it offer?

Now as to what the work of the social ecologist is: First of all, it means looking at society and community by asking these questions: "What changes have already happened that do not fit 'what everybody knows'?" "What are the 'paradigm changes'?" "Is there any evidence that this is a change and not a fad?" And, finally, one then asks: "If this change is relevant and meaningful, what opportunities does it offer?"

A simple example is the emergence of knowledge as a key resource. The event that alerted me to the fact that something was happening was the passage of the GI Bill of Rights in the United States after the Second World War. This law gave every returning war veteran the right to attend college, with the government paying the bill. It was a totally unprecedented development. These considerations led me to the question: "What impact does this have on expectations, on values, on social structure, on employment, and so on?" And once this question was asked—I first asked it in the late 1940s—it became clear that knowledge as a productive resource had attained a position in society as never before in human history. We were clearly on the threshold of a major change. Ten years later, by the mid-1950s, one could confidently talk of a "knowledge society," of "knowledge work" as the new center of the economy, and of the "knowledge worker" as the new, ascendant workforce.

ACTION POINT: Identify changes that have already taken place that do not fit "what everybody knows." Capitalize on the opportunities these present.

The Ecological Vision

Turbulent Times Ahead

In turbulent times, the first task of management is to make sure of the institution's capacity to survive a blow.

In turbulent times, the first task of management is to make sure of the institution's capacity for survival, to make sure of its structural strengths, of its capacity to survive a blow, to adapt to sudden change, and to avail itself of new opportunities. Turbulence, by definition, is irregular, nonlinear, erratic. But its underlying causes can be analyzed, predicted, managed.

What management should—and can—manage is the single most important new reality underlying a great deal of the turbulence around: the sea-change in population structure and population dynamics, and especially the shift in population structure and population dynamics in the developed countries of the West and Japan. These shifts are already changing the modes of economic integration throughout the world. They are likely to lead to a new "transnational confederation" based on production sharing and market control, replacing in many areas the old "multinational corporation" based on financial control. They are creating new consumer markets and realigning existing old consumer markets. They are drastically changing the labor force to the point where there will only be "labor forces," each with different expectations and different characteristics. They will force us to abandon altogether the concept of "fixed retirement age." And they will create a new demand on management—as well as a new opportunity—to make organized plans for redundancy.

ACTION POINT: Define the underlying causes of turbulence affecting your enterprise today. What steps should you take now to protect your organization and to allow it to thrive in the midst of turbulence?

Managing in Turbulent Times (Hardcover)

The New Entrepreneur

History moves in a spiral; one returns to the preceding position, but on a higher level, and by a corkscrew-like path.

We are again entering an era in which emphasis will be on entrepreneurship. However, it will not be an entrepreneurship of a century ago, that is, the ability of a single man to organize a business he himself could run, control, embrace. It will rather be the ability to create and direct an organization for the new. We need men and women who can build a new structure of entrepreneurship on the managerial foundations laid these last eighty years. History, it has often been observed, moves in a spiral; one returns to the preceding position, or to the preceding problem, but on a higher level, and by a corkscrew-like path. In this fashion we are going to return to entrepreneurship on a path that led out from a lower level, that of the single entrepreneur, to the manager, and now back, though upward, to entrepreneurship again. The businessperson will have to acquire a number of new abilities, all of them entrepreneurial in nature, but all of them to be exercised in and through a managerial organization.

ACTION POINT: Establish an entrepreneurial culture in your organization.

The Age of Discontinuity

Information on Cost and Value

We cannot achieve results until we have information on cost and value.

Basic structural information is focused upon the value that is created for customers and the resources used to do so. The concepts and tools of accounting are now in the throes of its most fundamental change. The new accounting tools are not just different views of recording transactions but represent different concepts of what business is and what results are. So even the executive far removed from any work in accounting, such as a research manager in a development laboratory, needs to understand the basic theory and concepts represented by these changes in accounting. These new concepts and tools include: activity-based costing, price-led costing, economic-chain costing, economic value added, and benchmarking.

Activity-based costing reports all the costs of a product or service until the customer actually buys the product, and provides the foundation for integrating cost and value into one analysis.

ACTION POINT: Pick up a book on Activity-Based Costing and become proficient with the strategic, conceptual, and procedural issues of this accounting concept.

Management Challenges for the 21st Century
From Data to Information Literacy (Corpedia Online Program)

Price-Led Costing

The problem is not with technology. It is with mentality.

Traditionally, Western companies have started with costs, put a desired profit margin on top, and arrived at a price. This is cost-led pricing. In price-led costing, the price the customer is willing to pay determines allowable costs, beginning with design costs and ending with service costs. Marketing provides information on the price the customer is willing to pay for the value the product or service provides.

A cross-functional team starts its analysis of costs by taking this price as a given. The team then subtracts the profit required to compensate the enterprise for capital investment and risk, and arrives at an allowable cost for a product or service. Then it proceeds to make the tradeoffs between the utility provided by a product and allowable costs. Under price-led costing, the entire economic framework focuses upon creating value for the customer and meeting cost targets while earning the necessary rate of return on investment.

ACTION POINT: Examine the cost-and-pricing procedures used in your organization. Are they cost-led pricing or price-led costing? Focus on creating value for your customer and implement price-led costing.

Management Challenges for the 21st Century
From Data to Information Literacy (Corpedia Online Program)

Activity Costing

Activity-based costing is a totally different way of thinking.

Traditional costing techniques are now rapidly being replaced by activity-based cost accounting. Traditional costing builds cost from the bottom up—labor, material, and overhead. It concentrates primarily on manufacturing-related costs, the so-called inventoriable costs. Activity-based costing starts from the end and asks, "Which activities and related costs are used in carrying out the complete value chain of activities associated with the cost object?" Activity-based costing includes the cost of quality and service.

By designing quality into products and services during the design stage, design costs may increase, but warranty and service costs are likely to decrease, thus overcoming any cost increase experienced at the front-end of the chain. And unlike traditional costing, it includes all costs of producing a product or service.

ACTION POINT: Activity-based costing is a totally different way of thinking, especially for accountants whose financial reports do not require activity costs. Tackle this issue with your accounting staff.

Management Challenges for the 21st Century
From Data to Information Literacy (Corpedia Online Program)

Obstacles to Economic-Chain Costing

Switching to economic-chain costing requires uniform accounting systems along the entire chain.

The real cost is the cost of an entire process, in which even the biggest company is just one link. Companies are therefore beginning to shift costing from including only what goes on inside their own organization to costing the entire economic process, the economic chain. There are obstacles in implementing economic-chain costing. For many businesses it will be painful to switch to economic-chain costing. Doing so requires uniform or at least compatible accounting systems of all businesses along the entire chain. Yet each one does its accounting in its own way, and each is convinced that its system is the only possible one. Moreover, economic-chain costing requires information sharing across companies; yet even within the same company, people tend to resist information sharing. Whatever the obstacles, economic-chain costing is going to be done. Otherwise, even the most efficient company will suffer from an increasing cost disadvantage.

ACTION POINT: Identify the obstacles to implementing economic-chain costing, overcome them, and implement economic-chain costing in your organization.

Management Challenges for the 21st Century
From Data to Information Literacy (Corpedia Online Program)

EVA as a Productivity Measure

Until a business returns a profit that is greater than its cost of capital, it does not create wealth, it destroys it.

Measuring total-factor productivity is one of the major challenges confronting the executive in the age of knowledge work. For manual work, measuring quantity is usually sufficient. In knowledge work, we have to manage both quantity and quality, and we do not know yet how to do that. We must try to assess total-factor productivity using the common denominator of revenues and expenses. By measuring the value added over all costs, including the cost of capital, EVA (economic value added analysis) measures, in effect, the productivity of all factors of production [or the true economic costs produced by all resources used].

Never mind that a business pays taxes as if it had earned a profit. It does not cover its full costs until reported profits exceed its cost of capital. Until a business returns a profit that is greater than its cost of capital, it operates at a loss. And this is why EVA is growing in popularity. It does not, by itself, tell us why a certain product or a certain service does not add value or what to do about it. It does show which products, services, operations, or activities have unusually high productivity and add unusually high value. Then we should ask ourselves, "What can we learn from these successes?"

ACTION POINT: Calculate the "economic value added" for your organization or for a product or service that you provide.

Management Challenges for the 21st Century
From Data to Information Literacy (Corpedia Online Program)

Benchmarking for Competitiveness

Benchmarking assumes that being at least as good as the leader is a prerequisite to being competitive.

EVA (economic value added analysis) is a good start to assess the competitiveness of an enterprise in the global marketplace, but to it we must add benchmarking. Benchmarking is a tool that helps a firm tell whether or not it is globally competitive. Benchmarking assumes, correctly, that what one company does another company can always do as well. "Best performers" are often found in identical services or functions inside an organization, in competitor organizations, but also in organizations outside the industry. Together, EVA and benchmarking provide the diagnostic tools needed to measure total-factor productivity and to manage it. They are examples of the new tools executives should understand to measure and manage what goes on inside the enterprise. Combined, they are the best measures we have so far available.

ACTION POINT: Instigate a benchmarking study by gathering data on a product, service, or process from a comparable organization, even from one outside your industry. Set performance measures to ensure that you are competitive with the best performers.

Management Challenges for the 21st Century
From Data to Information Literacy (Corpedia Online Program)

Resource-Allocation Decisions

The allocation of capital and people determine whether the organization will do well or poorly.

The allocation of capital and performing people converts into action all that management knows about its business—they determine whether the organization will do well or poorly. An organization should allocate human resources as purposefully and as thoughtfully as it allocates capital. To understand a capital investment, a company has to look at four measures: return on investment, payback period, cash flow, and discounted present value. Each of these four measures tells the executive something different about a prospective capital investment. Each looks at the investment through a different lens. Decision makers should not evaluate capital investments in isolation, but as part of a cluster of projects. They should then select the cluster that shows the best ratio between opportunity and risk. The results of capital spending should be assessed against expectations in the postaudit procedure. Information gathered from the procedure can then be used to help make decisions about future investments.

The decisions to hire, to fire, and to promote are among the most important decisions of the executive. They are more difficult than the capital allocation decision. An organization needs to have a systematic process for making people decisions that is just as rigorous as the one it has for making decisions about capital. Executives need to evaluate people against expectations.

ACTION POINT: Review your capital allocation decisions of the past year. Are they meeting your expectations? Review your hiring and promotion decisions of the past year. Are they meeting your expectations? Make changes to your resource allocation procedures based on feedback analysis.

Management Challenges for the 21st Century
From Data to Information Literacy (Corpedia Online Program).

Six Rules of Successful Acquisitions

Acquisitions should be successful, but few are, in fact.

Acquisitions should be successful, but few are, in fact. The reason for this nonperformance is always the same: disregard of the well-known and well-tested rules for successful acquisitions.

The six rules of successful acquisitions are:

1. The successful acquisition must be based on business strategy, not financial strategy.
2. The successful acquisition must be based on what the acquirer contributes to the acquisition.
3. The two entities must share a common core of unity, such as markets and marketing, or technology, or core competencies.
4. The acquirer must respect the business, products, and customers of the acquired company, as well as its values.
5. The acquirer must be prepared to provide top management to the acquired business within a fairly short period, a year at most.
6. The successful acquisition must rapidly create visible opportunities for advancement for both the people in the acquiring business and people in the acquired business.

ACTION POINT: Evaluate three acquisition prospects against these six rules. Which ones would you recommend that your organization pursue?

The Frontiers of Management
The Successful Acquisition (Corpedia Online Program).

Business Not Financial Strategy

"There ain't no bargains," and "You get at most what you pay for."

Successful acquisitions are based upon business plans, not financial analyses. Acquisition targets must fit the business strategies of the acquiring company; otherwise, the acquisition is likely to fail. The worst acquisition record of the last decades of the twentieth century was that of Peter Grace, the longtime CEO of W. R. Grace. He was a brilliant man. He set out in the 1950s to build a world-class multinational through financially-based acquisitions. He assembled the ablest group of financial analysts and had them scout all over the world for industries and companies with a low price/earnings ratio. He bought these companies at what he thought were bargain prices. The financial analysis of each Grace purchase was impeccable. But there was absolutely no business strategy.

By contrast, one of the most successful examples of company growth based on acquisitions was the one that underlined the stellar performance of General Electric during the tenure of Jack Welch as CEO from 1981 to 2001. The largest single cause of the company's growth in sales and earnings—and the resulting rise in the company's market value—was the acquisition-based expansion of GE Capital. Of course, not all of them panned out. In fact, there was one major failure, the acquisition of a brokerage firm. But otherwise the GE Capital acquisitions seem to have worked out magnificently. Underlying practically all of them was a sound business strategy.

ACTION POINT: Think through an acquisition made by your organization. What was the basis of the acquisition: strategic or financial? How has it worked out?

The Successful Acquisition (Corpedia Online Program)

What the Acquirer Contributes

The successful acquisition is based on what the acquiring company contributes to the acquisition.

An acquisition will succeed only if the acquiring company thinks through what it can contribute to the business it is buying, not what the acquired company will contribute to the acquirer, no matter how attractive the expected "synergy" may look. What the acquiring company contributes may vary. It may be management, technology, or strength in distribution. This contribution has to be something besides money. Money by itself is never enough.

The acquisition of Citibank by Travelers was successful because the acquiring company, Travelers, thought through and planned what it could contribute to Citibank that would make a major difference. Citibank had established itself successfully in practically every country of the world and had, at the same time, built a transnational management. But in its products and services Citibank was still primarily a traditional bank, and its distributive and management capacity way exceeded the products and services commercial banking can produce and deliver. And Travelers had a good many of these products and services. What it saw itself as being able to contribute was greatly to increase the volume of business the superb Citibank worldwide distribution system and management could sell, and at little or no extra cost.

ACTION POINT: Before making an acquisition, focus on contribution, not synergy.

The Frontiers of Management
The Successful Acquisition (Corpedia Online Program)

Common Core of Unity

There has to be a "common culture" or at least a "cultural affinity."

Successful diversification by acquisition, like all successful diversification, requires a common core of unity. The two businesses must have in common either markets or technology, though occasionally a comparable production process has also provided sufficient unity of experience and expertise, as well as a common language, to bring companies together. Without such a core of unity, diversification, especially by acquisition, never works; financial ties alone are insufficient.

One example is a big French company that has been built by acquiring producers of all kinds of luxury goods: champagne and high-fashion designers, very expensive watches and perfumes and handmade shoes. It looks like the worst kind of conglomerate. The products have seemingly nothing in common. But all of them are being bought by customers for the same reason, which, of course, is not utility or price. Instead, people buy them because they are "status." What all the acquisitions of this successful acquirer have in common is their customers' values. Champagne is being sold quite differently from high fashion. But it is being bought for much the same reason.

ACTION POINT: In any acquisition, make sure there is a common culture or a cultural affinity between the two entities.

The Frontiers of Management
The Successful Acquisition (Corpedia Online Program)

Respect for the Business and Its Values

The acquisition must be a "temperamental fit."

No acquisition works unless the people in the acquiring company have respect for the product, the markets, and the customers of the company they acquire. Though many large pharmaceutical companies have acquired cosmetic firms, none has made a great success of it. Pharmacologists and biochemists are "serious" people concerned with health and disease. Lipsticks and lipstick users are frivolous to them. By the same token, few of the big television networks and other entertainment companies have made a go of the book publishers they bought. Books are not "media," and neither book buyers nor authors—a book publisher's two customers—bear any resemblance to what the Nielsen rating means by "audience." Sooner or later, usually sooner, a business requires a decision. People who do not respect or feel comfortable with the business, its products, and its users invariably make the wrong decision.

ACTION POINT: Take an acquisition with which you are familiar. Was there a temperamental fit between the two companies? How did the companies respect, or fail to respect, each other's business?

The Frontiers of Management
The Successful Acquisition (Corpedia Online Program)

Provide New Top Management

The business these people sell is their "child."

Within a year or so, the acquiring company must be able to provide top management for the company it acquires. The buyer has to be prepared to lose the top incumbents in companies that are bought. Top people are used to being bosses; they don't want to be "division managers." If they were owners or part-owners, the merger has made them so wealthy they don't have to stay if they don't enjoy it. And if they are professional managers, without an ownership stake, they usually find another job easily enough. Then to recruit new top management is a gamble that rarely comes off.

This applies particularly to a CEO who originally built the company that he or she sold. Very often this CEO has actually initiated the acquisition. He or she typically expects the acquirer to make the changes that he or she has been reluctant to make—for instance, get rid of an old employee who is a close friend and has served the company faithfully as it grew but has been long outgrown by the job. But still, the business these people sell is their "child." And the moment it is owned by someone else, they become protective and see their job as defending the "child" against one of those unfeeling "foreigners" who now own it.

ACTION POINT: Investigate a recent acquisition by your company or another company. What happened to the top management of the acquired company?

The Frontiers of Management
The Successful Acquisition (Corpedia Online Program)

Promote Across Lines

Politically, the people in the acquired company become "us" determined to defend their business against "them."

Even if all the rules have been faithfully observed, many acquisitions end up failing or at least take forever before they live up to their expectations. Legally the acquired business is now part of the acquiring company. But politically, the people in the acquired company become "us" determined to defend their business against "them," the people in the acquiring company. And the people in the acquiring company similarly think and act in terms of "us" against "them." Sometimes it takes a whole generation before these invisible but impenetrable barriers come down. It is therefore imperative that, within the first few months after the acquisition, a number of people on both sides are promoted to a better job across the lines. This way both sides see the acquisition as a personal opportunity.

The goal is to convince managers in both companies that the merger offers them personal opportunities. This principle apples not only to executives at or near the top, but also to the younger executives and professionals, the people on whose dedication and efforts any business primarily depends. If they see themselves blocked as a result of an acquisition, they will "vote with their feet," and as a rule they can find new jobs even more easily than displaced top executives.

ACTION POINT: Make sure you promote people in the wake of an acquisition.

The Frontiers of Management
The Successful Acquisition (Corpedia Online Program)

Alliances for Progress

The practice of management will have to base itself on the new assumption that its scope is not legal but the entire economic chain.

Business growth and business expansion in different parts of the world will increasingly not be based on mergers and acquisitions or even on starting new, wholly owned businesses there. They will increasingly have to be based on alliances, partnerships, joint ventures, and all kinds of relations with organizations located in other political jurisdictions. They will increasingly have to be based on structures that are economic units and not legal—and therefore not political—units.

There are many reasons growth henceforth will be based on partnerships of all sorts rather than on outright ownership and command-and-control. One of the more compelling will be the need to operate in both a global world economy and a splintered world polity. A partnership is by no means a perfect solution to this problem. But at least the conflict between economic reality and legal reality is greatly lessened if the economic unit is not also a legal unit, but is a partnership, an alliance, a joint venture, that is a relationship in which political and legal appearance can be separated from economic reality.

ACTION POINT: A very successful U.S. company constructed a number of plants in South America. A less prominent U.S. company decided to form alliances with existing companies in South America. The first company failed miserably, whereas the second succeeded. What insights are provided by this reading as to why the second was successful and the first a failure?

Management Challenges for the 21st Century

Rules for Successful Alliances

Alliances tend to get into serious trouble when they succeed.

While their failure rate in early years is no higher than that of new ventures, alliances tend to get into serious trouble—sometimes fatal—when they succeed. Often when an alliance does well, it becomes apparent that the goals and objectives of the partners are not compatible.

The problems can be anticipated and largely prevented by following five rules.

1. Before the alliance is completed, all parties must think through their objectives and the objectives of the "child."
2. Equally important is advance agreement on how the joint enterprise should be run.
3. Next, there has to be careful thinking about who will manage the alliance.
4. Each partner needs to make provisions in its own structure for the relationship to the joint enterprise and the other partners. The best way, especially in a large organization, is to entrust all such "dangerous liaisons" to one senior executive.
5. Finally, there has to be prior agreement on how to resolve disagreements. The best way is to agree, in advance of any dispute, on an arbitrator whom all sides know and respect and whose verdict will be accepted as final by all of them.

ACTION POINT: Alliances have been portrayed as "dangerous liaisons." What is so dangerous about entering into an alliance?

Managing for the Future

The Temptation to Do Good

Public-service institutions are out to maximize rather than to optimize.

The most important obstacle to innovation is that public-service institutions exist, after all, to "do good." This means that they tend to see their mission as a moral absolute rather than as economic and subject to a cost/benefit calculus. Economics always seeks a different allocation of the same resources to obtain a higher yield. In the public-service institution, there is no such thing as a higher yield. If one is "doing good," then there is no "better." Indeed, failure to attain objectives in the quest for a "good" only means that efforts need to be redoubled.

"Our mission will not be completed," asserts the head of the Crusade Against Hunger, "as long as there is one child on the earth going to bed hungry." If he were to say, "Our mission will be completed if the largest possible number of children that can be reached through existing distribution channels get enough to eat not to be stunted," he would be booted out of office. But if the goal is maximization, it can never be attained. Indeed, the closer one comes toward attaining one's objective, the more efforts are called for. For, once optimization has been reached, additional costs go up exponentially while additional results fall off exponentially. The closer a public-service institution comes to attaining its objectives, therefore, the more frustrated it will be and the harder it will work on what it is already doing.

ACTION POINT: Prison Fellowship seeks to reduce the rate at which released prisoners are incarcerated again because of new crimes. Why would it be unwise for Prison Fellowship to try to eliminate so-called "recidivism?"

Innovation and Entrepreneurship

The Whistle-blower

Whistle-blowing is ethically ambiguous.

Today's ethics of organization debate pays great attention to the duty to be a "whistle-blower" and to the protection of the whistle-blower against retaliation or suppression by his boss or by his organization. This sounds high-minded. Surely, the subordinate has a right, if not indeed a duty, to bring to public attention and remedial action his superior's misdeeds, let alone violation of the law on the part of a superior or of his employing organization. But in the context of the ethics of interdependence, whistle-blowing is ethically quite ambiguous.

To be sure, there are misdeeds of the superior or of the employing organization that so grossly violate propriety and laws that the subordinate (or the friend, or the child, or even the wife) cannot remain silent. This is, after all, what the word "felony" implies; one becomes a partner to a felony and criminally liable by not reporting, and thus compounding it. But otherwise? It is not primarily that to encourage whistle-blowing corrodes that bond of trust that ties the superior to the subordinate. Encouraging the whistle-blower must make the subordinate lose trust in the superior's willingness and ability to protect people.

ACTION POINT: The Sarbanes-Oxley law encourages whistle-blowing from insiders in the case of corporate corruption. How will this legislation affect the bond between superior and subordinates?

The Ecological Vision

Limits of Social Responsibility

"It is not enough for business to do well; it must also do good." But in order to "do good," a business must first "do well."

Whenever a business has disregarded the limitation of economic performance and has assumed social responsibilities that it could not support economically, it has soon gotten into trouble.

Union Carbide was not socially responsible when it put its plant into Vienna, West Virginia, to alleviate unemployment there. It was, in fact, irresponsible. The plant was marginal to begin with. The process was obsolescent. At best the plant could barely keep its head above water. And this, inevitably, meant a plant unable to take on social responsibility, even for its own impacts. Because the plant was uneconomical to begin with, Union Carbide resisted so long all demands to clean it up. This particular demand could not have been foreseen in the late 1940s, when concern with jobs far outweighed any concern for the environment. But demands of some kind can always be expected. To do something out of social responsibility that is economically irrational and untenable is therefore never responsible. It is sentimental. The result is always greater damage.

ACTION POINT: Explain why this is true: In order for a business to "do good," it must first "do well," and indeed very well.

Management: Tasks, Responsibilities, Practices

23 DECEMBER

Spiritual Values

Only compassion can save—the wordless knowledge of my own responsibility for whatever is being done to the least of God's children. This is knowledge of the spirit.

Society needs a return to spiritual values—not to offset the material but to make it fully productive. However remote its realization for the great mass of mankind, there is today the promise of material abundance or at least of material sufficiency. Mankind needs the return to spiritual values, for it needs compassion. It needs the deep experience that the *Thou* and the *I* are one, which all higher religions share. In an age of terror, of persecution, and of mass murder, such as ours, the hard shell of moral callousness may be necessary to survival. Without it we might yield to paralyzing despair. But moral numbness is also a terrible disease of mind and soul, and a terrible danger. It abets, even if it does not condone, cruelty and persecution. We have learned that the ethical humanitarianism of the nineteenth century cannot prevent man from becoming beast.

The individual needs the return to spiritual values, for he can survive in the present human situation only by reaffirming that man is not just a biological and physiological being but also a spiritual being, that is, creature, and existing for the purposes of his Creator and subject to Him. Only thus can the individual know that the threat of instant physical annihilation of the species does not invalidate his own existence, its meaning, and its responsibility.

ACTION POINT: In the presence of the threat of instant annihilation, how can we maintain meaning and responsibility without spiritual values?

Landmarks of Tomorrow

Human Existence in Tension

For Kierkegaard, human existence is possible only in tension—in tension between man's simultaneous life as an individual in the spirit and as a citizen in society.

Disintegration of the rational character of society and the rational relationship between individual and society is the most revolutionary trait of our times.

Society must make it possible for man to die without despair if it wants him to be able to live exclusively in society. And it can do so in only one way: by making *individual* life meaningless. If you are nothing but a leaf on the tree of the race, a cell in the body of society, then your death is not really death; you had better call it a process of collective regeneration. But then of course your life is not a real life either; it is just a functional process within the life of the whole, devoid of any meaning except in terms of the whole. Thus an optimism that proclaims human existence in society leads straight to despair. And this despair can lead only to totalitarianism. Human existence *is* possible as existence not in despair, as existence not in tragedy; it is possible as existence in Faith. Faith is the belief that in God the impossible is possible, that in Him time and eternity are one, that both life and death are meaningful.

ACTION POINT: Reflect on the following: "Human existence is possible only in tension—in tension between man's simultaneous life as an individual in the spirit and as a citizen in society."

The Ecological Vision
The End of Economic Man

The Unfashionable Kierkegaard

Faith enables man to die; but it also enables him to live.

My *work* has indeed been totally in society. But I knew at once, in those far-back days of 1928, that my *life* would not and could not be totally in society, that it would have to have an existential dimension that transcends society. Still my work has been totally in society—except for this essay on Kierkegaard.

Though Kierkegaard's faith cannot overcome the awful loneliness, the isolation and dissonance of human existence, it can make it bearable by making it meaningful. The philosophy of the totalitarian creeds enables man to die. It is dangerous to underestimate the strength of such a philosophy; for, in a time of sorrow and suffering, of catastrophe and horror, it is a great thing to be able to die. Yet it is not enough. Kierkegaard's faith, too, enables man to die; but it also enables him to live. Faith is the belief that in God the impossible is possible, that in Him time and eternity are one, that both life and death are meaningful. Faith is the knowledge that man is creature—not autonomous, not the master, not the end, not the center—and yet responsible and free. It is the acceptance of man's essential loneliness, to be overcome by the certainty that God is always with man, even "unto the hour of our death."

ACTION POINT: Salvation by society has always failed in the end. Find a purpose that sustains you both in society and as a human being.

The Ecological Vision

Return of the Demons

If freedom is incompatible with security, the masses will decide for security.

The masses, then, have become prepared to abandon freedom if this promises to reestablish the rationality of the world. If freedom is incompatible with equality, they will give up freedom. If it is incompatible with security, they will decide for security. To be free or not has become a secondary question, since the freedom available does not help to banish the demons. Since the "free" society is the one that is threatened by the demons, it seems more than plausible to blame freedom and to expect delivery from despair through the abandonment of freedom.

ACTION POINT: The passage refers to the embrace by Europe of Nazism to escape the demons of war and depression. Why will society be more likely to embrace complete regimentation and totalitarianism in the absence of strong institutions?

The End of Economic Man

Integrating the Economic and Social

It is this absence of a functioning industrial society, able to integrate our industrial reality, that underlies the crises of our times.

Man in his social and political existence must have a functioning society just as he must have air to breathe in his biological existence. However, the fact that man has to have a society does not necessarily mean that he has it. Nobody calls the mass of unorganized, panicky, stampeding humanity in a shipwreck a "society." There is no society, though there are human beings in a group. Actually, the panic is directly due to the breakdown of a society; and the only way to overcome it is by restoring a society with social values, social discipline, social power, and social relationships.

Social life cannot function without a society; but it is conceivable that it does not function at all. The evidence of the last twenty-five years of Western civilization hardly entitles us to say that our social life functioned so well as to make out a prima-facie case for the existence of a functioning society.

ACTION POINT: The passage above was written during World War II. It recognized that after centuries of industrial advance there had not been a similar advance in other institutions of society. Should the economic dimension of society ever take supremacy over the human, social, and political dimensions?

The Future of Industrial Man

The Family-Managed Business

The majority of businesses everywhere are family controlled and family managed.

The majority of businesses everywhere—including the United States and all other developed countries—are family controlled and family managed. And family management is by no means confined to small and medium-sized firms—families run some of the world's largest companies. DuPont, controlled and managed by family members for 170 years (since its founding in 1802 until professional management took over in the mid-1970s), grew into the world's largest chemical company. And two centuries after a still obscure coin dealer began to send out his sons to establish banks in Europe's capitals, financial firms bearing the Rothschild name and run by Rothschilds are still among the world's premier private bankers.

Yet management books and management courses deal almost entirely with the publicly owned and professionally managed company—they rarely as much as mention the family-managed business. Of course, there is no difference whatever between professionally managed and family-managed businesses in respect to all functional work: research or marketing or accounting. But with respect to management, the family business requires its own and very different rules. These rules have to be stringently observed. Otherwise, the family-managed business will not survive, let alone prosper.

ACTION POINT: Less than 30 percent of family-owned companies survive into the second generation, while only 10 percent make it to the third generation, and just 4 percent to the fourth generation (*Family Magazine*, Web site, June 2004). Speculate as to why family businesses have such difficulty transitioning from generation to generation.

Managing in a Time of Great Change

Rules for the Family-Managed Business

The controlling word in "family-managed business" is not "family." It has to be "business."

The first rule is that family members do not work in the business unless they are at least as able as any nonfamily employee, and work at least as hard. The second rule is equally simple: No matter how many family members are in the company's management, and how effective they are, one top job is always filled by an outsider who is not a member of the family. Typically, this is either the financial executive or the head of research—the two positions in which technical qualifications are most important. Rule three is that family-managed businesses, except perhaps for the very smallest ones, increasingly need to staff key positions with nonfamily professionals. The knowledge and expertise needed, whether in manufacturing or in marketing, in finance, in research, in human resource management, have become far too great to be satisfied by any but the most competent family member.

Even the family-managed business that faithfully observes the preceding three rules tends to get into trouble—and often breaks up—over *management succession.* Then what the business needs and what the family wants tend to collide. There is only one solution: Entrust the succession decision to an outsider who is neither part of the family nor part of the business.

ACTION POINT: Get to know the top management of a family-owned business. Ask members how they plan to handle the problem of management succession "into the next generation." Determine whether the plans are being driven by business issues or family issues, or by a combination of the two.

Managing in a Time of Great Change

Innovations for Maximum Opportunities

What is lacking to make effective what is already possible?

The characteristic of the innovator is the ability to envisage as a system what to others are unrelated, separate elements. It is the successful attempt to find and to provide the smallest missing part that will convert already existing elements. To find areas where innovation would create maximum opportunities, one asks: "What is lacking to make effective what is already possible? What one small step would transform our economic results? What small change would alter the capacity of the whole of our resources?"

To describe the need is not to satisfy it. But describing the need gives a specification for the desirable results. Whether they are likely to be obtained can be decided. Innovation is applicable to finding business potential and to making the future.

ACTION POINT: Ask yourself the three questions above.

Managing for Results

31 DECEMBER

From Data to Information Literacy

The executive and the knowledge worker have only one tool—information.

Information is what holds an organization together and information is what makes individual knowledge workers effective. Enterprises and individuals will have to learn what information they need and how to get it. They will have to learn how to organize information as their key resource.

In moving from data literacy to information literacy, you need to answer two principal questions: "What information does my enterprise need?" and "What information do I need?" To answer these questions you have to rethink:

- What your job is, and what it should be
- What your contribution is, or should be
- What the fundamentals are of your organization

You will need three different types of information, each with its own concepts. The three primary types of information are: external information, internal information, and cross-organizational information. Your success and the success of your organization depend upon getting these answers right.

ACTION POINT: Answer these questions: "What is my job? What should be my contribution?" and "What are the fundamentals of the organization?" Then answer: "What information does my organization need?" and "What information do I need?"

Management Challenges for the 21st Century
From Data to Information Literacy (Corpedia Online Program)

ANNOTATED BIBLIOGRAPHY

The End of Economic Man; Transaction Publishers 1995 (originally published by John Day Company, NY, 1939)

The End of Economic Man is Drucker's first full-length book. It is a diagnostic study of the totalitarian state and the first book to study the origins of totalitarianism. He describes the reasons for the rise of fascism and the failures of established institutions that led to its emergence. Drucker develops an understanding of the dynamics of the totalitarian society and helps us to understand the causes of totalitarianism in order to prevent such a catastrophe in the future. Developing social, religious, economic, and political institutions that function effectively will prevent the emergence of circumstances that frequently encourage the totalitarian state.

The Future of Industrial Man; Transaction Publishers 1995 (originally published by John Day Company, NY, 1942)

Drucker describes the requirements for a functioning society by developing a social theory of society in general and of the industrial society in particular. In *The Future of Industrial Man*, Peter Drucker presents the requirements for any society for it to be both legitimate and functioning. Such a society must give status and function to the individual. The book addresses the question: "How can individual freedom be preserved in an industrial society in light of the dominance of managerial power and the corporation?" Written before the entrance of the U.S. into World War II, it is optimistic about post–World War II Europe and reaffirms its hopes and values through a time of despair. The book dared to ask, "What do we hope for the postwar world?"

Concept of the Corporation; Transaction Publishers 1993 (originally published by John Day Company, NY, 1946)

This classic book is the first to describe and analyze the structure, policies, and practices of a large corporation, General Motors. The book looks upon a "business" as an "organization," that is, as a social structure that brings together human beings in order to satisfy economic needs and the wants of a community. It establishes the "organization" as a distinct entity, and management of an organization as a legitimate subject of inquiry. The book represents a link between Drucker's first two books on society and his subsequent writings on management. Detailed information is provided regarding such management practices as decentralization, pricing, and the roles of profits and of labor unions. Drucker looks at General Motors' managerial organization and attempts to understand what makes the company work so effectively. Certain questions are addressed, such as: "What are the company's core principles, and how do they contribute to the success of the organization?" The principles of organization and management at General Motors described in this book became models for organizations worldwide. The book addresses issues that go beyond the borders of the business corporation, and considers the "corporate state" itself.

The New Society; Transaction Publishers 1993 (originally published by Harper & Row Publishers, NY, 1950)
In *The New Society,* Peter Drucker extends his previous works *The Future of Industrial Man* and *Concept of the Corporation* into a systematic, organized analysis of the industrial society that emerged out of World War II. He analyzes large business enterprises, governments, labor unions, and the place of the individual within the social context of these institutions. Following publication of the of *The New Society,* George G. Higgins wrote in *Commonweal,* "Drucker has analyzed, as brilliantly as any modern writer, the problems of industrial relations in the individual company or 'enterprise.' He is thoroughly at home in economics, political science, industrial psychology, and industrial sociology, and has succeeded admirably in harmonizing the findings of all four disciplines and applying them meaningfully to the practical problems of the 'enterprise.' " Drucker believes that the interests of the worker, management, and corporation are reconcilable with society. He advances the idea of "the plant community" in which workers are encouraged to take on more responsibility and act like "managers." He questions whether unions can survive in their present form if the worker is encouraged to act as a manager.

The Practice of Management; HarperCollins 1993 (originally published by Harper & Row Publishers, NY, 1954)
This classic is the first book to define management as a practice and a discipline, thus establishing Drucker as the founder of the discipline of modern management. Management has been practiced for centuries, but this book systematically defines management as a discipline that can be taught and learned. It provides a systematic guide for practicing managers who want to improve their effectiveness and productivity. It presents Management by Objectives as a genuine philosophy of management that integrates the interests of the corporation with those of the managers and contributors to an organization. Illustrations come from such companies as Ford; GE; Sears, Roebuck & Co.; GM; IBM; and AT&T.

America's Next Twenty Years; Out of Print HarperCollins (originally published by Harper & Row Publishers, NY, 1957)
In this collection of essays, Peter Drucker discusses the issues that he believes will be significant in America, including the coming labor shortage, automation, significant wealth in the hands of a few individuals, college education, American politics, and perhaps most significantly, the growing disparity between the "haves" and the "have nots." In these essays Drucker identifies the major events that "have already happened" that will "determine the future." "Identifying the future that has already happened" is a major theme of Drucker's many books and essays.

Landmarks of Tomorrow; Transaction Publishers 1996 (originally published by Harper & Brothers Publishers, NY, 1957)

Landmarks of Tomorrow identifies "the future that has already happened" in three major areas of human life and experience. The first part of the book treats the philosophical shift from a Cartesian universe of mechanical cause to a new universe of pattern, purpose, and configuration. Drucker discusses the need to organize men of knowledge and of high skill for joint effort, and performance as a key component of this change. The second part of the book sketches four realities that challenge the people of the free world: an educated society, economic development, the decline of the effectiveness of government, and the collapse of Eastern culture. The final section of the book is concerned with the spiritual reality of human existence. These are seen as basic elements in late-twentieth-century society. In his new introduction, Peter Drucker revisits the main findings of *Landmarks of Tomorrow* and assesses their validity in relation to today's concerns.

Managing for Results; HarperCollins 1993 (originally published by Harper & Row Publishers, NY, 1964)

This book focuses upon economic performance as the specific function and contribution of business and the reason for its existence. The effective business, Peter Drucker observes, focuses on opportunities rather than problems. How this focus is achieved in order to make the organization prosper and grow is the subject of this companion to his classic, *The Practice of Management*. The earlier book was chiefly concerned with how management functions as a discipline and practice; this volume shows what the executive decision-maker must do to move his enterprise forward. One of the notable accomplishments of this book is its combining of specific economic analysis with the entrepreneurial force in business prosperity. For though it discusses "what to do" more than Drucker's previous works, the book stresses the qualitative aspect of enterprise: every successful business requires a goal and spirit all its own. *Managing for Results* was the first book to describe what is now widely called "business strategy" and to identify what are now called an organization's "core competencies."

The Effective Executive; HarperCollins 2002 (originally published by Harper & Row Publishers, NY, 1966, 1967)

The Effective Executive is a landmark book that develops the specific practices of the executive that lead to effectiveness. It is based on observations of effective executives in business and government. Drucker starts by reminding executives that the measure of effectiveness is the ability to "get the right things done." This involves five practices: (1) managing one's time, (2) focusing on contribution rather than problems, (3) making strengths productive, (4) establishing priorities, and (5) making effective decisions. A major portion of the book is devoted to the process of making effective decisions and the criteria for effective decisions. Numerous examples are provided of executive effectiveness. The book concludes by emphasizing that effectiveness can be learned and must be learned.

The Age of Discontinuity; Transaction Publishers 2003 (originally published by Harper & Row Publishers, NY, 1968, 1969)

Peter Drucker focuses with great clarity and perception on the forces of change that are transforming the economic landscape and creating tomorrow's society. He discerns four major areas of discontinuity underlying contemporary social and cultural reality: (1) the explosion of new technologies resulting in major new industries; (2) the change from an international to a world economy; (3) a new sociopolitical reality of pluralistic institutions that poses drastic political, philosophical, and spiritual challenges; and (4) the new universe of knowledge work based on mass education along with its implications. *The Age of Discontinuity* is a fascinating and important blueprint for shaping a future already very much with us.

Men, Ideas, and Politics; Out of Print HarperCollins (originally published by Harper & Row Publishers, NY, 1971)

This book is a compilation of thirteen essays addressing the issues of society—people, politics, and thought. Included are essays on Henry Ford, Japanese management, and effective presidents. Two articles in particular show aspects of Drucker's thinking that are especially important. One is an essay on "The Unfashionable Kierkegaard," which encourages the development of the spiritual dimension of humankind. The other is on the political philosophy of John C. Calhoun, describing the basic principles of America's pluralism and how they shape government policies and programs.

Technology, Management, and Society; Out of Print HarperCollins (originally published by Harper & Row Publishers, NY, 1970)

Technology, Management, and Society presents an overview of the nature of modern technology and its relationships with science, engineering, and religion. The social and political forces, which increasingly impinge on technological development, are analyzed within the framework of broad institutional change. Peter Drucker's critical perspective will be welcomed by scholars and students troubled by society's growing reliance on technological solutions to complex social and political problems.

Management: Tasks, Responsibilities, Practices; HarperCollins 1993 (originally published by Harper & Row Publishers, NY, 1973)

This book is a compendium of Drucker on management. It updates and expands upon *The Practice of Management*. It is an essential reference book for executives. Management is an organized body of knowledge consisting of managerial tasks, managerial work, managerial tools, managerial responsibilities, and the role of top management. According to Peter Drucker, "This book tries to equip the manager with the understanding, the thinking, the knowledge, and the skills for today's and also tomorrow's jobs." This management classic has been developed and tested during more than thirty years of management teaching in universities, executive programs, seminars, and through the author's close work with managers as a consultant for large and small businesses, government agencies, hospitals, and schools.

The Pension Fund Revolution; Transaction Publishers 1996 (originally published as *The Unseen Revolution,* by Harper & Row Publishers, NY, 1976)

In this book, Drucker describes how institutional investors, especially pension funds, have become the controlling owners of America's large companies, and the country's "capitalists." He explores how ownership has become highly concentrated in the hands of large institutional investors, and that through the pension funds, "ownership of the means of production" has become "socialized" without becoming "nationalized." Another theme of this book is the aging of America. Drucker points to the new challenges this trend will pose with respect to health care, pensions, and social security's place in the American economy and society; and how, altogether, American politics would increasingly become dominated by middle-class issues and with the values of elderly people. In the new epilogue, Drucker discusses how the increasing dominance of pension funds represents one of the most startling power shifts in economic history, and examines their present-day impact.

Adventures of a Bystander; John Wiley & Sons 1997 (originally published by Harper & Row Publishers, NY, 1978)

Adventures of a Bystander is Drucker's collection of autobiographical stories and vignettes, in which he paints a portrait of his life, and of the larger historical realities of his time. Drucker conveys his life story—from his early teen years in Vienna through the interwar years in Europe, the New Deal era, World War II, and the postwar period in America—through intimate profiles of a host of fascinating people he's known through the years. Along with bankers and courtesans, artists, aristocrats, prophets, and empire-builders, we meet members of Drucker's own family and close circle of friends, among them such prominent figures as Sigmund Freud, Henry Luce, Alfred Sloan, John Lewis, and Buckminster Fuller. Shedding light on a turbulent and important era, *Adventures of a Bystander* also reflects Peter Drucker himself as a man of imaginative sympathy and enormous interest in people, ideas, and history.

Managing in Turbulent Times; HarperCollins 1993 (originally published by Harper & Row Publishers, NY, 1980)

This important and timely book concerns the immediate future of business, society, and the economy. We are, says Drucker, entering a new economic era with new trends, new markets, a global economy, new technologies, and new institutions. How will managers and management deal with the turbulence created by these new realities? This book, as Drucker explains it, "is concerned with action, rather than understanding, with decisions, rather than analysis." It deals with the strategies needed to adapt to change and to turn rapid changes into opportunities, to turn the threat of change into productive and profitable action that contributes positively to our society, the economy, and the individual. An organization must be structured to withstand a blow caused by environmental turbulence.

Toward the Next Economics; Out of Print HarperCollins
(originally published by Harper & Row Publishers, NY, 1981)
These essays cover a wide-ranging collection of topics on business, management, economics, and society. They are all concerned with what Drucker calls "social ecology" and especially with institutions. These essays reflect "the future that has already happened." The essays reflect Drucker's belief that in the decade of the 1970s there were genuine changes in population structure and dynamics, changes in the role of institutions, changes in the relation between sciences and society, and changes in the fundamental theories about economics and society, long considered as truths. The essays are international in scope.

The Changing World of the Executive; Out of Print Truman Talley Books
(originally published by Truman Talley Books, NY, 1982)
These essays from the *Wall Street Journal* explore a wide variety of topics. They deal with changes in the workforce—its jobs, its expectations—with the power relationships of a "society of employees," and with changes in technology and in the world economy. They discuss the problems and challenges facing major institutions, including business enterprises, schools, hospitals, and government agencies. They look anew at the tasks and work of executives, at their performance and its measurement, and at executive compensation. However diverse the topics, these chapters have one common theme, the changing world of the executive—changing rapidly within the organization; changing rapidly with respect to the visions, aspirations, and even characteristics of employees, customers, and constituents; changing outside the organization, as well, economically, technologically, socially, politically.

Innovation and Entrepreneurship; HarperCollins 1993 (originally published by Harper & Row Publishers, NY, 1985)
The first book to present innovation and entrepreneurship as a purposeful and systematic discipline. It explains and analyzes the challenges and opportunities presented by the emergence of the entrepreneurial economy in business and public-service institutions. It is a major contribution to functioning management, organization, and economy. The book is divided into three main sections: (1) The Practice of Innovation, (2) The Practice of Entrepreneurship, and (3) Entrepreneurial Strategies. The author presents innovation and entrepreneurship as both practice and discipline, choosing to focus on the actions of the entrepreneur as opposed to entrepreneurial psychology and temperament. All organizations, including public-service institutions, must become entrepreneurial to survive and prosper in a market economy. The book provides a description of entrepreneurial policies and windows of opportunity for developing innovative practices in both emerging and well-established organizations.

The Frontiers of Management; Truman Talley Books 1999 (originally published by Truman Talley Books, NY, 1986)

This book is a collection of thirty-five previously published articles and essays, twenty-five of which have appeared on the editorial page of the *Wall Street Journal.* Featuring a new introduction, Drucker forecasts the business trends of what was then the next millennium. *The Frontiers of Management* is a clear, direct, lively, and comprehensible examination of global trends and management practices. There are chapters dealing with the world economy, hostile takeovers, and the unexpected problems of success. Jobs, younger people, and career gridlock are also covered. Throughout this book, Drucker stresses the importance of forethought and of realizing that "change is opportunity" in every branch of executive decision-making.

The New Realities; Transaction Publishers 2003 (originally published by Harper & Row Publishers, NY, 1989)

This book is about the "next century." Its thesis is that the "next century" is already here, indeed that we are well advanced into it. In this book, Drucker writes about the "social superstructure"—politics and government, society, economy and economics, social organization, and the new knowledge society. He describes the limits of government and dangers of "charisma" in leadership. He identifies the future organization as being information-based. While this book is not "futurism," it attempts to define the concerns, the issues, and the controversies that will be realities for years to come. Drucker focuses on what to do today in contemplation of tomorrow. Within self-imposed limitations, he attempts to set the agenda on how to deal with some of the toughest problems we are facing today that have been created by the successes of the past.

Managing the Non-Profit Organization; HarperCollins 1992 (originally published by HarperCollins, NY, 1990)

The service, or nonprofit, sector of our society is growing rapidly (with more than 8 million employees and more than 80 million volunteers), creating a major need for guidelines and expert advice on how to lead and manage these organizations effectively. This book is an application of Drucker's perspective on management to nonprofit organizations of all kinds. He gives examples and explanations of mission, leadership, resources, marketing, goals, people development, decision making, and much more. Included are interviews with nine experts that address key issues in the nonprofit sector.

Managing for the Future; Truman Talley/E.P. Dutton 1992

Bringing together the most exciting of Drucker's many recent essays on economics, business practices, managing for change, and the evolving shape of the modern corporation, *Managing for the Future* offers important insights and lessons for anyone trying to stay ahead of today's unremitting competition. Drucker's universe is a constantly expanding cosmos composed of four regions in which he demonstrates mastery: (1) the economic forces affecting our lives and livelihoods, (2) today's changing workforce and workplaces, (3) the newest management concepts and practices, and (4) the shape of the organization, including the corporation, as it evolves and responds to ever-increasing tasks and responsibilities. Each of this book's chapters explores a business or corporate or "people" problem, and Drucker shows how to solve it or use it as an opportunity for change.

The Ecological Vision; Transaction Publishers 1993
The thirty-one essays in this volume were written over a period of more than forty years. These essays range over a wide array of disciplines and subject matter. Yet they all have in common that they are "Essays in Social Ecology" and deal with the man-made environment. They all, in one way or another, deal with the interaction between individual and community. And they try to look upon the economy, upon technology, upon art, as dimensions of social experience and as expressions of social values. The last essay in this collection, *The Unfashionable Kierkegaard,* was written as an affirmation of the existential, the spiritual, the individual dimension of the Creature. It was written by Drucker to assert that society is not enough—not even for society. It was written to affirm hope. This is an important and perceptive volume of essays.

Post-Capitalist Society; Transaction Publishers 2005 (originally published by HarperCollins, NY, 1993)
In *Post-Capitalist Society,* Peter Drucker describes how every few hundred years a sharp transformation has taken place and greatly affected society—its worldview, its basic values, its business and economics, and its social and political structure. According to Drucker, we are right in the middle of another time of radical change, from the Age of Capitalism and the Nation-State to a Knowledge Society and a Society of Organizations. The primary resource in the post-capitalist society will be knowledge, and the leading social groups will be "knowledge workers." Looking backward and forward, Drucker discusses the Industrial Revolution, the Productivity Revolution, the Management Revolution, and the governance of corporations. He explains the new functions of organizations, the economics of knowledge, and productivity as a social and economic priority. He covers the transformation from Nation-State to Megastate, the new pluralism of political systems, and the needed turnaround in government. Finally, Drucker details the knowledge issues and the role and use of knowledge in the post-capitalist society. Divided into three parts—Society, Polity, and Knowledge—*Post-Capitalist Society* provides a searching look into the future as well as a vital analysis of the past, focusing on the challenges of the present transition period and how, if we can understand and respond to them, we can create a new future.

Managing in a Time of Great Change; Truman Talley/E.P. Dutton 1995
This book compiles essays written by Drucker from 1991 to 1994 and published in the *Harvard Business Review* and the *Wall Street Journal.* All of theses essays are about change: changes in the economy, society, business, and in organizations in general. Drucker's advice on how managers should adjust to these tectonic shifts centers around the rise of the now-ubiquitous knowledge worker and the global economy. In this book, Drucker illu-

minates the business challenges confronting us today. He examines current management trends and whether they really work, the implications for business in the reinvention of the government, and the shifting balance of power between management and labor.

Drucker on Asia; Out of Print Butterworth-Heinemann 1995 (first published by Diamond, Inc., Tokyo, 1995)
Drucker on Asia is the result of an extensive dialogue between two of the world's leading business figures, Peter F. Drucker and Isao Nakauchi. Their dialogue considers the changes occurring in the economic world today and identifies the challenges that free markets and free enterprises now face, with specific reference to China and Japan. What do these changes mean to Japan? What does Japan have to do in order to achieve a "third economic miracle"? What do these changes mean to society, the individual company, the individual professional and executive? These are the questions that Drucker and Nakauchi address in their brilliant insight into the future economic role of Asia.

Peter Drucker on the Profession of Management; Harvard Business School Press 1998
This is a significant collection of Peter Drucker's landmark articles from the *Harvard Business Review*. Drucker seeks out, identifies, and examines the most important issues confronting managers, from corporate strategy to management style to social change. This volume provides a rare opportunity to trace the evolution of great shifts in our workplaces, and to understand more clearly the role of managers in the ongoing effort to balance change with continuity, the latter a recurring theme in Drucker's writings. These are strategically presented here to address two unifying themes: the first examines the "Manager's Responsibilities," while the second investigates "The Executive's World." Containing an important interview with Drucker on "The Post-Capitalist Executive," as well as a preface by Drucker himself, the volume is edited by Nan Stone, longtime editor of the *Harvard Business Review*.

Management Challenges for the 21st Century; HarperCollins 1999
In his first major book since *The Post-Capitalist Society*, Drucker discusses the new paradigms of management—how they have changed and will continue to change our basic assumptions about the practices and principles of management. Drucker analyzes the new realities of strategy, shows how to be a leader in periods of change, and explains the "New Information Revolution," discussing the information an executive needs and the information an executive owes. He also examines knowledge-worker productivity, and shows that changes in the basic attitude of individuals and organizations, as well as structural changes in work itself, are needed for increased productivity. Finally, Drucker addresses the ultimate challenge of managing oneself while meeting the demands on the individual during a longer working life and in an ever-changing workplace.

Managing in the Next Society; St. Martin's Press 2002
In this compilation of essays culled from published magazine articles and a lengthy essay appearing in the *Economist* in November 2001, and interviews during the period of

1996 to 2002, Drucker has expertly anticipated our ever-changing business society and ever-expanding management roles. In this book, Drucker identifies the reality of the "Next Society," which has been shaped by three major trends: the decline of the young portion of the population, the decline of manufacturing, and the transformation of the workforce (together with the social impact of the Information Revolution). Drucker also asserts that e-commerce and e-learning are to the Information Revolution what the railroad was to the Industrial Revolution, and thus, an information society is developing. Drucker speaks of the importance of the social sector (that is, nongovernmental and nonprofit organizations), because NPOs can create what we now need: communities for citizens and especially for highly educated knowledge-workers, who increasingly dominate developed societies.

ANTHOLOGIES

The Essential Drucker; HarperCollins 2001
The Essential Drucker offers, in Drucker's words, "a coherent and fairly comprehensive 'Introduction to Management' and gives an overview of my management work and thus answers the question I've been asked again and again: 'Which writings are Essential?' " The book contains twenty-six selections on management in the organization, management and the individual, and management in society. It covers the basic principles and concerns of management and its problems, challenges, and opportunities, giving managers, executives, and professionals the tools to perform the tasks that the economy and society of today and tomorrow will demand of them.

A *Functioning Society*; Transaction Publishers 2003
In these essays, Drucker has brought together selections from his vast writings on community, society, and the political structure. Drucker's primary concern is with a functioning society in which the individual has status and function. Parts I and II identify the institutions that could recreate community, the collapse of which produced totalitarianism in Europe. These selections were written during World War II. Part III deals with the limits of governmental competence in the social and economic realm. This section is concerned with the differences between big government and effective government.

NOVELS

The Last of All Possible Worlds	1982	Out of Print HarperCollins
The Temptation to Do Good	1984	Out of Print HarperCollins

E-LEARNING MODULES

MANAGING ONESELF AND OTHERS

Module 8101: *Managing Oneself*	2001	Corpedia Education
Module 8102: *People Decisions*	2001	Corpedia Education
Module 8103: *Managing the Boss*	2001	Corpedia Education
Module 8104: *The Elements of Decision Making*	2001	Corpedia Education
Module 8105: *Knowledge Worker Productivity*	2002	Corpedia Education

BUSINESS STRATEGIES ESSENTIALS

Module 8106: *The Successful Acquisition*	2001	Corpedia Education
Module 8107: *Alliances*	2001	Corpedia Education
Module 8108: *The Five Deadly Business Sins*	2001	Corpedia Education
Module 8109: *Permanent Cost Control*	2001	Corpedia Education
Module 8110: *Entrepreneurial Strategies*	2001	Corpedia Education

LEADING CHANGE

Module 8114: *The Next Society*	2004	Corpedia Education
Module 8115: *From Data to Information Literacy*	2004	Corpedia Education
Module 8116: *Driving Change*	2003	Corpedia Education

SOURCES BY BOOK OR INTERNET MODULE

Adventures of a Bystander
February 12, April 21, April 22, April 25, June 23

The Age of Discontinuity
January 2, January 4, January 18, February 1, February 4, February 19, May 6, May 10, May 30, October 22, October 23, October 24, October 25, November 1, December 3

Concept of the Corporation
February 16, May 27, June 25, October 20, November 18, November 29

Drucker on Asia
January 24, January 25, June 7, June 22, August 31, October 1

The Ecological Vision
January 2, January 17, January 21, January 22, January 26, February 10, February 20, March 9, March 15, March 18, April 27, April 28, May 21, May 31, June 2, June 3, June 4, June 5, August 7, August 8, November 17, December 1, December 21, December 24, December 25

The End of Economic Man
January 20, June 28, October 17, October 18, December 24, December 26

The Essential Drucker
April 8, April 18

The Effective Executive
January 5, January 15, April 7, September 1, September 2, September 3, September 4, September 5, September 6, September 8, September 16, September 20, October 2, October 3, October 4, October 5, October 7, October 8, October 9, October 10, October 11, October 13, October 14

The Frontiers of Management
January 27, March 2, March 4, April 1, May 11, June 6, September 22, October 26, November 27, November 28, November 30, December 11, December 13, December 14, December 15, December 16, December 17

A *Functioning Society*
January 31, March 19, April 12, April 13, April 18, October 28, November 18

The Future of Industrial Man
January 19, January 31, February 13, February 17, February 24, October 16, December 27

Innovation and Entrepreneurship
February 10, March 6, July 12, July 13, July 14, July 15, July 16, July 17, July 18, July 19, July 20, July 21, July 22, July 29, August 4, August 6, August 10, August 11, August 12, August 13, August 16, August 17, August 18, August 19, August 20, August 21, August 22, August 23, August 24, December 20

Landmarks of Tomorrow
March 29, April 4, December 23

Management: Tasks, Responsibilities, Practices
January 1, January 10, January 16, January 28, February 27, February 28, February 29, March 7, March 13, March 29, April 2, April 3, April 6, April 9, April 16, April 29, June 20, June 21, June 27, July 1, July 3, July 23, July 26, August 1, August 2, August 3, August 28, September 10,

January 29, February 21, March 9, March 12, March 16, March 17, November 13, November 15

SOURCES BY CORPEDIA INTERNET MODULE

Driving Change (Module 8116)
July 14, July 15, July 16, July 17, July 19, July 20

The Elements of Decision Making (Module 8104)
October 5, October 7, October 8, October 9, October 10, October 11, October 12, October 14

Entrepreneurial Strategies (Module 8110)
August 16, August 17, August 18, August 19, August 20, August 21, August 22, August 23, August 24

The Five Deadly Business Sins (Module 8108)
March 24, July 24, July 27

From Data to Information Literacy (Module 8115)
March 3, March 25, July 7, November 2, November 3, December 4, December 5, December 6, December 8,December 9, December 10, December 31

Knowledge Worker Productivity (Module 8105)
January 8, May 24, May 25, May 28

Managing Oneself (Module 8101)
June 1, September 12, September 13, September 14, September 15, September 17

Managing the Boss (Module 8103)
September 16

The Next Society (Module 8114)
January 9, March 14, March 23, March 27, May 3, May 14, May 15, May 16, May 17, June 14, August 9, September 19

People Decisions (Module 8102)
April 18, April 19, September 21

Permanent Cost Control (Module 8109)
July 28, July 29, July 30, July 31

The Successful Acquisition (Module 8106)
December 11, December 12, December 13, December 14, December 15, December 16, December 17

SOURCES BY DAY AND PARALLEL PASSAGES

Unless indicated otherwise, the page references provided in "Sources by Day" refer to the latest edition of each book. The status of each reference is contained in the "Annotated Bibliography."

		Source Page Number
January 1	*Management: Tasks, Responsibilities, Practices* (Hardcover)	462–463
January 2	*The Ecological Vision*	450–451
	The Age of Discontinuity	37
January 3	*The Practice of Management*	4
January 4	*The Age of Discontinuity*	193, 194, 195
January 5	*The Effective Executive*	104
	Managing in Turbulent Times	45
	Managing in a Time of Great Change	33
	Management Challenges for the 21st Century	75
January 6	*Management Challenges for the 21st Century*	74–75
January 7	*Management Challenges for the 21st Century*	148–149
January 8	*Management Challenges for the 21st Century*	146
	Knowledge Worker Productivity (Corpedia Module 8105)	
January 9	*Managing in the Next Society*	287
	The Next Society (Corpedia Module 8114)	
January 10	*Management: Tasks, Responsibilities, Practices* (Hardcover)	ix–x
January 11	"Teaching the Work of Management," *New Management* (Winter 1985)	5
January 12	*The New Realities*	ix–x
January 13	*The New Realities*	223
January 14	*The New Society*	158
January 15	*The Practice of Management*	144, 145
	The Effective Executive	40, 78
January 16	*Management: Tasks, Responsibilities, Practices*	17
January 17	*The Ecological Vision*	143–145
January 18	*Post-Capitalist Society*	49
	The Age of Discontinuity	189–190, 211
January 19	*The Future of Industrial Man*	29
January 20	*The End of Economic Man*	45
January 21	*The Ecological Vision*	111–112
January 22	*The Ecological Vision*	75–76
January 23	*The Practice of Management*	390–391
January 24	*Drucker on Asia*	108–109

January 25	*Drucker on Asia*	98–101
January 26	*The Ecological Vision*	441–442
	The Age of Discontinuity	441–442
January 27	*The Frontiers of Management*	9
January 28	*Management: Tasks, Responsibilities, Practices*	380–381
January 29	*The Practice of Management*	9–10
January 30	*Managing in the Next Society*	xii–xiii
January 31	*A Functioning Society*	xv–xvii
	The Future of Industrial Man	27, 28
February 1	*The New Realities*	3
	Post-Capitalist Society	1
	The Age of Discontinuity	Preface
February 2	*Managing in Turbulent Times*	6
February 3	*Post-Capitalist Society*	33, 40, 42
February 4	*The Age of Discontinuity*	38, 351, 352
February 5	*Management in the Next Society*	235–236, 247
February 6	"The Global Economy and the Nation-State," *Foreign Affairs, 75th Anniversary Edition* (September/October 1997)	168–169
February 7	*Post-Capitalist Society*	212–213
February 8	*Management Challenges for the 21st Century*	90–92
February 9	*Post-Capitalist Society*	60–62
February 10	*Managing in a Time of Great Change*	77
	The Ecological Vision	445
	Innovation and Entrepreneurship	253–254
February 11	*The New Realities*	220–221
February 12	*Adventures of a Bystander*	1, 6
February 13	"The Freedom of Industrial Man," *The Virginia Quarterly Review* (Vol. 18, No. 4, Autumn 1942)	482–483
February 14	*The New Realities*	100–104
February 15	*Post-Capitalist Society*	13
February 16	*Concept of the Corporation*	17
February 17	*The Future of Industrial Man*	196, 197
February 18	*Post-Capitalist Society*	159–160
February 19	*The Age of Discontinuity*	234, 236–238
February 20	*The Ecological Vision*	149–150
February 21	*The Practice of Management*	22–23
February 22	*Post-Capitalist Society*	125–126, 133–134
February 23	*Post-Capitalist Society*	145–148, 159
February 24	*The Future of Industrial Man*	95–96
February 25	*Management Challenges for the 21st Century*	158–159
February 26	*Managing in the Next Society*	287–288
February 27	*Management: Tasks, Responsibilities, Practices*	77, 79

February 28	*Management: Tasks, Responsibilities, Practices*	80–82
February 29	*Management: Tasks, Responsibilities, Practices*	84–86
March 1	*Management Challenges for the 21st Century*	73, 93
	Managing in the Next Society	295
March 2	*The Frontiers of Management*	262
	Management Challenges for the 21st Century	86
March 3	*Management Challenges for the 21st Century*	22–25
	From Data to Information Literacy (Corpedia Module 8115)	
March 4	*The Frontiers of Management*	261–262
March 5	*Managing for Results*	173, 174, 183
March 6	*Innovation and Entrepreneurship*	139–140
March 7	*Management: Tasks, Responsibilities, Practices*	398–399
March 8	*The "How to" Drucker, American Management Association, 1977*	22–24
	Managing in Turbulent Times	41–71
March 9	*Managing in a Time of Great Change*	69
	The Practice of Management	70
	The Ecological Vision	146
	Management Challenges for the 21st Century	92–93
March 10	*Managing in the Next Society*	74–75
March 11	*Management Challenges for the 21st Century*	86–88
March 12	*The Practice of Management*	39–40
March 13	*Management: Tasks, Responsibilities, Practices*	128
March 14	"Management's New Paradigms," *Forbes*, October 5, 1998	174
	Management Challenges for the 21st Century	73–93
	The Next Society (Corpedia Module 8114)	
March 15	*The Ecological Vision*	116
	Management Challenges for the 21st Century	179
March 16	*The Practice of Management*	62–63
March 17	*The Practice of Management*	76–77
March 18	*The Ecological Vision*	112–113
March 19	*A Functioning Society*	131, 133–134
March 20	*Managing in Turbulent Times*	67–71
March 21	*Managing in the Next Society*	3–4, 19–20
March 22	*Managing in the Next Society*	30–31
March 23	*Managing in the Next Society*	60–61
	The Next Society (Corpedia Module 8114)	
March 24	*Managing in a Time of Great Change*	45–50
	The Five Deadly Business Sins (Corpedia Module 8108)	
March 25	*Management Challenges for the 21st Century*	114–115
	From Data to Information Literacy (Corpedia Module 8115)	
March 26	*Managing in the Next Society*	241–242
March 27	*Managing in the Next Society*	274–275
	The Next Society (Corpedia Module 8114)	

March 28	*Management Challenges for the 21st Century*	121–123
March 29	*Landmarks of Tomorrow*	6
	Management: Tasks, Responsibilities, Practices	508
March 30	*The New Realities*	157–159
March 31	*The New Realities*	252–254
April 1	*The Frontiers of Management*	226–227
April 2	*Management: Tasks, Responsibilities, Practices*	284
	second paragraph from a letter to Jack Beatty, *The World According to Peter Drucker*, Jack Beatty (Free Press, 1998)	79
April 3	*Management: Tasks, Responsibilities, Practices*	455–456
April 4	*Landmarks of Tomorrow*	109–110
April 5	*Managing the Non-Profit Organization*	16–17
April 6	*Managing the Non-Profit Organization*	3
	Management: Tasks, Responsibilities, Practices	463
April 7	*The Effective Executive*	98–99
April 8	*The Leader of the Future*, Francis Hesselbein, et al., eds. (Jossey-Bass, 1996)	xi–xiv
	The Essential Drucker	268–271
	Managing the Non-Profit Organization	9–27
April 9	*Management: Tasks, Responsibilities, Practices*	462
April 10	*Managing the Non-Profit Organization*	9
April 11	*Managing the Non-Profit Organization*	20–21, 27
April 12	*A Functioning Society*	35–36
April 13	*A Functioning Society*	35–36
April 14	*Management Cases* (Part Five, Case No. 2)	95–97
April 15	*Managing the Non-Profit Organization*	145–146
April 16	*Management: Tasks, Responsibilities, Practices*	108–109
April 17	*Managing the Non-Profit Organization*	149
April 18	*The Essential Drucker*	127–135
	People Decisions (Corpedia Module 8102)	
April 19	*Managing the Non-Profit Organization*	145–153
	People Decisions (Corpedia Module 8102)	
April 20	*Managing the Non-Profit Organization*	154–155
April 21	*Adventures of a Bystander*	280–281
April 22	*Adventures of a Bystander*	281
April 23	*Managing for Results*	223
April 24	*Managing in a Time of Great Change*	84
April 25	*Adventures of a Bystander*	292–293
April 26	"An Interview with Peter Drucker," *The Academy of Management Executive* (Vol. 17, No. 3, August 2003)	11
April 27	*The Ecological Vision*	196–197, 199
April 28	*The Ecological Vision*	199–202
April 29	*Management: Tasks, Responsibilities, Practices*	366, 368–369

April 30	*The New Society*	200–201
May 1	*Management Challenges for the 21st Century*	21
	Managing in the Next Society	23–24
May 2	*Managing in a Time of Great Change*	65–66, 68–69, 72
May 3	*Management Challenges for the 21st Century*	61, 63
	The Next Society (Corpedia Module 8114)	
May 4	*Managing in the Next Society*	237–238
May 5	*The New Realities*	78–79
May 6	*The Age of Discontinuity*	268
	Management Challenges for the 21st Century	149–150
	Managing in the Next Society	238–239
May 7	*Managing in a Time of Great Change*	76, 250
	Post-Capitalist Society	215
May 8	*Managing in the Next Society*	262–263
May 9	*Managing in a Time of Great Change*	77, 226, 234
May 10	*The Age of Discontinuity*	213–214
May 11	*The Frontiers of Management*	66, 68
	The New Realities	121–122
May 12	*Managing in the Next Society*	263, 264–265, 266, 268
May 13	*Management Challenges for the 21st Century*	62
	The New Realities	xiii
	Managing in the Next Society	268
May 14	*Managing in the Next Society*	118–122
	The Next Society (Corpedia Module 8114)	
May 15	*Managing in the Next Society*	114–118, 276
	The Next Society (Corpedia Module 8114)	
May 16	*Managing in the Next Society*	292–294
	The Next Society (Corpedia Module 8114)	
May 17	*Managing in the Next Society*	283–284
	The Next Society (Corpedia Module 8114)	
May 18	*Managing in the Next Society*	286
May 19	*Managing in a Time of Great Change*	350–351
May 20	*Management Challenges for the 21st Century*	136–137, 141
May 21	*The Ecological Vision*	228–230
May 22	*Post-Capitalist Society*	93–95
	Managing for the Future	275
May 23	*Management Challenges for the 21st Century*	142
May 24	*Management Challenges for the 21st Century*	143–146
	Knowledge Worker Productivity (Corpedia Module 8105)	
May 25	*Management Challenges for the 21st Century*	147
	Knowledge Worker Productivity (Corpedia Module 8105)	
May 26	*Management Challenges for the 21st Century*	146–148
May 27	*Concept of the Corporation*	296–297

May 28	*Management Challenges for the 21st Century*	146
	Knowledge Worker Productivity (Corpedia Module 8105)	
May 29	*Post-Capitalist Society*	192–193
May 30	*Post-Capitalist Society*	56, 64
	The Age of Discontinuity	276–277
May 31	*The Ecological Vision*	99
June 1	*Management Challenges for the 21st Century*	163
	Managing Oneself (Corpedia Module 8101)	
June 2	*The Ecological Vision*	349–350
June 3	*The Ecological Vision*	350–351
June 4	*The Ecological Vision*	351
June 5	*The Ecological Vision*	352–353
June 6	*The Frontiers of Management*	204, 206–207
June 7	*Drucker on Asia*	107–108
June 8	*Managing the Non-Profit Organization*	201–202
June 9	*Managing the Non-Profit Organization*	189–190, 192–193, 200
June 10	*Management Challenges for the 21st Century*	178
June 11	*Managing the Non-Profit Organization*	195–196
June 12	"An Interview with Peter Drucker," *The Academy of Management Executive* (Vol. 17, No. 3, August 2003)	10–12
June 13	*Managing in the Next Society*	281–282
June 14	*Managing in the Next Society*	288–289
	The Next Society (Corpedia Module 8114)	
June 15	*Post-Capitalist Society*	76
June 16	*The Pension Fund Revolution*	71–72
June 17	*The Pension Fund Revolution*	81–82
June 18	*Managing for the Future*	236, 248
June 19	*The Pension Fund Revolution*	195
June 20	*Management: Tasks, Responsibilities, Practices*	334–335
June 21	*Management: Tasks, Responsibilities, Practices*	181–182, 185
June 22	*Drucker on Asia*	103–104
June 23	*Adventures of a Bystander*	273
June 24	*Managing in the Next Society*	225, 231–232
June 25	*Concept of the Corporation*	152–153
June 26	"Meeting of the Minds," *Across the Board: The Conference Board Magazine* (Nov/Dec 2000)	21
June 27	*Management: Tasks, Responsibilities, Practices*	807–811
June 28	*The End of Economic Man*	36–37
June 29	*Managing in a Time of Great Change*	273–274, 277–278
June 30	*Managing for the Future*	204
July 1	*Management: Tasks, Responsibilities, Practices*	74
	Managing in a Time of Great Change	29–30
July 2	*Managing in a Time of Great Change*	30

July 3	*Management: Tasks, Responsibilities, Practices*	96–97
	Managing in a Time of Great Change	29–30
July 4	*Managing in a Time of Great Change*	31–32
July 5	*Managing in a Time of Great Change*	37–38
July 6	*Managing for Results*	117–118
July 7	*Management Challenges for the 21st Century*	97–132
	From Data to Information Literacy (Corpedia Module 8115)	
July 8	*Management Challenges for the 21st Century*	118–119
July 9	*Management Challenges for the 21st Century*	119
July 10	*Management Challenges for the 21st Century*	82–83
July 11	*Management Challenges for the 21st Century*	80–81
July 12	*Innovation and Entrepreneurship*	34–36
July 13	*Innovation and Entrepreneurship*	37–39, 50
July 14	*Innovation and Entrepreneurship*	49–50, 153
	Driving Change (Corpedia Module 8116)	
July 15	*Innovation and Entrepreneurship*	57
	Driving Change (Corpedia Module 8116)	
July 16	*Innovation and Entrepreneurship*	69, 73
	Driving Change (Corpedia Module 8116)	
July 17	*Innovation and Entrepreneurship*	76, 85
	Driving Change (Corpedia Module 8116)	
July 18	*Innovation and Entrepreneurship*	88–89, 92, 96–98
July 19	*Innovation and Entrepreneurship*	99
	Driving Change (Corpedia Module 8116)	
July 20	*Innovation and Entrepreneurship*	36, 119, 132
	Driving Change (Corpedia Module 8116)	
July 21	*Innovation and Entrepreneurship*	177
July 22	*Innovation and Entrepreneurship*	183
July 23	*Management: Tasks, Responsibilities, Practices*	105–107
July 24	*Managing in a Time of Great Change*	45–46
	The Five Deadly Business Sins (Corpedia Module 8108)	
July 25	*Managing for the Future*	251–255
July 26	*Management: Tasks, Responsibilities, Practices*	64–65
July 27	*Managing in a Time of Great Change*	47–48
	The Five Deadly Business Sins (Corpedia Module 8108)	
July 28	*Permanent Cost Control* (Corpedia Module 8109)	
	Managing for Results	68–110
July 29	*Permanent Cost Control* (Corpedia Module 8109)	
	Innovation and Entrepreneurship	143–176
July 30	*Permanent Cost Control* (Corpedia Module 8109)	
July 31	*Permanent Cost Control* (Corpedia Module 8109)	
August 1	*Management: Tasks, Responsibilities, Practices*	674, 679
August 2	*Management: Tasks, Responsibilities, Practices*	664, 666, 668

August 3	*Managing in Turbulent Times*	48
	Management: Tasks, Responsibilities, Practices	774
August 4	*Innovation and Entrepreneurship*	162–163
August 5	*Managing for the Future*	281–282
August 6	*Innovation and Entrepreneurship*	189–192
August 7	*The Ecological Vision*	177–179
August 8	*The Ecological Vision*	179
August 9	*Managing in the Next Society*	277–279
	The Next Society (Corpedia Module 8114)	
August 10	*Innovation and Entrepreneurship*	193
August 11	*Innovation and Entrepreneurship*	193–194
August 12	*Innovation and Entrepreneurship*	194–195
August 13	*Innovation and Entrepreneurship*	198–199
August 14	*Managing for Results*	151
August 15	*Managing for Results*	171–172
August 16	*Innovation and Entrepreneurship*	viii, 19, 209
	Entrepreneurial Strategies (Corpedia Module 8110)	
August 17	*Innovation and Entrepreneurship*	210–211
	Entrepreneurial Strategies (Corpedia Module 8110)	
August 18	*Innovation and Entrepreneurship*	220–221
	Entrepreneurial Strategies (Corpedia Module 8110)	
August 19	*Innovation and Entrepreneurship*	225–227
	Entrepreneurial Strategies (Corpedia Module 8110)	
August 20	*Innovation and Entrepreneurship*	243, 247
	Entrepreneurial Strategies (Corpedia Module 8110)	
August 21	*Innovation and Entrepreneurship*	233–236
	Entrepreneurial Strategies (Corpedia Module 8110)	
August 22	*Innovation and Entrepreneurship*	236–240
	Entrepreneurial Strategies (Corpedia Module 8110)	
August 23	*Innovation and Entrepreneurship*	240–242
	Entrepreneurial Strategies (Corpedia Module 8110)	
August 24	*Innovation and Entrepreneurship*	241
	Entrepreneurial Strategies (Corpedia Module 8110)	
August 25	*Management Cases* Harper & Row, 1977 (Part One, Case No. 3)	8–9
August 26	*Management Cases* Harper & Row, 1977 (Part One, Case No. 3)	9
August 27	*Management Cases* Harper & Row, 1977 (Part One, Case No. 3)	9–10
August 28	*Management: Tasks, Responsibilities, Practices*	88, 106
August 29	"Meeting of the Minds," *Across the Board: The Conference Board Magazine* (Nov/Dec 2000)	21
August 30	"Meeting of the Minds," *Across the Board: The Conference Board Magazine* (Nov/Dec 2000)	20
August 31	*Drucker on Asia*	101

September 1	*The Effective Executive*	25, 51
September 2	*The Effective Executive*	35–37
September 3	*The Effective Executive*	29–31, 49–51
September 4	*The Effective Executive*	22–25
September 5	*The Effective Executive*	52–53
	Management Challenges for the 21st Century	182–183
September 6	*The Effective Executive*	85–86
September 7	*Managing the Non-Profit Organization*	147–149
September 8	*The Effective Executive*	173–174
September 9	*Managing in a Time of Great Change*	5–7
September 10	*Management: Tasks, Responsibilities, Practices*	456–457
September 11	*Management Challenges for the 21st Century*	182–183
September 12	*Management Challenges for the 21st Century*	164–168
	Managing Oneself (Corpedia Module 8101)	
September 13	*Management Challenges for the 21st Century*	164–168
	Managing Oneself (Corpedia Module 8101)	
September 14	*Management Challenges for the 21st Century*	164–168
	Managing Oneself (Corpedia Module 8101)	
September 15	*Management Challenges for the 21st Century*	183–188
	Managing Oneself (Corpedia Module 8101)	
September 16	*The Effective Executive*	93–95
	Managing the Boss (Corpedia Module 8103)	
September 17	*Management Challenges for the 21st Century*	188–193
	Managing Oneself (Corpedia Module 8101)	
September 18	*Management Challenges for the 21st Century*	194–195
September 19	*Management Challenges for the 21st Century*	192–193
	The Next Society (Corpedia Module 8114)	
September 20	*The Effective Executive*	71, 72–73, 75, 87
September 21	*People Decisions* (Corpedia Module 8102)	
	Management: Tasks, Responsibilities, Practices	409–410
September 22	*The Frontiers of Management*	147
September 23	*Management: Tasks, Responsibilities, Practices*	494–495
September 24	*Management: Tasks, Responsibilities, Practices*	496
September 25	*Management: Tasks, Responsibilities, Practices*	497
September 26	*Management: Tasks, Responsibilities, Practices*	497–498
September 27	*Management: Tasks, Responsibilities, Practices*	504–505
September 28	*Management: Tasks, Responsibilities, Practices*	398–399
September 29	*Management: Tasks, Responsibilities, Practices*	431
September 30	*Management: Tasks, Responsibilities, Practices*	434–436
October 1	*Drucker on Asia*	104
October 2	*The Effective Executive*	130
October 3	*The Effective Executive*	134–135
October 4	*The Effective Executive*	134–135

October 5	*The Effective Executive*	136–139
	The Elements of Decision Making (Corpedia Module 8104)	
October 6	*Management: Tasks, Responsibilities, Practices*	472–474
October 7	*The Effective Executive*	113–142
	The Elements of Decision Making (Corpedia Module 8104)	
October 8	*The Effective Executive*	155–156
	The Elements of Decision Making (Corpedia Module 8104)	
October 9	*The Effective Executive*	123–130
	The Elements of Decision Making (Corpedia Module 8104)	
October 10	*The Effective Executive*	126–128
	The Elements of Decision Making (Corpedia Module 8104)	
October 11	*The Effective Executive*	126–128
	The Elements of Decision Making (Corpedia Module 8104)	
October 12	*Management: Tasks, Responsibilities, Practices*	466–470
	The Elements of Decision Making (Corpedia Module 8104)	
October 13	*The Effective Executive*	141
October 14	*The Effective Executive*	139–142
	The Elements of Decision Making (Corpedia Module 8104)	
October 15	*Management: Tasks, Responsibilities, Practices*	543–545
October 16	*The Future of Industrial Man*	28, 32
October 17	*The End of Economic Man*	xx–xxi
October 18	*The End of Economic Man*	37–38
October 19	*Managing in the Next Society*	149–150
October 20	*Concept of the Corporation*	242–243
October 21	*Post-Capitalist Society*	120, 122–123
October 22	*The Age of Discontinuity*	229, 233
October 23	*The Age of Discontinuity*	233–234, 241
October 24	*The Age of Discontinuity*	236, 240–241
October 25	*The Age of Discontinuity*	225
	The New Realities	129–130
October 26	*The Frontiers of Management*	210, 212–213
October 27	*The New Realities*	22–23
October 28	*A Functioning Society*	143
October 29	*Managing the Non-Profit Organization*	4, 53–54
October 30	*Managing the Non-Profit Organization*	56
October 31	*Managing the Non-Profit Organization*	157–158
November 1	*The Age of Discontinuity*	192–193
November 2	*Management Challenges for the 21st Century*	122–123
	From Data to Information Literacy (Corpedia Module 8115)	
November 3	*Management Challenges for the 21st Century*	123–126
	From Data to Information Literacy (Corpedia Module 8115)	
November 4	*Management Challenges for the 21st Century*	128–130
November 5	*Management Challenges for the 21st Century*	88–89

November 6	*Managing the Non-Profit Organization*	59
November 7	*Managing the Non-Profit Organization*	71
November 8	*Managing in a Time of Great Change*	39–40
	Management: Tasks, Responsibilities, Practices	125–126
November 9	*Management: Tasks, Responsibilities, Practices*	122–123
November 10	*Management Challenges for the 21st Century*	79–80
November 11	*Management: Tasks, Responsibilities, Practices*	719–720
November 12	*Management: Tasks, Responsibilities, Practices*	398–402
November 13	*The Practice of Management*	130–132
November 14	*Management: Tasks, Responsibilities, Practices*	101–102
November 15	*The Practice of Management*	129–130
	Management: Tasks, Responsibilities, Practices	438–439
November 16	*Management Challenges for the 21st Century*	12–13, 16–17
	Management: Tasks, Responsibilities, Practices	523
November 17	*The Ecological Vision*	451–452
November 18	*Concept of the Corporation*	141–142
	Management Challenges for the 21st Century	11
	A Functioning Society	137–138
November 19	*Post-Capitalist Society*	53
November 20	*The New Society*	269, 270
November 21	*Management: Tasks, Responsibilities, Practices*	574–575
November 22	*Management: Tasks, Responsibilities, Practices*	577–580
November 23	*Management: Tasks, Responsibilities, Practices*	577–578
November 24	*Management: Tasks, Responsibilities, Practices*	585–586, 589
November 25	*Management: Tasks, Responsibilities, Practices*	530–532, 535
November 26	*Management: Tasks, Responsibilities, Practices*	483–484, 486–488, 490
November 27	*The Frontiers of Management*	194–196
November 28	*The Frontiers of Management*	196–197
November 29	*Concept of the Corporation*	95–96
November 30	*The Frontiers of Management*	200–202
December 1	*The Ecological Vision*	453–454
December 2	*Managing in Turbulent Times* (Hardcover)	1–2
December 3	*The Age of Discontinuity*	43
December 4	*Management Challenges for the 21st Century*	110–113
	From Data Information Literacy (Corpedia Module 8115)	
December 5	*Management Challenges for the 21st Century*	115–116
	From Data to Information Literacy (Corpedia Module 8115)	
December 6	*Management Challenges for the 21st Century*	111–113
	From Data to Information Literacy (Corpedia Module 8115)	
December 7	*Management Challenges for the 21st Century*	115
	From Data to Information Literacy (Corpedia Module 8115)	
December 8	*Management Challenges for the 21st Century*	117
	From Data to Information Literacy (Corpedia Module 8115)	

December 9	*Management Challenges for the 21st Century*	117
	From Data to Information Literacy (Corpedia Module 8115)	
December 10	*Management Challenges for the 21st Century*	120–121
	From Data to Information Literacy (Corpedia Module 8115)	
December 11	*The Frontiers of Management*	257–260
	The Successful Acquisition (Corpedia Module 8106)	
December 12	*The Successful Acquisition* (Corpedia Module 8106)	
December 13	*The Frontiers of Management*	257–258
	The Successful Acquisition (Corpedia Module 8106)	
December 14	*The Frontiers of Management*	258
	The Successful Acquisition (Corpedia Module 8106)	
December 15	*The Frontiers of Management*	258
	The Successful Acquisition (Corpedia Module 8106)	
December 16	*The Frontiers of Management*	259–260
	The Successful Acquisition (Corpedia Module 8106)	
December 17	*The Frontiers of Management*	259
	The Successful Acquisition (Corpedia Module 8106)	
December 18	*Management Challenges for the 21st Century*	34, 37, 67
December 19	*Managing for the Future*	288–291
December 20	*Innovation and Entrepreneurship*	179–180
December 21	*The Ecological Vision*	210–211
December 22	*Management: Tasks, Responsibilities, Practices*	345
December 23	*Landmarks of Tomorrow*	264–265
December 24	*The Ecological Vision*	429, 435, 437
	The End of Economic Man	55
December 25	*The Ecological Vision*	425, 437, 439
December 26	*The End of Economic Man*	78–79
December 27	*The Future of Industrial Man*	25–26
December 28	*Managing in a Time of Great Change*	51–52
December 29	*Managing in a Time of Great Change*	52–57
December 30	*Managing for Results*	148
December 31	*Management Challenges for the 21st Century*	97–102
	From Data to Information Literacy (Corpedia Module 8115)	

READINGS BY TOPIC